Christology

Christology

A Global Introduction

Veli-Matti Kärkkäinen

Baker Academic
Grand Rapids, Michigan

Published by Baker Academic
a division of Baker Publishing Group
P.O. Box 6287, Grand Rapids, MI 49516-6287
www.bakeracademic.com

Printed in the United States of America

Library of Congress Cataloging-in-Publication Data
Kärkkäinen, Veli-Matti.
    Christology : a global introduction / Veli-Matti Kärkkäinen.
        p.   cm.
    Includes bibliographical references and indexes.
    ISBN 978-0-8010-2621-8 (pbk.)
    ISBN 10: 0-8010-2621-0 (pbk.)
    1. Jesus Christ—Person and offices. 2. Jesus Christ—History of doctrines.
I. Title.
BT203.K37 2003
232′.09—dc21   2002038573

Contents

Acknowledgments

Textbooks usually grow out of teaching experience, and the present book is no exception to that rule. I am grateful to my students, past and present, on three different continents—Europe, Asia, and North America—for giving me an opportunity to learn about Christology in many different colors. My current teaching position at Fuller Theological Seminary, with students from more than seventy countries representing all Christian traditions, provides a unique experience to learn what it means to interpret the significance of Jesus Christ for the global world.

Melinda Van Engen at Baker Book House, with her keen eye and many editorial questions, helped make the book more reader and classroom friendly. To Robert N. Hosack at Baker I am deeply indebted for his continuing interest in and support of producing globally relevant theology textbooks.

Susan Wood at the Fuller Faculty Publications Office deserves once again a big thank you. During the past two years as we have worked together on a number of texts, she has not only transformed my Finnish-English into proper language but has also taught me much about how to make theological texts both understandable and accurate.

I am so grateful to my family, my wife, Anne-Päivi, and two wonderful daughters, Nelli and Maiju, for giving me time to write and also letting me use one corner of our dining room table as my research spot. Nothing is more inspiring for an academic writer than sounds of music, smells from the kitchen, and loving hugs every now and then. Therefore, I could not imagine locking myself into a study and doing my writing all alone.

Introduction

Jesus' question to his first disciples—"Who do you say I am?"—is addressed also to us. Just as his early followers tried to answer this question in the context of their times, we today must try to give as adequate an answer as possible in the context of our times. How should we speak of Jesus at the beginning of the twenty-first century? As God incarnate? As the Man for others? As the forerunner of a new humanity/community/creation?[1]

These different views, held by men and women theologians from all continents and Christian traditions, reveal the continuing task of Christology: to interpret the significance and meaning of Jesus Christ for our own times in light of biblical and historical developments. Beginning in the biblical period and traveling through two thousand years of winding theological roads, Christian theology has tried to make sense of the person and work of Jesus Christ, the founder of Christianity and the most hotly debated figure of religious history. Every generation of theologians and Christians has responded to Christ's person and influence in the context in which it has found itself.

The person of Jesus Christ stands at the center of Christian faith and theology. For this reason, the study of Christology needs no prolonged justification in regard to the study of theology or an introduction to Christian faith. "While no theology can confine itself exclusively to Christology, no Christian theology would be complete without serious reflection on Jesus Christ."[2] In

1. William R. Barr, "The Significance of Jesus Christ: Introducing the Issue," in *Constructive Christian Theology in the Worldwide Church,* ed. William R. Barr (Grand Rapids: Eerdmans, 1997), 287.

2. J. P. Galvin, "Jesus Christ," in *Systematic Theology: Roman Catholic Perspectives,* 2 vols., ed. Francis Schüssler Fiorenza and John P. Galvin (Minneapolis: Fortress, 1991), 251.

this sense, no study comes closer to the core of Christian life and theology than Christology. Jesus' brief life on earth, his death on the cross, and his disciples' claims regarding the resurrection and ascension lay the historical and religious foundations for Christianity. "Over the years Christology has been a perennial object of fascination, for it is the keystone of theology for serious Christians."[3]

The Spectrum of Christologies

From the beginning of Christianity there arose a variety of interpretations of who Christ is. At no time was one picture of Jesus dominant. In fact, the New Testament itself contains several complementary interpretations of Jesus Christ. The existence of four Gospels—Matthew, Mark, Luke, and John—provides an everlasting reminder of the plurality of the Christian canon. Moreover, the pictures painted by Paul and other New Testament writers should be added to the distinctive testimonies of the evangelists of the New Testament. The New Testament, therefore, contains a myriad of pictures, silhouettes, and appropriations of Jesus Christ. What binds them together is the common core, a conviction that something crucial happened in the person of this One who is confessed as the Lord and Savior by all Christians at all times.

Along with the establishment of the biblical canon in the fourth century, Christian theology, in the form of the classical creeds of Nicea in the fourth century and Chalcedon in the fifth century, attempted to formulate a definitive understanding of Christ in light of the existing cultural milieu. Much was achieved by the exact formulations concerning Christ's divinity and humanity, but even more was left open. Basically, what the early creeds said was in the negative. In other words, they combated views regarded as heretical. During subsequent centuries up until our own time, theology has taken its point of departure from these early formulations and has refined them. Still, the work continues.

The blossoming of christological study and reflection, beginning at the turn of the twentieth century and culminating in the emergence of so-called contextual or intercultural Christologies in the 1960s and since, has produced a fascinating rainbow of christological interpretations. In Protestant theology, Christology has been the focus of debate for nearly two centuries, beginning with the famous quest of the historical Jesus. That goal was never achieved, but the enthusiasm of that quest gave impetus to the rise of a myriad of rich interpretations. Roman Catholic theology has witnessed a resurgence of Christology during the past three or four decades. The most exciting feature

3. William J. LaDue, *Jesus among the Theologians: Contemporary Interpretations of Christ* (Harrisburg, Pa.: Trinity Press, 2001), vii.

of the current scene is the rise of contextual and/or intercultural Christologies that attempt to speak to specific local needs (for example, in Africa or Asia) or needs of specific groups of people (such as women or the poor). Some contextual Christologies are also linked with specific philosophical or worldview movements, such as process philosophy. The end result has been the emergence of African, Asian, Latin American, liberation, black, feminist, and process Christologies.

It is the task of this book to offer a comprehensive, even if not exhaustive, introduction to Christology in three different moments. Part 1 surveys the main biblical approaches to the person of Christ as they are presented by the Gospel writers and Paul. Part 2 inquires into historical developments, focusing on two crucial, defining phases: early developments during the first five centuries that laid the foundation for the rest of Christology, and the quest of the historical Jesus, which in conjunction with the radical transformation of the intellectual climate as a result of the Enlightenment definitively changed the study of Christology. Parts 3 and 4 examine the current landscape of international Christology in its various forms: contemporary interpretations in the West and several contextual approaches that have been developed not only in Europe and North America but also in Asia, Africa, and Latin America.

The Person and Work of Christ

In works of Christology written before the twentieth century, there was often a sharp distinction between "the person of Christ" (Christology proper) and "the work of Christ" (soteriology, the doctrine of salvation). Nowadays, the distinction is less clear, and there are both philosophical and practical reasons for a less sharp division (though a clear distinction is helpful for educational purposes).

One of the early Eastern fathers, Athanasius, argued that Christ had to be both human and divine in order to save us: divine in order to save and human in order to identify with us. His insight into the full divinity and humanity did not grow out of a sustained abstract philosophical reflection but out of Jesus' role as Savior. Usually it is the salvation and healing brought about by Christ that leads a person to ask about the person of Christ. When Jesus of Nazareth healed a crippled man in John 5, the man did not know who the healer was. In the temple, he learned who Jesus was.

Philip Melanchthon, a colleague of Martin Luther in the Protestant Reformation, is attributed with the saying, "To know Christ is to know his benefits." That is, apart from soteriology, the doctrine of salvation, there is no access to the person of Christ. In fact, Melanchthon and many others have wondered whether there is really any other avenue to understanding who

Christ is. He is the Savior. That is the approach of the Bible. The New Testament nowhere enters into a sophisticated philosophical discussion about Christ's person but rather focuses on the salvation brought about by Christ.

The famous philosopher Immanuel Kant of the eighteenth century, who inquired into the conditions of our knowledge, maintained that in general we cannot know things directly but only insofar as we can perceive their impact. The identity of Jesus, therefore, is known through his impact on us. In the same spirit, Albrecht Ritschl, one of the founders of classical liberalism, argued that it is improper to separate Christology and soteriology because the only way to receive knowledge of something is to observe its effects on us.[4]

These foundational perspectives concerning the integral link between the person and the work of Christ have led theologians to a growing realization of the connection between "functional" (what Christ has done for us) and "ontological" (who Christ is in his person) Christologies. Yet at the same time, works of Christology tend to focus on one or the other, and this book is no exception. The focus here is on the person of Christ, and therefore, soteriological questions will be addressed only insofar as they are intertwined with that inquiry.

But should we speak of "Jesusology" rather than "Christology"? After all, Jesus is the first name of the divine-human person. This question takes us to the most foundational methodological question in Christology.

Christology "from Below" and "from Above"

There are two options, in principle, for inquiry into the person and work of Christ. Conveniently, these have been labeled "from above" and "from below." Christology from above begins with the confession of faith in the deity of Christ as expressed in the New Testament. Christology from below begins with an inquiry into the historical Jesus and the historical basis for belief in Christ. In other words, the approach from above takes the theological interpretation of Jesus Christ as found in the New Testament as its point of departure for determining the meaning of Christ for our own times. A theologian who uses the approach from below goes behind the theological interpretation of the evangelists, Paul, and other New Testament writers and attempts to ascertain for himself or herself the historical and factual foundation of christological claims. It is important to note that this is not a distinction between "conservative" and "liberal" but one of method. (Although most conservatives work from above, many notable theologians in the from above category are

---

4. Albrecht Ritschl, *The Christian Doctrine of Justification and Reconciliation* (Edinburgh: T & T Clark, 1900), 385–484.

liberal. Other theologians advocate a from below method but still hold to a "high" view of Christ as truly divine.)

Understandably, from above was the dominant orientation of the earliest centuries. There was no question about the historical reliability of the Gospel records; the Gospel narratives were taken for granted. The development of christological tradition before the time of the Enlightenment was simply an interpretation of the New Testament confession of faith in Christ and an attempt to express it in precise philosophical and theological terms. The from above method also had its proponents in the twentieth century, though their motivation was vastly different from the pre-Enlightenment orientation. Theologians associated with neo-orthodoxy (a movement examined in part 3), such as Emil Brunner and Karl Barth, and those with existentialist leanings (see also part 3), such as Rudolf Bultmann, argued that the basis for understanding Christ is not the historical Jesus but the *kērygma* (Greek, "preaching," "proclamation"), the church's proclamation of Christ. In the words of Brunner:

> We are bound to oppose the view that the Christian faith springs out of historical observation, out of the historical picture of Jesus of Nazareth. Christendom itself has always known otherwise. Christian faith springs only out of the witness to Christ of the preached message and the written word of the Scriptures.[5]

In this view, preference is given to Paul and John over the Synoptic Gospels (Mark, Matthew, and Luke), because Paul and John were not interested in the details of Jesus' earthly life but in the meaning of the Jesus event for the Christian life and church. Consequently, this contemporary from above method argues that faith in Christ is not based on historical or rational proof, and it cannot be scientifically proven. Brunner made a distinction between "Christ in the flesh," who is God become incarnate as confessed in the New Testament documents, and "Christ after flesh," the Christ known by a historian with his or her methods of research. Brunner thinks the believer knows more than the researcher because the believer knows Christ "in the flesh." Bultmann contended that faith in the "kerygmatic" Christ, based on the preaching of the New Testament authors, cannot with certainty be connected with the actual earthly life of Jesus. Whatever one believes about the earthly, historical Jesus is secondary to one's own existential view of Christ.

The main orientation of Christology since the time of the Enlightenment, however, has been from below. This is understandable given some of the developments associated with the Enlightenment (part 2 discusses in detail the implications of the Enlightenment for Christology): All religious, philosophical, and other authorities were replaced by independent individual judgment

5. Emil Brunner, *The Mediator* (London: Lutterworth, 1934), 158.

and the right to form one's own opinion. Why should one rely on the faith confession of people from the past rather than try to decide for oneself the meaning of Christ? The most appropriate candidate for such a methodological approach is naturally the quest of the historical Jesus. Theologians involved in this quest attempt to go beyond the biblical authors' confessions and ascertain for themselves who Jesus of Nazareth was. They study the historical person of Jesus Christ as any other figure of history. In this sense, the nineteenth-century searches for the historical Jesus were "Jesusologies" rather than Christologies because they focused on the human person Jesus rather than on the divine Christ confessed by the early church.

A leading from below approach proponent, one who differs from the scholars of the quest of the historical Jesus, has been Wolfhart Pannenberg, whose *Jesus, God and Man*[6] and later systematic theology attempted to find a historically and scientifically reliable basis for the study of Christology. Pannenberg maintains that the task of Christology is to offer rational support for belief in the divinity of Jesus. Since from above methods presuppose it rather than argue for it, they cannot be judged as valid methods. A from above approach tends to neglect the history of Jesus and therefore avoids tackling the obvious question as to the reliability of the sources on Jesus. Pannenberg argues that historical inquiry is both necessary and possible. If we rest our faith on *kērygma* alone and not on historical facts, we risk creating "our own Christs" rather than following the one witnessed to in the Bible.

As a stalwart defender of the necessity of historical-critical study of the Gospels and Jesus tradition, Pannenberg also firmly believes it is important not to limit historical study as the nineteenth-century and later traditions did by not allowing miracles and other supernatural events. Historical sources talk about the miracles associated with the life of Jesus, the greatest of which is, of course, the resurrection. When conducting critical study into the origins and historical basis of Christology, according to Pannenberg, one should not decide beforehand which events are historically possible. Even though historical study in itself may never lead one to a final commitment of faith in the divinity of the person of Jesus Christ, for Pannenberg, it is absolutely necessary to take the critical and historical examination to its end until one is convinced, for example, that Jesus' claim for resurrection is valid, or at least probable. Faith in the divinity of Christ, therefore, is a result of historical study and not a blind "leap of faith" as in neo-orthodoxy and existentialism.

In the final analysis, one may not need to choose either of these methodological approaches in a way that excludes the other. One can take a both-and approach. The basic problem of the from above approach is the foundation of faith: How do we know we believe in the right Jesus? What about other figures with similar claims? The basic problem with the from below approach

6. Wolfhart Pannenberg, *Jesus, God and Man* (Philadelphia: Westminster, 1968).

is that faith might be dependent on changing results of historical study, and objective certainty is difficult to reach. For academic purposes, one should depend mainly on the from below approach, which can also serve the faith commitment of the individual. Finally, however, belief in the divinity and related claims of Christ is a personal worldview commitment that cannot be argued with academic reasoning alone.

A Christological Profile

From early on, various traditions or emphases concerning Christ began to emerge. As mentioned above, the brief life of Jesus of Nazareth on earth, his suffering and death, and his subsequent resurrection and ascension form the foundation for Christian theology in general and Christology in particular. The various moments of Christ's life form the basis for the major approaches that have shaped and continue to shape Christology. "The life, death and resurrection of Jesus are to some degree the iconographic corner-points from which Christology can be retold time and again."[7] A different central perspective opens up on Jesus Christ depending on which of the three corner-points one begins with. Three major approaches have been presented recently, to which a fourth can be added to give a fuller account. These four[8] may be summarized as follows:

1. the incarnational Christology of the early church and Catholicism
2. the theology of the cross of Protestantism, especially of the Lutheran tradition
3. the resurrection and ascension Christology of Eastern Orthodoxy
4. the empowerment Christology of Pentecostalism and the Charismatic movements

The early church focused on the incarnation of the preexistent Son of God in the form of Jesus of Nazareth on the basis of John 1:14, "The Word became flesh," and a host of other passages. Belief in the incarnation of God in Jesus Christ made Mary "the mother of God," with the child Jesus the symbol of Catholic piety. From the central perspective of the incarnation, death was the necessary consequence, and the resurrection completed this earthly career of the Savior.

7. Volker Küster, *The Many Faces of Jesus Christ: Intercultural Christology* (Maryknoll, N.Y.: Orbis, 2001), 29–30.
    8. Ibid., 30–32, mentions the first three.

Martin Luther and other Reformers did not downplay the idea of incarnation, but they did shift the focus from the incarnation to the suffering and death on the cross of the One who was condemned for our sins and for our justification. Luther's "theology of the cross," the controlling principle of his whole theology, maintained that God can be found only in the shame and suffering of the cross. There follows a piety of the remembrance of the passion of Christ and a willingness to follow the path of the despised Messiah.

The Orthodox Church's piety, which focuses on icons and liturgy, looks, so to speak, to heaven, where the resurrected Christ sits at the right hand of the Father. Not guilt but the need for immortality has been the driving force of Orthodox theology and Christology with its idea of salvation as divinization, becoming like God, even god. The incarnation and the cross are but the beginning of the way of salvation, which culminates in glorious victory over death. The splendid liturgy of the church on earth is but an icon of the heavenly liturgy.

The newest and in many ways the most controversial christological model is associated with Pentecostalism and later Charismatic movements. While such believers do not ignore the incarnation, cross, and resurrection, they look to Christ especially as the miracle worker and baptizer with the Holy Spirit who is the source of power and empowerment, be it for physical healing, freedom from evil powers, or charismatic gifts such as prophecy. In contrast to what many outsiders think, these movements are not centered on the Holy Spirit more than on Christ, even though their spirituality is charismatic and spiritualistic. The classical "five-fold gospel," or as it soon came to be known, "full gospel," of Pentecostalism depicted Jesus Christ in his role as Savior (or justifier), baptizer with the Spirit, sanctifier, healer, and soon-coming King.

These basic orientations regarding various moments of Christ's life highlight the richness and complementary nature of the biblical witness to Christ. They also add to the plurality of basic interpretation paradigms. These various paradigms of Christology have a bearing on the rest of theology, for Christology literally stands at the center of theology. As a result, Christology is related to other topics such as the doctrine of the church and revelation. The church is the body of Christ; the self-revelation of God can be known only in the person of Jesus Christ; eschatology, the doctrine of the last things, is about the coming of the kingdom in the person of Jesus Christ; and so on. In other words, what one believes about Christ has implications for the rest of one's theology.

*also thru other humans + the natural world — Ignatius "finding God in all things."

Part 1

Christ in the Bible

The foundational document for the Christian church is the Bible, the canonical books of the Old and New Testaments. Even though it is the task of Christian theology, especially systematic theology, to go beyond the Bible when inquiring into the meaning and significance of Jesus Christ for people living in various contexts in the third millennium—asking many questions the Bible did not ask—the foundational material for all Christian theology is the Bible. Therefore, a survey of biblical perspectives on Jesus Christ requires no prolonged justification.

But which parts of the Bible highlight the significance of the person and work of Jesus Christ? Obviously, the Gospels of the New Testament seem to be the first choice in that they offer an interpretation of Jesus. The Gospels, naturally, are the main focus of the present book. But the Gospels are not the only documents of the New Testament. The writings of St. Paul, a major early interpreter of Christian faith, are also rich in Christology.

There is much more to be found about Christ in the New Testament, from writers such as James, the author of the Book of Hebrews (the name of whom we do not know), and Peter. For a survey such as this, however, we have to be selective. The Gospels and the writings of Paul, therefore, will serve as representatives of New Testament interpretations.

What about the Old Testament? It is also a part of the Christian canon and therefore a normative guide for the Christian church and theology. In the past, much was made of its prophecies and predictions concerning Jesus Christ. The current way of doing theology, however, while giving due attention to the significance of the Old Testament as a background to the New Testament (and providing, for example, much of the conceptual apparatus of the New Testament), does not too easily "christianize" the Old Testament. Rather, theologians now let the Old Testament stand first as the Bible of the people of Israel. Testimonies, prophecies, and expectations concerning the Messiah are indeed found in the Old Testament, but determining how to relate them to the Christ of the New Testament is a demanding task that goes well beyond the confines of an introductory survey in Christology.

Therefore, part 1 of this introductory text delves into interpretations concerning the person of Jesus Christ in the four Gospels and in the main writings of the apostle Paul.

1

The Many Faces of Christ in the Bible

The Plurality of the Biblical Testimony

Who is Jesus Christ? The most obvious way to answer this question would be simply to refer to the Bible, the book that virtually all Christians have regarded as the highest and normative source of doctrine. Fundamentally, that is the correct answer. Apart from the Bible, there is no comprehensive information available regarding Jesus Christ, even though an occasional extra-biblical reference to Christ can be found. But mere reference to the Bible as the defining source for determining who Jesus Christ is does not go far enough. The fact is that not even the Bible contains a single overriding description of Christ. Rather, it contains a myriad of pictures, images, and testimonies to his person.

Because of the way the Bible was written, mainly in the form of a story, it does not contain a systematized outline of the person and work of Christ. The teaching on Jesus Christ is given through symbols and stories, and the accent is on his deeds. In this sense, we could perhaps describe biblical Christology as a sort of "lived" Christology rather than a schematized doctrine.

The fact that there are various complementary faces of Christ in the New Testament is illustrated most aptly by the existence of four Gospels. Why four Gospels? Why not just one? This fact has been acknowledged and pondered by Christians for centuries. Already in the second century, attempts were made to harmonize the four Gospels into one whole in order to make the story of Christ more coherent. Even the first Bible readers noticed that having four stories not only added to the richness of the overall story but also created problems such as contradictions between various details related to the same story. The church and Christian theology, however, decided in favor of a plurality of testimonies at the expense of harmony in every detail.

The most popular approach to biblical Christology has involved focusing on the various titles given to Jesus Christ. There is an old Latin saying, *nomen est omen,* which means "name is an omen." In ancient cultures, as well as in many cultures in today's two-thirds world, the name given to a person reflects either a distinctive personal characteristic or significant events related to that person. Clearly, various titles given to Christ serve that function. The more recent method of New Testament Christology involves reading each book as it stands without necessarily trying to pull all the differing materials into a coherent whole. In other words, the specific contribution of each of the Gospels is appreciated on its own terms. Thus, there is a Christology of Matthew, Mark, Luke, and John.

Various Christological Trajectories

Not all scholars have been content with either of these approaches, namely, describing the various titles of Christ or focusing on each of the Gospels independently. There are those who think that the best gateway into the Gospel writers' understanding of Christology is to look at the various New Testament trajectories and to discern what kind of Christology is related to each of them.

Reginald H. Fuller, in his *Foundations of New Testament Christology,*[1] suggested a three-stage division among Palestinian Judaism, Hellenistic Judaism, and the Hellenistic Gentile world; to each environment corresponded particular christological patterns. The Palestinian church, the earliest phase of the church, focused on the past word and work of Jesus and his future coming in glory. The second stratum, Hellenistic Judaism,[2] transformed the primitive *kērygma* ("preaching," "proclamation") into a proclamation of Jesus' present work as exalted Lord and Christ; there was more interest in Jesus' function as Savior than in his being and personhood. For the Hellenistic Gentile mission, Christology was conceived in a three-stage framework of preexistence, incarnation, and exaltation. Similar to Greek culture and philosophies, which focused on ontological questions, it focused on Jesus' being and personhood. Fuller's scheme may have some truth to it, but the sharp division between the

1. Reginald H. Fuller, *The Foundations of New Testament Christology* (London: Collins, 1965).
2. Hellenistic Judaism refers to that part of Jewish religion and culture that was shaped by the Hellenistic (i.e., Greek) culture prevalent at the time of Jesus. These Jews read the Old Testament in the Greek translation called the Septuagint (LXX).

Palestinian and Hellenistic spheres has been questioned, and Greek influence was present in Israel during the centuries before Jesus' birth.

Yet another orientation to the study of Christ was taken by Helmut Koester, who identified four basic christological trajectories that arose independently of one another in different Christian circles in the years between Jesus' death and the writing of the New Testament.[3] Each of these trajectories, not mutually exclusive of one another, shed light on various aspects of Christ's person and work. ①

The most primitive of these trajectories is the idea of Jesus as Son of Man and coming Lord (the following sections analyze in detail the meaning of christological titles such as Son of Man; therefore, this section merely assumes the basic meanings). Focusing on eschatology, this trajectory continued Jesus' own future-oriented preaching, as is evident, for example, in Mark 13 and Matthew 25. The Pauline teaching in 1 Thessalonians 4 also stands in the same tradition. As is often the case in eschatologically minded communities that look forward to the coming world end, there was a sharp separation between Jesus' followers and society. ②

The second trajectory identified by Koester is the idea of Jesus as miracle worker. This type looked to events in Jesus' public life, especially his miracles and exorcisms, and depicted Jesus as a sort of powerful "divine man." This orientation is visible in Acts 2:22, where Jesus of Nazareth is depicted as "a man attested to you by God with mighty works and wonders and signs" (RSV). Naturally, many passages in the Gospels (e.g., Mark 1:23–45) stand in this tradition. This trajectory emphasized the piety of individual Christians rather than the coming eschatological transformation. ③

The third type of Christology is wisdom Christology, which also looked at the public life of Jesus but saw him as a teacher, an envoy of wisdom, rather than as a miracle worker. Passages such as Matthew 11:25–30 and many others in the Gospels (Luke 11:49–51; John 1:1–18) and in the writings of Paul (Col. 2:6–23) represent this tradition. This is what can be called a "parable tradition" or a "theological school" model. ④

Lastly, a fourth christological model directed its attention to Jesus as crucified and raised from the dead. Early creedal formulations such as 1 Corinthians 15:3–8 and liturgical traditions (1 Cor. 11:23–26) highlight the all-important role of the death and resurrection of Christ. This trajectory is sometimes called "paschal Christology" (from the Hebrew and Greek terms that refer to the Passover, the feast in which sacrificial lambs were slaughtered). It was promoted especially by Paul, who, for example in 1 Corinthians 5:7, talks about Christ as the "Passover lamb." This image was familiar to the

---

3. Helmut Koester, "The Structure and Criteria of Early Christian Beliefs," in *Trajectories through Early Christianity,* ed. James M. Robinson and Helmut Koester (Philadelphia: Fortress, 1971), 205–31.

Gospel writers, as shown in the phrase "Lamb of God" (John 1:29, 36). This type takes seriously the reality of Jesus' human life and sufferings, and while not ignoring Jesus' roles as miracle worker and teacher, looks to him as the sufferer. These four christological models are equally valid, but in the canon the last one seems to dominate.

Yet another crucial perspective needs to be mentioned before beginning a detailed examination of individual titles given to Jesus, namely, the challenge posed by James Dunn, a leading New Testament scholar. In his book *Unity and Diversity in the New Testament*,[4] the title of which reveals its basic orientation, he argues that rather than trying to identify a single Christology of the Gospels, let alone of the entire New Testament, we should acknowledge and affirm that the New Testament contains several legitimate pictures and theological interpretations of Jesus. Since there is no one definitive view of Jesus, we should cherish the plurality of pictures. At the same time, though, there is a common foundation, a unifying core that all New Testament writers share: In and through Jesus something decisive for human salvation occurred.

New Testament scholarship has had a difficult time keeping the balance and therefore at times has identified Paul and John as "more theological" interpreters of Jesus over against the Synoptic Gospels. Other times the Synoptics have been read on their own terms and have been regarded as "historically more reliable." The richness of the New Testament traditions concerning the person and work of Christ might be an important clue: Rather than arguing for the priority of this or that type, we are in a place to appreciate the various needs and contexts out of which Christology arose in the New Testament and therefore are better prepared to address the various multicultural, local, and contextual needs of the ever changing postmodern, global world in the third millennium.

Having surveyed the various approaches to the study of Christology in the New Testament, especially with regard to the four Gospels, we will now focus in more detail on two complementary approaches: examining the titles of Christ in the Gospels and examining each of the Gospels and their Christologies (chap. 2).

The famous New Testament scholar Oscar Cullmann, in *The Christology of the New Testament,* written in the 1950s,[5] classified the various titles given to Christ in four main categories. He also summarized the background of each title in Judaism and Hellenism and traced the history of its application to Jesus. Cullmann's proposal included:

1. Jesus' earthly work: prophet, servant, high priest
2. future work: Messiah, Son of Man

4. James D. G. Dunn, *Unity and Diversity in the New Testament* (Philadelphia: Westminster, 1977); see also his *Christology in the Making* (Philadelphia: Westminster, 1980).
5. Oscar Cullmann, *The Christology of the New Testament* (London: SCM, 1957).

3. present work: Lord, Savior
4. preexistence: Word, Son of God, God

Ferdinand Hahn's *Titles of Jesus in Christology: Their History in Early Christianity*[6] followed a similar path, even though Hahn focused on fewer titles: Son of Man, Lord, Christ, Son of David, Son of God (the appendix also includes a treatment of an eschatological prophet).

The following discussion focuses on the titles most frequently used in the New Testament, providing a detailed account of the content of christological labels: Christ/Messiah, Son of God, Son of Man, and Lord. Other significant New Testament titles, namely, God, Son of David, and *Logos,* will also be mentioned.

Christ/Messiah   *The Anointed One*

One of the most important christological titles is Christ, which appears over five hundred times in the New Testament. Christ *(Christos)* is the Greek equivalent of the Hebrew Messiah *(mashiach),* which means literally "the anointed one." While *Christos* had no special religious significance in Greek culture prior to the influence of ancient Jewish and Christian usage, it had a special religious meaning in the Old Testament. The Old Testament contains three categories of persons who were anointed with oil and appointed to a specific task: prophets, priests, and kings. Kings especially were considered to be appointed by God, and anointing was the public sign of God's appointment, as in the case of the first king of Israel, Saul (1 Samuel 9–10). In postexilic Old Testament texts, one finds hope for a renewed Davidic monarchy, often pictured with grandiose dimensions and qualities (e.g., Hag. 2:20–23; Zech. 9:9–10). Thus, the idea of messiahship was related to the future of Israel, her deliverance from foreign tyranny, and the introduction of a righteous rule.

Jesus was regarded by some as a political liberator. Several self-appointed "Christs" had the vision of deliverance, but Jesus Christ did not want to identify with those expectations. In fact, Jesus never permitted his followers to use the term Messiah. William Wrede, a nineteenth-century pioneer of research into the Gospels, especially Mark, called this the "messianic secret": Rather than encouraging his followers to spread the good news of the Messiah who had come, Jesus forbade those he healed, for example, to tell anyone. Jesus did not want to identify with this primarily political messianic expectation and wanted to avoid conflict with the political and religious establishment until the time had come for him to die. If Jesus regarded himself as Messiah, it was

6. Ferdinand Hahn, *The Titles of Jesus in Christology: Their History in Early Christianity* (Cleveland: World, 1969).

not in the political or nationalistic sense. Moreover, the people expected a victorious Messiah; the crucified Jesus was a disappointment.

It is worth noting that while all the Gospel writers, each one in his own distinct way, appropriates the title Christ, Paul uses the term by far the most frequently: Of the 530 occurrences of the term, 383 are in the Pauline corpus (270 in the seven letters whose authorship is virtually undisputed today: Romans, 1 and 2 Corinthians, Galatians, Philippians, 1 Thessalonians, Philemon). The heavy concentration of the term in Paul's letters, the earliest New Testament writings, suggests that very early the term became an important part of the vocabulary of Christian faith. Christ is undoubtedly Paul's favorite title for Jesus.

Close examination of *Christos* in Paul's letters shows that he uses the term almost as a name, or as part of the name for Jesus, and not characteristically as a title. Thus, for example, it appears in the following formulae: Christ Jesus, Jesus Christ, the Lord Jesus Christ, and so on. This has led many to ask whether Paul connected the term to an understanding of Jesus as Messiah or whether he used Christ more as a name, a convenient way of referring to Jesus. While *Christos* was not immediately meaningful as a religious term to ancient Gentiles unfamiliar with Jewish messianic expectations, Paul as a Jew was completely familiar with the Hebrew/Judaic tradition. In fact, in Romans 9:5, Paul makes explicit reference to "the Christ," not merely a name but a title, and often he connects the term Christ with Jesus' crucifixion and resurrection (Rom. 5:6–7; 1 Corinthians 15; Gal. 3:13).

It is also worth noting that especially in 1 Peter the title Christ is connected with the sufferings of Jesus (1:11, in fulfillment of the Old Testament prophecies; 2:21; 3:18; etc.). This connection between the term *Christos* and suffering demonstrates the early Christian understanding that Jesus' crucifixion was a messianic event.

Even though Jesus fulfilled the hopes of Israel's Messiah in a way that was not compatible with the dreams of a majority of the people, he still was and is Israel's Messiah, not merely the Messiah of the Gentiles (in biblical terminology, all non-Jews are Gentiles). People have too often lost sight of this perspective throughout history, resulting in unfortunate implications for Christian-Jewish relations.

Son of God

Two parallel names have become part of Christian theology's vocabulary, namely, Son of God and Son of Man. Naturally, one would assume that the former refers to Jesus' divinity and the latter to his humanity. This was, in fact, taken for granted until the twentieth century, when a more careful exegesis of biblical texts created ambiguity regarding these two titles. In fact, exegetically, both assumptions—that Son of God denotes divinity and Son of Man denotes humanity—are inaccurate.

The basic meaning of son of God in the Old Testament is "belonging to God," as in the case of the people of Israel (Exod. 4:22) or King David and his successors (2 Sam. 7:14).[7] In both the Old and New Testaments, the concept of sonship carries a variety of meanings, including commissioning to special work, obedience, intimate fellowship, knowledge, likeness, and the receiving of blessing and gifts. The Old Testament does not speak explicitly of the Messiah or of a specifically messianic figure as the Son of God.

The name Son of God appears 124 times in the New Testament and is found especially in Paul's writings and Hebrews. According to Romans 1:4, Jesus had "been declared Son of God" on account of the resurrection.

Jesus used the term rarely, but according to the Synoptic Gospels, Jesus did understand himself and his mission according to the idea of divine sonship and clearly implied that he was the Son of God. Some scholars have questioned the authenticity of those rare passages in which Jesus refers to himself as the Son, but the majority of scholars think that at least some of the sayings come directly from Jesus (Matt. 11:27; Mark 12:6; 13:32; Luke 10:22). An examination of the authentic sayings of Jesus regarding the "Father" and the "Son" reveals the following emphases. First, Jesus claimed personal intimacy with the Father. This comes to the fore especially in the *abba* sayings of Jesus (Mark 14:36); this Aramaic term denotes a warm, close address similar to "daddy." Second, the use of "Son" signified obedience to the will of God, as is evident especially in Jesus' prayer in Gethsemane (Mark 14:32–42). Finally, "Son" referred to the uniqueness of his status. Jesus' relation to the Father as Son is exclusive. This becomes evident in the distinction Paul makes between Jesus' sonship and our sonship, using two different Greek terms: Believers are adopted and called sons or children *(tekna),* but Jesus is the Son *(huios).*

One of the concerns of our day is the question of inclusive language: Should *son* be replaced by *child* in order to be inclusive? The New Testament usage of *son* is not sexist: It includes both sexes. Chapter 22 delves into this problem as it discusses feminist interpretations of Christ.

Son of Man

The Old Testament term *ben adam* ("Son of man," literally "Adam"; the Hebrew term refers to both the proper name Adam and the noun denoting

7. The notion of divine sonship appears in the Old Testament with regard to three persons or groups: angels (Job 1:6), Israel (Hosea 11:1), and the king (Ps. 2:7).

the human person) is used in three contexts. In the Book of Ezekiel, the term appears over one hundred times as a form of address to Ezekiel. It is also used to emphasize the frailty of human nature, as in the famous saying in Psalm 8:4. Christologically, the most significant usage is that of Daniel 7:13–14, which talks about "one like a son of man, coming with the clouds of heaven," approaching "the Ancient of Days" [God], to whom was given "authority, glory and sovereign power," and who was worshiped by all peoples. Christian theology has seen in the Son of Man of Daniel the Messiah, who came in the person of Jesus of Nazareth. Rudolf Bultmann disagreed and claimed that the Son of Man of Daniel 7 and Jesus were originally not the same person; the early church merged the two. Bultmann's suggestion has not won support.

Son of Man is used more frequently than any other title to refer to Jesus in the Gospels. What is distinctive about its usage, though, is that it occurs in all four Gospels and only there. The only exception to the rule is Acts 7:56. The other distinctive feature of the title is that only Jesus uses it in the Gospels (except in John 12:34, when the people quote Jesus' phrase back to him). Clearly, Son of Man is the preferred self-designation of Jesus.

The expression is used in much the same way in each of the Synoptic Gospels. New Testament scholarship basically agrees that as a christological title, Son of Man in the Synoptic Gospels is related to the following:

1. Jesus' present authority (e.g., Mark 2:10, 28; par. in Matthew and Luke)
2. his suffering and resurrection (e.g., Mark 8:31; 9:9; 10:33; par. in Matthew and Luke)
3. his glorious coming (e.g., Mark 8:38; 13:26; par. in Matthew and Luke)

What is remarkable about the authority sayings is that the Son of Man assumes for himself the authority of God, for example, over the Sabbath, a holy ordination for the people of God. With regard to sufferings, the sayings make it clear that Jesus as the Son of Man comes to serve others and to give his life as a ransom for many. The sayings that refer to the future coming of the Son of Man "in clouds with great power and glory" (Mark 13:26) are associated with his being seated on the right hand of God. Mark 13:26 and 14:62 are clearly reminiscent of Daniel 7:13–14, revealing that the Son of Man of the Gospels identifies himself with the figure presented in Daniel 7. It is also clear that sayings such as Mark 9:12 and 10:45 portray the Son of Man as the "righteous sufferer" of Psalms (e.g., 22; 69) and the Servant of Yahweh (Isa. 52:13–53:12) who suffers but is vindicated by God. It is also notable that when Jesus is identified as "Christ" (e.g., Mark 8:29–30), he responds by speaking of what "the Son of Man" will do (v. 31).

The title Son of Man has a distinctive usage in John's Gospel: It is used with the expression "be lifted up," which may refer either to the cross or to Christ's exaltation (John 3:14; 8:28; 12:34). Perhaps the author preserved the ambiguity on purpose, wanting his readers to make both connections. John also contains the unique sayings about the Son of Man coming down from heaven (3:13) and ascending to where he formerly was (8:28).

Lord

The early Christian confession was "Jesus is Lord" (Rom. 10:9). Surprisingly, this attributes to Jesus the same name that in the Old Testament was applied to God, *kyrios,* "Lord."[8] That was a highly special name, and according to the Jewish historian Josephus, the Jews refused to call the emperor by that name even though the emperor at that time was worshiped as a semi-god. This kind of reverence is the background for the New Testament use of *kyrios* in reference to Jesus.

The term *kyrios* had a wide variety of uses in the New Testament era, both in religious and secular contexts. The mystery religions, especially in the East (Egypt, Syria, Asia Minor, and elsewhere), frequently used the term *kyrios* or its female equivalent, *kyria,* to refer to gods and goddesses such as Isis, Serapis, or Osiris. The Roman emperor, as early as the time of Nero, was also called *kyrios,* with the sense of divinity. Yet even though he was divinized, the emperor was also known to be a human being. It is quite likely that the early church deliberately and polemically ascribed to Jesus titles that had already been applied to the emperor to challenge the people's desire to offer worship to an earthly lord. The lordship of Jesus is also illustrated by the application of the term "slaves" *(doulos)* to Christians, in contrast to the more neutral "servant" *(diakonos)* who, unlike *doulos,* had certain rights and privileges. The task of the slave was to pledge absolute allegiance to the lord; this terminology was common in various Eastern religions to express the relationship of the adherent to the deity.

The most explicit passage in which Jesus applies the title *kyrios* to himself is Mark 12:35–37, which is based on Psalm 110:1: "The LORD says to my Lord: 'Sit at my right hand.'" If this passage is an authentic saying of Jesus, and there is no compelling reason to deny that it is, it means that Jesus considered himself equal to the Old Testament Lord Yahweh; sitting at the right hand is the place of highest status and honor.

8. *Kyrios* is a translation from the Hebrew term YHWH, the tetragrammaton that denotes the name of God. The Hebrew Old Testament was translated into Greek, a translation called the Septuagint, literally "seventy," and abbreviated LXX.

A noteworthy observation about the use of *kyrios* with regard to Jesus in Matthew is that it is only the disciples who use this address; outsiders prefer the neutral term *teacher* or *rabbi*. It took spiritual insight to see who Jesus was. The title Lord was not loosely used.

The main passage in the Pauline corpus is Philippians 2:10–11, which most scholars believe is a pre-Pauline hymn. The passage says that as a result of his obedience to the Father, Christ was granted the title Lord, which implies equality with God.

Other Titles

God. The New Testament was written against the backdrop of the strict monotheism of Israel. Therefore, to call someone other than God God was blasphemous. Yet the New Testament applies the term God to Jesus in instances such as John 1:1, where *Logos,* the "Word," is named God, obviously in reference to Jesus; John 20:28, the confession of Thomas; and Hebrews 1:8. Furthermore, several indirect, functional sayings in the New Testament imply that Jesus is God: He is called the Savior of humanity (Matt. 1:21; Luke 2:11; Acts 4:12; Heb. 2:10); worship is given to Jesus (Rom. 1:23; 1 Cor. 1:2); and Jesus reveals God (John 14:9).

Son of David. When used as a christological title, Son of David points to Jesus as the royal Messiah in the line of David, the premier and foremost king of Israel. In his person and ministry, Jesus fulfills the promises of God given to the Davidic dynasty in the Old Testament (2 Sam. 7:12–16, etc.). Of course, against the popular political expectations, Jesus refused to claim political power; rather, as the Suffering Servant, he laid down his life and died for his people to gain salvation. In comparison to major New Testament christological titles, Son of David is used much less frequently and always in reference to Jesus' earthly life. It appears only eleven times and only in the Synoptics. Matthew uses the title the most, probably because it is important for Matthew to establish Jesus' Davidic lineage (1:1–17).

Logos. This title is the transliteration of a common Greek word that generally means "word," "speech," "story," "principle," perhaps also "wisdom." As a christological title, it occurs only in John, with the main references in the beginning of the Gospel (1:1; 1:14). Several proposals have been made as to the origin and source of the concept. These point to the philosophy of Plato, Hellenism, and the Old Testament concept of the "word" (of God; *davar* means not only "word" but also "action"); no scholarly consensus yet exists. John 1:1 contains an obvious allusion to the beginning of the Old Testament, to the creative word of Yahweh. John says that in the beginning of creation the *Logos* existed. The *Logos* was not only with God but also was God. John

1:14 describes the incarnation of the *Logos.* John also identifies the incarnate *Logos* as the "unique one" of God *(monogenēs theos).*

Having discussed the main christological titles in the New Testament, we turn in the next chapter to the distinctive features of Christology in each of the four Gospels. The main method of current New Testament scholarship and theology is to appreciate the specific contribution of each of the New Testament books in general and the Gospels in particular in order to do justice to the rich pluralism of the biblical witness to Christ. The next chapter follows the order in which scholarship believes the Gospels were written: Mark, Matthew, and Luke, which are the Synoptic Gospels, and then John.

2

Christ in the Gospels

The Suffering Servant in Mark

For centuries, Mark's Gospel, the shortest one, was regarded as not much more than an abridged version of Matthew and Luke. In the twentieth century, however, its own distinctive contribution to the theology and life of Jesus was rediscovered. There is agreement that Mark's Gospel provides the outline for the rest of the Synoptic Gospels and was written first. Therefore, it is an appropriate starting point for a study of the Gospels' Christologies.

The Gospel of Mark presents a fast-paced narrative that begins with the appearance of John the Baptist, the forerunner of Christ, and climaxes in the conflict between Jesus and the religious and political leaders. Characteristic of Mark's narrative, the disciples of Christ consistently fail to acknowledge and recognize the true meaning of their leader.

Mark's Gospel is a narrative, not a theology book in the sense of presenting an orderly system. Consequently, "the Christology of Mark's Gospel is in the story it tells."[1] The story identifies Jesus as the Messiah, the Son of God, whose destiny is to suffer, die, rise from the dead, and return as the glorious Son of Man to gather the elect.

The Christocentrism of Mark comes to focus in the very first sentence: "the beginning of the gospel about Jesus Christ, the Son of God" (1:1). Mark's Gospel is also christologically structured. Jesus' ministry in public

---

1. Frank J. Matera, *New Testament Christology* (Louisville: Westminster, 1999), 24.

30

runs to 8:29, which is the turning point. The latter part focuses on the death of Jesus. The fact that Jesus is God's Anointed One, the Messiah, is confirmed at his baptism with the voice from heaven (1:11). This echo of the coronation psalm (2:7) points to the royal coronation of Jesus as the anointed king. At the same time, the voice from heaven also declares Jesus to be the Suffering Servant whom God equips with the Spirit (Isa. 42:1). The deeds and miracles of the Messiah reveal him as the inaugurator of the kingdom. After the turning point of 8:29, in which Jesus is confessed as the Messiah, the Jewish high priest asks whether he is "the Christ, the Son of the Blessed One" (14:61), and Pilate asks whether he is "the king of the Jews" (15:1).

Mark, more than any other Gospel writer, highlights the role of Jesus as miracle worker and healer. Even in the first three chapters, Jesus appears as exorcist, healer, and overcomer of infirmities that bind people. After he teaches in chapter 4, Jesus continues his ministry of deliverance. In the words of Frank Matera:

> The Messiah is the Spirit-anointed Son of God who proclaims the arrival of God's kingdom in word and deed. He heals the sick, expels demons, and even extends his ministry to Gentiles. Most important, he gives his life as a ransom for the many. Having suffered, died, and risen from the dead, he will return as the glorious Son of Man.[2]

The presence of miracles and wonders in Jesus' ministry, however, is ambiguous. After encountering initial enthusiasm, the Messiah faces increasing opposition. No amount of miracles will stop people, especially the religious leaders, from getting angry at his person and claims. However, this opposition to the Messiah propels the story to the climax that defines the Messiah's identity in Mark.

The defining feature in Mark is that Jesus' identity as Messiah can be clearly understood only in light of the cross. As soon as Peter identifies him as the Messiah (8:29), Jesus announces that the Son of Man must suffer, be killed, and rise again after three days (8:31). The disciples' reaction demonstrates the incongruity of such a fate for the Messiah (8:32), and Jesus rebukes them for it. It comes as no surprise, therefore, that after making several predictions about his impending death, Jesus makes the only explicit affirmation of his identity as the Messiah before the Sanhedrin (14:61–62). It is only after Jesus has explained what kind of Messiah he is that he dares to confess to be the Messiah. The title Messiah, therefore, becomes visible in the latter part of the Gospel, where the shadow of Jesus' approaching death looms over the narrative. In fact, after the opening words of 1:1, *Christos* does not appear in

2. Ibid., 24–25.

Mark until 8:29–30. Thereafter, it is used more frequently, especially with regard to Jesus' approaching clash with the religious leaders and the cross.

Even though the suffering Messiah motif is perhaps the leading idea of Mark, the prominence of the address Son of God is equally important. This expression appears already in the opening clause (although some textual traditions omit it). The theme of identifying Jesus as the Son of God runs through the Gospel: from 1:1, where the author uses the phrase; to 1:11, where the Father calls Jesus "my son"; to 1:24, where the demons use the address; to 15:39, where the Roman centurion makes a confession of faith. In between, significant events, such as the transfiguration (9:7) and Jesus' *abba* prayer of agony in Gethsemane (14:36), confirm this role.

Even though Mark begins his narrative by identifying Jesus as the Son of God and Messiah, Christ, the most frequent designation is Son of Man. Appearing only twice in the first part of the Gospel, it appears no less than thirteen times in the latter. Three times Jesus uses Son of Man to refer to his future coming as the judge (8:38; 13:26; 14:62), and two of these references appear in the context of Jesus' impending death. Five others are also linked in one way or another with passion motifs. Three occur within predictions about his suffering and death (8:31; 9:31; 10:33). It follows, therefore, that the Son of Man references in Mark primarily have to do with suffering and death. Interestingly, however, the title Son of Man also highlights his authority (2:10, 28).

While Jesus is reserved in his use of Christ and Son of God as self-designations, he freely uses the designation Son of Man publicly. Why did Jesus prefer this title, which at best is ambiguous? Perhaps the reason lies in the ambiguity: Jesus did not want his audience to understand his role clearly until he was ready to suffer and die. This brings us to the age-old problem of the "messianic secret." William Wrede, in his epoch-making work *The Messianic Secret,* noted that Jesus forbade several persons and groups to reveal his messianic personhood: demons (1:25), disciples (8:30), and the healed (1:40–45).[3] The reason for this silencing is that Jesus' true messiahship could be understood only in light of the cross. Mark accents Jesus' suffering and death as the essential part of the Messiah's identity. Jesus' silence has nothing to do with a refusal to reveal who he is but with a need to qualify that understanding, which eventually enhances its significance. In other words, it is essential for Mark that people recognize the correct Messiah, since there are several self-appointed Christs—"Look, here is the Christ!"—and many "false Christs" are deceiving people (13:21–22).

Matera summarizes in a helpful way the distinctive Markan picture of Jesus:

3. William Wrede, *The Messianic Secret* (Cambridge: Mowbrays, 1971), 5–7.

For Mark, Jesus is the Messiah, the Son of God, because he fulfills the destiny of the Son of Man. Were Jesus not to fulfill this destiny, he would not be God's messianic Son. Markan Christology, then, can be summarized in the terms "Messiah," "Son of God," "the Son of Man." And yet, none of these can be understood adequately apart from Mark's narrative; for the Christology is in the story, and through the story we learn to interpret the titles.[4]

The King of the Jews in Matthew

Matthew, the first Gospel in the New Testament canon, follows carefully the narrative of Mark. Yet it also presents a highly distinctive theology in general and Christology in particular. While Matthew makes substantial additions to Mark's Gospel, such as the opening genealogy and extensive teaching blocks concerning the kingdom of God (5–7, 10, 13, 18, 24–25), Matthew is faithful to the major themes of Mark's Christology. Matthew presents Jesus as the Messiah, the Son of God, whose fate is the destiny of the Son of Man.

While theologians have put forth several proposals concerning the structure of Matthew's Gospel, most agree that the defining theme is the kingdom of God, for which Matthew prefers the term kingdom of "heaven" in compliance with the Jewish refusal to use God's name. Matthew bases his story mainly on the materials in Mark, incorporating most of Mark and following Mark's order for the most part (when he does not, Luke does). Typical of Matthew's structure is the intertwining of narrative and discourse and its orderly, systematic nature. Matthew is characterized by a Jewish style and material pertinent to Jews.

If Mark is mainly interested in the miracles and deeds of the Messiah, Matthew has an eye on Jesus' teachings. It is in this Gospel that many of Jesus' famous teachings are found, such as the Sermon on the Mount (chaps. 5–7), the demands of discipleship (chap. 10), the parables of the kingdom (chap. 13), his teaching on eschatology (chaps. 24–25), and so on. Jesus' most prominent activity in Matthew's Gospel is teaching. As God's Son, he uniquely knows the Father's will and can reveal it to others (11:25–30). The way Jesus chooses to convey his teachings is mainly in the form of parables, which are meant to hide the "secret" of the kingdom from those who are not yet in the kingdom (13:11). The Sermon on the Mount is a constitution for the kingdom, and the Beatitudes (5:3–12) establish the conditions of entry into the kingdom. Jesus teaches the citizens of the kingdom how to pray to their "Father in heaven"; the theme of "Father in heaven" runs through the sermon (5:16, 45; 6:1, 4, 18; etc.).

4. Matera, *New Testament Christology*, 26.

As the premier Teacher, Jesus reveals God's will in his public ministry, but his teaching and preaching are largely ignored or rejected. It is ironic, therefore, that only non-disciples describe Jesus as teacher (8:19; 9:11; 19:16; etc.). The disciples of Jesus never call him teacher but rather Lord and similar titles. For Matthew, Jesus, the revealer of God's will, is not only a teacher but also a preacher of the gospel of the kingdom of heaven (4:17; 9:35), a message requiring repentance and obedience to God's will. In the tradition of the prophets, Jesus experiences rejection as did the prophets of old (5:10–12; 26:3–5) and John the Baptist (14:1–13).

While it is true that Matthew highlights Jesus' teaching, he does not ignore the deeds of the Messiah. In fact, he records a myriad of healings, exorcisms, and nature miracles (such as walking on the sea and multiplying food). For example, in chapters 8 and 9, he recounts no less than eight healings and several other miracles. With the same kind of authority with which Jesus taught the Sermon on the Mount (chaps. 5–7), he heals and frees people from all kinds of needs. The one powerful in word is also powerful in deed.

The opening of the Gospel shows how the Markan understanding of Jesus as Son of David and Son of God is distinctively influenced by the Torah, the Bible of the Jews and our Old Testament, and by an interaction with Pharisaic Judaism. The infancy narratives (chaps. 1–2) identify Jesus as the Son of David. Matthew establishes not only the Davidic line but also Jesus' link with the whole history of Israel going back to Abraham. The Gospel contains several references to David not found in Mark (9:27; 12:3, 23; 15:22; 20:30–31). The Davidic connection is made most explicit at Jesus' entry into Jerusalem, when Jesus is identified as the king and "Son of David" (21:5, 9, 15). Several aspects of the infancy account, such as the escape to Egypt and the killing of babies (2:13–23), also echo the exodus story of the Old Testament and help create the image of Jesus as a Mosaic figure who will save his people (cf. Exod. 3:10). Like Moses of old, the new Moses teaches on the mountain (chaps. 5–7, the Sermon on the Mount; cf. Exodus 20–24, the giving of the law through Moses on Mount Sinai).

It is no wonder, then, that Matthew emphasizes the fulfillment of the Old Testament. He cites Scripture directly fifty-seven times. From these passages we learn that Jesus is God's Son (2:15; cf. Hosea 11:1), he is a Nazarene (2:23; cf. Judg. 13:5, a person totally devoted to God and God's service), he was born in Bethlehem as a ruler of the people (2:6; cf. Micah 5:2), and so on. He will also proclaim justice to the Gentiles[5] (12:18; cf. Isa. 42:1–4).

The Matthean Jesus, the Son of God, is Immanuel (Hebrew, "God among us"). This line runs through the Gospel. In the infancy narrative, Jesus is identified as "God with us" (1:23), in the promise to the church Jesus promises

---

5. In the biblical language, all non-Jews are Gentiles.

his presence forever (18:20), and the Great Commandment to spread the good news of the kingdom is backed up by the same promise (28:20).

Matthean scholars have taken various approaches to determining the specific shape of his Christology. Many interpreters regard the titles that Matthew ascribes to Jesus as the decisive clues. This approach usually revolves around the centrality of Son of God. Another tradition has argued that while Son of God is a central title, it must be supplemented by additional ideas to achieve a comprehensive and accurate portrayal of Matthew's Christology. Yet another approach highlights the "royal Christology" of Matthew, focusing on Jesus as Messiah King and Son of God. These various emphases need not, of course, be at variance with one another; they may even be complementary to a large extent. What can be said safely is that the royal emphasis is visible in that Matthew wants to introduce his readers, Jews and non-Jews alike, to the Messiah King. This emphasis appears at the beginning of the Gospel when the magi ask about the birth of the "king of the Jews" (2:1–4).

Matthew's main title for Jesus is Messiah; it occurs a number of times (1:1; 2:4; 11:2; 16:16; 27:17; etc.). For the Jews, the term Messiah implies a confession that in Jesus the Old Testament promises of restoration and salvation are coming to pass. The Messiah fulfills the Old Testament in his person and ministry. The Messiah is the new Moses, he brings the fulfillment of the law and prophets (3:15; 5:17–48; etc.), and he is the suffering and rejected Servant of Yahweh (3:17; 8:17; 13:14–15; 23:37; 27:5–10; etc.). In Matthew 8:17, Jesus' healing ministry is seen as a fulfillment of Isaiah 53:4, "He took up our infirmities and carried our sorrows," while in Matthew 12:15–21, Jesus' withdrawal from public attention is understood in light of the first Servant Song, Isaiah 42:1–4.[6]

As the Messiah, Jesus is described at several crucial junctures in the Gospel of Matthew as the Son of God. This title is perhaps even more crucial to the first Gospel than Messiah, yet there is no need to put them at odds with each other. In 3:17, the Father announces publicly his identification of Jesus as "my Son"; in 4:3, the devil addresses Jesus as God's Son; in 11:27, Jesus refers to his special relationship with God as that of a son to a father; in 14:33, the men in the boat confess Jesus as God's Son; and so on. In light of later christological developments, it is interesting to note that even though Matthew connects Jesus' divine sonship to his virginal conception (1:18–25), he does not develop the notion of the divine nature of Jesus. He focuses instead on

6. Four passages in Isaiah 40–55, usually called "Second Isaiah" by scholars (indicating that this part of the book comes from a later period and another hand than the first thirty-nine chapters), are conventionally designated the "Servant Songs" because they together present a distinctive vision of a particular "Servant of Yahweh" or "Suffering Servant" to whom is entrusted a special mission on behalf of his people. This figure has traditionally been identified with Jesus in the New Testament.

more functional aspects of Jesus' sonship. Jesus is God's Son primarily in the sense that he perfectly obeys the will of his Father, especially the will of God that the Messiah must suffer and die.

As the Messiah, Jesus is also the destined king of Israel, though the crucified one. For Matthew, to be the Messiah is to be the king of Israel (2:2; 21:5). But even though Jesus is the king of Israel, he is a unique king because he is God's Son and reigns through his sufferings (27:11).

The title Son of Man occurs often in Matthew, over thirty times, and basically follows the usage of Mark. Matthew emphasizes the role of the Son of Man as the coming Savior and Judge (13:41; 19:28), as well as his eschatological role.

Against the framework of Matthew's Gospel, the centrality of the idea of the kingdom of heaven, Jesus also acts as the inaugurator of the kingdom. This he accomplishes in three moments: in his public ministry, in his passion, and in his vindicating resurrection. After the resurrection, the disciples of Christ are sent into the world to preach the good news of the gospel and to invite all nations to obedience to the master, teacher, and king (28:18–20). This emphasis on the universal scope of Jesus' ministry culminates in the last verses of the Gospel, but it runs through the narrative as a dominant theme, beginning with the visit of the Gentile magi to the newborn king of the Jews in chapter 2.

The Friend of All in Luke

As in Matthew, Markan material serves as the basis for the Gospel of Luke, but Luke arranges and edits it creatively. A basic difference between Luke and the other Synoptic Gospels is that Luke's narrative is divided into two parts: the Gospel and the Book of Acts. Mark, therefore, describes events following Jesus' resurrection to which Mark and Matthew allude but never describe. The Lukan narrator thus extends the story of Jesus by recounting the vital role the risen Lord plays in the life of the early church.

Although Luke writes with Gentiles in view, his two-volume work presents one of the most traditional Christologies of the New Testament. The Gospel of Luke begins with a prologue in which the narrator explains his purpose, namely, to provide his readers with assurance about the events concerning Jesus. The narrator has done a thorough, critical survey of existing materials about Jesus and offers his best account. The manner in which Luke orders the events of his story produces a narrative with a plot that can be summarized as follows:

The Messiah of God comes to his people Israel as the Spirit-anointed Son of God with a gracious offer of salvation: the forgiveness of sins. Despite this gracious offer, Israel does not repent. Nonetheless, its rejection of the Messiah paradoxically fulfills God's plan that the Messiah must suffer in order to enter into his glory so that repentance and forgiveness can be preached in his name to all nations.[7]

Luke structures his Gospel story around two significant phases in the life of Jesus: the Galilean ministry during which Jesus as the anointed Messiah is introduced (4:14–9:50) and the journey of the Messiah to Jerusalem, where he is rejected (9:51–19:44). Luke 9:51 is the crucial turning point in which Jesus turns his face toward Jerusalem to begin his way to the cross, where he will be slain (19:45–24:53).

Jesus and deliverance stand at the center of the divine plan of God. Questions such as Who is Jesus? What does he bring? and How do we know he is God's chosen? are central christological questions for Luke. In the first two introductory chapters, Jesus is introduced as a regal figure. Both the announcement to Mary and the remarks of Zechariah make explicit his Davidic connection (1:31–33, 69). The royal image is enhanced in his kingly entry into the city of David (19:38). Similar to Matthew, Luke also makes explicit the connection between Jesus and the history and hopes of Israel. In 2:25–32, Simeon encounters the "consolation of Israel" and sees his hopes fulfilled. The final Lukan affirmation of Jesus' messiahship appears in 24:26–27 (and 44–47), where the risen Jesus identifies himself as "the Christ," whose sufferings and subsequent glory were predicted in the Old Testament. At the same time, Jesus corrects the earthly expectations of his followers and "opens their minds" to the Old Testament so they can see that Jesus' suffering was predicted (24:27, 45).

The idea of Jesus as a prophet emerges in his inaugural sermon at Nazareth, his hometown (4:16–30). His first sermon is based on the messianic passage of Isaiah 61:1, which talks about the Messiah, the Anointed One, being sent to preach the good news, offer forgiveness, heal the blind, and set captives free. The Old Testament prophets Elijah and Elisha are depicted as parallels to Jesus (4:25–27), and people soon recognize Jesus as a prophet (7:16; 9:7–9, 19). In the tradition of the Old Testament prophets, Jesus the prophet pronounces woes against the scribes (11:47–51) and mourns for Jerusalem (13:34–35). In the conversation on the Emmaus road, the two men connect Jesus' person with the Old Testament prophetic tradition and the law (24:19, 21).

One distinctive feature in Luke's portrait of Jesus is Luke's interest in Jesus' prayer life. Jesus is depicted as praying at every critical turn in his ministry, beginning at his baptism (3:21; see also 6:12; 9:18; 23:46; etc.). In Acts, Jesus' followers pray for guidance and for power (Acts 1:14; 2:42; 10:9; 14:23; etc.).

---

7. Matera, *New Testament Christology*, 51.

Luke applies a rich variety of titles to Jesus that highlight his ministry and personhood: Jesus is Savior (2:11), the Son of David (18:38), and King (19:38). He is the Son of the Father (1:35; 9:35) but also of Adam (3:38). He is compared to Jonah of old and to Solomon (11:29–32). As the Son of Man, he not only suffers and is exalted but also ministers (5:24) and shares the lot of those who are marginalized and outcasts (9:58). Another frequent title is teacher (7:40; 22:11).

Above all, Jesus reaches out to and is a friend of all kinds of people: women, the poor, the sick, the despised, and others who are in danger of being ignored by the religious and political establishment. Jesus' love is universal and all-inclusive. Women especially receive a great deal of attention in this Gospel (7:12, 36–50; 8:40–56; 10:38–42; 13:10–13; 15:8–10; 18:1–8; 21:1–4; 23:55–56).

Jesus as the Son of Man is introduced as early as 5:24, and the title appears frequently in Luke, as it does in Mark and Matthew. Luke highlights the role of the Son of Man in his mission to save the lost (19:10) and to suffer and die for sinners (chap. 24). This theme and Jesus' status as Lord become the focus of dispute later in the Gospel (20:41–44; 22:67–71).

Even though the title Son of God appears quite often in Luke, Jesus' divine sonship receives relatively less attention in Luke than in the other Gospels. Still, Luke establishes the basic contours of Jesus' divine sonship. The fact that Jesus was conceived by the Holy Spirit (1:32–35) forms the basis for Jesus' intimate personal relationship with God, a central theme in this Gospel (2:49; 10:21–22). By having Jesus address God as "Father" on the cross, Luke indicates that even at that point in Jesus' life, his intimate fellowship with God continues unabated (23:34, 46). Furthermore, as the Son of God, Jesus inherits the kingdom that God promised to the Son of David. Also, as the Son of God, Jesus is holy, set apart for the special service of bringing salvation (1:68–69; 19:9–10).

While all the Gospel writers portray the resurrection as the pivotal event of salvation history, only Luke mentions and develops the ascension, an event that for him provides the link between Luke 24 and Acts 1. A risen Savior is one who can both rule and consummate his promise. He is the one who can forgive and signify forgiveness by bestowing blessings (see Acts 2:21; 10:43). Luke sets forth the Abrahamic promise of blessing to the peoples of the earth as realized in Jesus (see Acts 3:22–26). Jesus also fulfills the Davidic hopes (Luke 1:31–33).

Jesus' miracles, indicating the arrival of the new era, also authenticate Jesus' role in the divine plan (7:22; see also Acts 2:22–24). In fact, the scope of Jesus' works of healing shows the breadth of Jesus' authority. He heals those suffering from a flow of blood, a withered hand, blindness, deafness, paralysis, epilepsy, and so on, and he exorcises evil spirits. He even resuscitates the dead and exercises power over nature.

Thus far we have focused on Luke's Christology as it is presented in his Gospel. In his second volume, Luke finishes the christological portrait of Jesus begun in the Gospel by completing themes introduced in the Gospel. For example, at the announcement of Jesus' birth, the angel Gabriel told Mary that God would give her son the throne of David, and he would reign over the house of Jacob forever (1:32–33). At the end of the Gospel, this promise still awaits its fulfillment. But in Acts, readers discover Jesus' messianic enthronement and exaltation at God's right hand. The Gospel focuses on the earthly Jesus, while Acts focuses on the ascended Christ.

The Pentecost speech of Peter in chapter 2 of the Book of Acts shows evidence that Jesus, having been raised from the dead, has been exalted to God's right hand, according to the prophecy of David. Peter's next speech in the following chapter is replete with christological themes: Jesus is God's servant, the holy and just one, the leader of life, the Messiah who has been designated for Israel, the prophet of whom Moses spoke. Those who reject this prophet will be cut off from the restored people of Israel, whereas those who repent will experience the forgiveness of sins and times of refreshment.

The Word of Life in John

> Jesus did many other miraculous signs in the presence of his disciples, which are not recorded in this book. But these are written that you may believe that Jesus is the Christ, the Son of God, and that by believing you may have life in his name.
>
> John 20:30–31

In this passage, the purpose of the fourth Gospel is stated explicitly, and its focus is on Christ and his ministry and significance. That signs should lead to belief and belief to life is clear enough. The ambiguity comes in the precise meaning of the Greek phrase "that you may believe": Does it mean "that you may believe" as a result of conversion, or "that you might go on believing," with reference to those already in the faith. Most commentators opt for the latter, although the two explanations might not be mutually exclusive. Clearly, this Gospel is preeminently a work of Christology since Jesus is the focal point of its many signs and discourses. This Christology goes beyond anything in the Synoptic Gospels. Most notably, John portrays Jesus as the incarnation of God's preexistent Word.

Current scholarship reminds us that the Gospel of John more than likely went through several revisions, for John's writing is a result of decades of reflection on who Jesus is. Because of these successive revisions, the Gospel contains christological strata: For example, it contains traditional Christologies that present Jesus as the expected Messiah and more developed ones that present him as the Son of Man who has descended from heaven. The Christologies are most fully developed in John (cf. Mark) and are almost put in juxtaposition.

John is different from the Synoptic Gospels first in both chronology and geography. In John, Jesus' ministry centers in Judea, not in Galilee, and his ministry lasts three years, not one. Further, in John, Jesus' ministry is intimately connected to the observance of the great pilgrimage feasts of Judaism, and even though Jesus is the Messiah of Israel, there is an irreconcilable conflict between the Jews and Christ. Among many other differences, it is highly significant that the Johannine Jesus does not cast out evil spirits. The number of healings is meager; three altogether and one resuscitation (Lazarus, chap. 11). His actions are called "signs" and have an obvious symbolic importance. The Jesus of the fourth Gospel does not teach in parables; in contrast to the Synoptics, in John, Jesus is a monologist. John records many miracles, but they often differ from those in Mark, Matthew, and Luke. Even the entire structure of the Gospel of John is unique compared to the other Gospels: After the prologue about the Word (1:1–18), the first part, the "Book of Signs" (1:19–12:50), contains miracles and speeches, and the second part, the "Book of Glory" (chaps. 13–20), tells about the farewell speeches of Jesus, his suffering on the cross, and his subsequent resurrection. A later appendix is attached to the Gospel (chap. 21).

John's prologue is unique among the Gospels. Whereas Mark makes no reference to Jesus' earthly beginnings, Matthew and Luke begin with infancy accounts that trace Jesus' origins to Abraham (Matthew) and even to Adam (Luke). John, however, begins by placing Jesus in the very bosom of God (1:1), in eternity. The prologue introduces the main themes about Jesus to be developed during the course of the Gospel such as light, life, truth, and so on. The most distinctive feature is the application of the title *Logos* to Christ, which connects Jesus with both the Old Testament beginning, the Word as creative force in Genesis 1, and with the Greek concept of wisdom. This prologue sets the Jesus story in eternity before the Word was made flesh. Before creation, the Word was already with God. The Word was with God and was God. All things were made through the Word, and the Word was life and light (1:1–5). This *Logos,* who became flesh and dwelt among human beings, was full of grace and truth (1:14). He is unique in that he is the only begotten Son of the Father. In him, and only in him, we see who the Father is (1:18).

From the first chapter on, John begins to compile a list of titles, images, and characterizations of Jesus: the Lamb of God who takes away the sins of the world (1:29, 36), Rabbi (1:38), Messiah (1:41), "the one Moses wrote about in the Law, and about whom the prophets also wrote—Jesus of Nazareth, the son of Joseph" (1:45), Son of God and King of Israel (1:49).

Typical of John is his dual emphasis on the humanity and the divinity of Jesus. John's Gospel is in many ways the most human portrayal of Jesus: Jesus experiences fatigue (4:6) and anguish (12:27); he weeps (11:33) and changes his mind (7:1–10). On the other hand, Jesus is "God's Word," the *Logos*. He speaks as no man has ever spoken (7:46); he is the one who reveals the Father (1:18).

John's Gospel is full of symbolic material and contains much less action than the Synoptics. Almost everything about Jesus is conveyed through images and symbols. Names (1:42), numbers (2:1; 21:11), especially the number seven, which denotes perfection to the Jews, and personality portraits such as that of Nicodemus, who stands for all teachers of the Jews, are symbolic.

A central theme in John's Christology is the intimate relationship between the Father and the Son (chap. 5), and this becomes the central issue in the debate between Jesus and the Jews. The first christological debate is occasioned by a Sabbath healing in Jerusalem when, following that incident, Jesus claims equality with his Father. The narrator makes explicit Jesus' claims of equality with God: The Father has shown him all things and has given him authority to do what God does, even to grant life and to judge. Yet even as an equal, Jesus is totally dependent on the Father (5:30). To honor the Son, whom the Father has sent, is to honor the Father. To Jews, this is a blasphemous claim because it seems to compromise the core of their confession of faith, monotheism. Following the miracle of feeding in chapter 6, Jesus claims to be the bread of life who gives life to the world. His flesh and blood are to be eaten. Jesus goes to the extreme by saying that he was before Abraham, the forefather of faith and of the people of Israel (8:58). After such statements, the opposition grows stronger, and already in chapter 8 people are ready to silence him.

Interestingly enough, even Jesus' death and resurrection are put in ambiguous, mysterious terms: John talks about Jesus "being glorified" (7:39; 8:54; etc.) and "being lifted up" (12:34)—yes, lifted up to the cross but also put down to death, to be raised to life immortal.

It was already mentioned that the Johannine Jesus performs miracles called "signs." Jesus performs seven signs, perhaps corresponding to the seven days of the new creation, and they are carefully timed: In the first part of the Gospel, Jesus' "time has not yet come" (2:4; 7:30; 8:20); then suddenly in 12:23 "the hour has come," and from this point on it is also made clear that the expression refers to the hour of his death.

But the function of the signs is ambiguous to say the least. The more Jesus performs these signs, the more confusion he creates, so that from early on the people start asking, "What miraculous sign can you show us to prove your authority?" (2:18) and "What miraculous sign then will you give that we may see it and believe you?" (6:30). The signs by themselves may fascinate and even lead to superficial assent, but they do not lead to full commitment of faith. This becomes clear to the author, and he quotes the prophet Isaiah (Isa. 6:10), who was also rejected by his people, to make explicit that all Jesus' signs did not lead to belief in him (12:40).

The most distinctive feature of Jesus' self-designation is the list of "I am" sayings, seven altogether, corresponding to the seven signs. The ambiguous "I am" phrase goes back to the self-revelation of Yahweh in the first part of the Old Testament when God names himself "I AM" in response to Moses' request (Exod. 3:14). Each of those sayings is connected to its context, either a sign, a speech, or a feast:

1. "I am the bread of life" (6:35, 48), after multiplying the loaves.
2. "I am the light of the world" (8:12; 9:5), at the Feast of Booths, in which a huge torch is lit to give light; following the feast, Jesus opens the eyes of a man born blind.
3. "I am the gate for the sheep" (10:7).
4. "I am the good shepherd" (10:11).
5. "I am the true vine" (15:1); these three self-designations highlight the importance of the relationship between Jesus and his followers.
6. "I am the resurrection and the life" (11:25), as a response to the sisters of the dead Lazarus, whom Jesus would raise from the dead.
7. "I am the way and the truth and the life. No one comes to the Father except through me" (14:6), in reference to the queries of his disciples, who were confused about Jesus' teaching and future destiny.

In addition to these seven "I am" statements, there are also more mysterious open-ended self-designations without an attribute (4:26; 6:20; etc.); these could be translated in English as "I am he," obviously referring to his divine status as God.

Of all the various titles, images, and symbols applied to Jesus in the Gospel of John, two seem to be the most important: Messiah and Son of God. These are major confessional titles for John. At the beginning of the Gospel, John the Baptist denies he is the Messiah, thereby confirming that Jesus is (1:20). Then Andrew claims to have found the Messiah in Jesus (1:41). Soon after, Jesus names himself the Messiah (4:26), which is extraordinary given that the Synoptics' Jesus is hesitant to do so. As do the other evangelists, John also qualifies his understanding of the Messiah. For John, Jesus is the Messiah because he is the one whom God sent into the world, the Son of Man who came from above, God's Word made flesh.

John contains fewer references to Jesus as the Son of God, but it is another crucial way of identifying Jesus. At the beginning of the Gospel, John testifies that Jesus is the Son of God, and Nathanael confesses, "Rabbi, you are the Son of God" (1:49). In fact, he is "God's one and only Son" (3:18). In 5:25, Son of God appears in a section that otherwise refers to Jesus as "the Son" (5:19, 21, etc.). Speaking of the power the Father has given him, Jesus says that "the dead will hear the voice of the Son of God and those who hear will live" (5:25). Jesus' claim to be God's Son ultimately brings about his death sentence: "We have a law, and according to that law he must die, because he claimed to be the Son of God" (19:7).

The existence of four Gospels in the canon is an everlasting testimony to the richness and legitimate plurality of the biblical picture of Jesus Christ. While they all share a common historical and theological basis, they do not have a forced uniformity. Rather, like a rainbow with many colors, the four Gospels highlight various aspects of the life, death, and resurrection of the One who was and is confessed as Lord and Savior.

3

Pauline Christology

The Shape of Pauline Christology

Readers of the New Testament need to be reminded that although the Synoptic Gospels are the first three writings in the order of the canon, they are not the earliest writings. Ten to fifteen years before the composition of these Gospels, the apostle Paul had already written most, if not all, of his letters. Nevertheless, because the Synoptic Gospels and the Gospel of John offer the most detailed narratives of Jesus' life and ministry, it is appropriate to place them first among the various New Testament writings.

Paul is the premier theologian of the New Testament. Traditionally, all "Pauline" letters were regarded as written by Paul. Current New Testament scholarship agrees that some letters in the Pauline corpus represent the thought forms of Paul's theology but most likely were not written by him. They were perhaps written by his students and younger colleagues. Letters that most scholars consider authentic (meaning they were written by Paul himself) are Romans, 1 and 2 Corinthians, Galatians, Philippians, 1 Thessalonians, and Philemon. A majority of scholars also believes that Colossians and Ephesians were written by Paul, even though Ephesians was most likely a circular letter rather than a letter addressed specifically to the church in Ephesus. The Pastoral Letters (1 and 2 Timothy and Titus) and 2 Thessalonians are regarded as later literary products in the line of Pauline theology.

To do justice to Paul's Christology, one has to take into consideration the special nature of his writings. Paul's writings are letters, epistles, not theological treatises. In fact, all the letters of Paul are pastoral, missionary, and theological responses to existing needs and problems in the young Christian congregations. They are occasional in nature. Paul nowhere presents a systematic Christology or theology, and no one letter can be regarded as a comprehensive presentation.

From what did Paul's Christology stem? On what sources did he base it? These questions shed light on the shape and content of his thinking about Christ. Understandably, several proposals have been presented among scholars. Because Paul was a Jew, even a Jewish Pharisee, a religious teacher, it would be most natural to locate the origin of his Christology in Judaism. However, even though Pauline theology, like the rest of the New Testament, is embedded in Judaism for the simple reason that the Bible of the early church was the Old Testament, the origin of Paul's Christology lies elsewhere. This was the view of the so-called History of Religions School, which maintained that the Christology of Paul stems from ideas in the Greco-Roman world, particularly those found in its various forms of pagan religions. But this proposal has not met with much acceptance either.

There is no doubt that part of Paul's Christology stems from his Judaic background and that he occasionally borrowed from the secular or religious environment of the Greco-Roman world, but these influences do not explain the main roots and origins of Paul's Christology. The most viable origin of Paul's Christology is his conversion experience, his subsequent call, and the early Christian tradition. In his conversion and call to preach the gospel, Paul received what he calls "the gospel of Christ" (Gal. 1:7, 11–23 is the most extensive account of Paul's call and subsequent events). Paul says that "God . . . was pleased to reveal his Son to me" (Gal. 1:15–16). As a result of his conversion and call, Paul learned that Jesus was risen from the dead and exalted at the right hand of the Father. He claims to have seen the risen Lord (1 Cor. 9:1).

In Romans 1:4, Paul testifies that Jesus was vindicated to be the Son of God in power by his resurrection from the dead. Paul argues that while we once viewed Jesus from a purely human point of view, we do so no longer (2 Cor. 5:16). In other words, he and all those "in Christ" now view Jesus as the Son of God. Paul appropriates in his writings early christological confessions, for example, the famous Christ hymn in Philippians 2:5–11. But even the sections in his writings that are not based on previously existing hymns and confessions reveal a Christology growing out of the emerging tradition among the Christian churches.

With that in mind, how should we uncover the Christology that Paul develops in his letters? One standard approach has been to study the titles of

Christ in the same way practiced in the study of the Gospels. Indeed, the titles highlight many important aspects of Paul's Christology, but two points have to be taken into consideration. First, individual titles do not offer a complete picture unless a person relates them to one another and to the whole. Second, Paul is more interested in soteriology, the benefits of salvation, than in titles, and so at best the titles he uses reveal only part of his Christology. Therefore, one could also approach Paul's Christology by examining soteriological concepts, such as sanctification, liberation, and forgiveness, and working backward to the person of Christ. For example, the one who sanctifies is the Holy One. But again, the soteriological concepts must be related to one another to avoid the danger of fragmentation. Yet another approach to Paul's Christology has been a systematization of christological topics, not unlike the method used in systematic theology. Here a danger is also evident: If one regards Paul's occasional pastoral responses as theological treatises, their distinctive nature is not honored.

The preferred approach in current New Testament studies is to appreciate the narrative framework and nature of Paul's letters. Theologians, rather than trying to synthesize Paul's Christology, examine the underlying narrative plot of the letters. This means a careful study of each individual letter in the same way that current Gospel study proceeds. A good case can be made for the claim that for Paul, his own personal story, the story of Israel, and the story of God's saving plan for the world are intertwined with the story of Christ. In other words, this is "the story of God's dealings with Israel and the Gentiles in light of what God has done in his Son, Jesus Christ."[1] Each of Paul's letters offers a distinctive, context-related response to an aspect of this story in light of the needs and problems faced by a young first-century church.

Because various approaches are seldom exclusive of one another but rather complementary, we will first examine the main christological titles in Paul's writings and then will look at the way in which each of his main letters approaches the person and work of Christ.

How Paul Names Christ

Christ/Messiah

Paul's extraordinarily frequent use of the term *Christos* calls for a closer scrutiny. It seems as if Paul often used the term as a second name for Jesus, even though he was no doubt aware of the larger context of the title. Scholarship agrees that Paul frequently used the title because he had received a tradition that associated the term Christ with the core of the early Christian mes-

---

1. Frank J. Matera, *New Testament Christology* (Louisville: Westminster, 1999), 85.

sage: the death and resurrection of Jesus, as 1 Corinthians 15:3–4 mentions (this is one of the oldest pieces in the New Testament). Earlier I mentioned, for example, that the Markan Jesus made it clear that Jesus' messiahship, rather than being political-nationalistic, was that of the suffering and dying One. Now, Paul continues and deepens this tradition, and he tends to mention messianic titles in contexts that speak of death, the cross, and resurrection. *Christ* is a highly theological term for Paul, and he uses it mainly in connection with Jesus' death, resurrection, and *parousia* (the return of Christ). When he talks about salvation, his preferred expression is "in Christ."

The fact that Paul makes frequent use of the term Christ already in his earliest letters points to the fact that this title had already become a virtual name for Jesus and would be recognized as such by the first Christians. In 1 Thessalonians, one of Paul's earliest letters, if not the earliest, Paul speaks of the "Lord Jesus Christ" (1:1), "Christ" (2:6), and "in Christ Jesus" (2:14).

A summary of Paul's theology of Christ can be found in 2 Corinthians 5:14–21, where he presents the divine plan for reconciliation of the world in Christ. Christ is the one who died and was raised so that those whom he redeemed might live for him. Christ is the reconciler of humans and the world to God and of humans to one another. Paul's interest in the death of Jesus as Christ makes him use a daring expression: "Christ crucified" (1 Cor. 1:23). This must have shocked his Jewish listeners for whom the idea of a dead Messiah was virtually inconceivable. Moreover, crucifixion was a punishment reserved for the worst criminals. For Jews, crucifixion also denoted God's curse (Deut. 21:23).

Careful study of the way Paul uses the term Christ reveals that he is thinking less in Old Testament categories of the Messiah as an anointed Davidic King and more in terms of Jesus as a crucified and risen Christ who was exalted at the right hand of God and was given authority over the powers and principalities. Especially in his salutations at the beginning of his letters, Paul exalts Christ to an equal position with the Father, and for Jews this fact must not have been overlooked. Yet Paul is aware of the Old Testament background of the term Messiah and gladly affirms, for example, Jesus' Davidic ancestry (Rom. 1:3). Paul never forgets that Jesus is the Messiah of the Jewish hopes, even though the door to salvation has now been opened to Gentiles. While Paul's use of the title Christ usually refers to Jesus' exalted state, Paul does not ignore the fully human character of Christ (Rom. 5:17–19; 8:3; Phil. 2:7).

The phrase "in Christ" appears over 160 times in Paul's chief letters. This number is remarkable given that the phrase is almost completely absent from the rest of the New Testament. Paul never uses the term Christian; his preferred substitute is "in Christ." A good example of Paul's usage is 2 Corinthians 5:17: "If anyone is in Christ, there is a new creation."[2] Not only individuals but also entire congregations are said to be "in Christ" in the same way they are said to be "in God" (Phil. 1:1; 1 Thess. 1:1). Paul also says that Christ is in the believer (Gal. 2:20) but does so rarely.

Ephesians and Colossians contain the idea of the "mystery of Christ," revealing a further development of Paul's understanding of Christ. This mystery is that God in Christ has provided salvation and reconciliation for all people, Jews and Gentiles alike, and even for the entire cosmos. The cosmic orientation of Paul's Christology becomes visible in his focus on the ongoing rule of the exalted Christ. Christ is not only the Savior of individuals but also a cosmic ruler. According to Ephesians 1:22, Christ rules over the cosmos for the church, and in Ephesians 5:23, the mystery relates to the relationship between Christ and his church.

Lord

In the New Testament, the Greek term *kyrios* is usually translated "Lord," which in the Septuagint (the Greek translation of the Hebrew Old Testament) is the standard name for God. "The Lord" is a major christological title used by Paul. The early Christian tradition used the term Lord in reference to Jesus; therefore, Paul uses it frequently without any explanation, assuming that his readers are already familiar with it.

Sometimes Paul applies to Christ Old Testament passages that originally quite clearly referred to Yahweh (e.g., Rom. 10:13; Joel 2:32). In other words, Paul equates the Old Testament God and Jesus. Often the title Lord appears in creedal passages, that is, passages reflecting early expressions of Christian faith in Christ. An example of a creedal statement is 1 Corinthians 12:3, which argues that only by the Holy Spirit can one confess that "Jesus is Lord."

Quite often Paul uses the title Lord in fixed formulas referring to Christ, such as "Jesus Christ our Lord" (e.g., Rom. 1:4), "our Lord Jesus Christ" (e.g., Rom. 5:1), "the Lord Jesus" (e.g., Rom. 14:14), and so on. Paul also frequently uses *kyrios* alone as the designation for Jesus: simply "the Lord" (e.g., Rom. 14:6).

As with any other title, the Lord is also often used in particular contexts. Three are most important: in parenetic passages in which Paul admonishes and encourages the believers (e.g., Rom. 14:1–12), in eschatological passages that are linked to the hope of the return of Christ (e.g., 1 Thess. 4:15–17), and in liturgical contexts that highlight the worship life of the church (e.g., the Lord's Supper, 1 Cor. 11:20).

---

2. This translation is currently accepted by a majority of scholars, but the older rendering, "If anyone is in Christ, that person is a new creation," also has good attestation.

Son of God

The divine sonship of Jesus is a major component of Paul's Christology even though the term Son of God is overshadowed by the terms Lord and Christ. Son of God appears less than twenty times in the Pauline corpus, and even then most occurrences use the form "his Son" (e.g., Rom. 1:3). Most of the references are in Romans and Galatians.

Even though the term Son of God conveys the idea of divine sonship, essentially it communicates Jesus' unique status and intimate relationship with God; neither in the Old Testament nor in Paul's writings (in contrast to John) does the title Son necessarily mean divinity. Son primarily means a special standing, status, and favor with God. Clearly for Paul, though, Jesus as God's Son participates in God's attributes and roles. He shares in the divine glory and, most importantly, is worthy to receive veneration with God in the churches.

In several passages, Paul portrays Jesus as having a royal role and status. He does so by drawing on Old Testament Davidic traditions and applying them to Jesus as the royal messianic Son. Romans 1:3–4, for example, is based on the promises made to King David in 2 Samuel 7:12–14. In addition to its royal connotation, the title Son also refers to the cross: The sacrificial Son is destined to die for others (Rom. 8:32). This reference is based on the typology of Isaac in Genesis 22, where Abraham is asked by God to offer Isaac, his only son, as a sacrifice to the Lord.

Last Adam

In two passages, Romans 5 and 1 Corinthians 15, Paul draws an analogy between Adam and Christ. Here Adam, rather than being an individual, is a typological or figurative character set over against Jesus Christ. First Corinthians 15 is a discussion of the resurrection of the dead in which Paul explains the meaning of Christ's resurrection for the hope of the resurrection of the believer. "For since death came through a man [Adam], the resurrection of the dead comes also through a man [Jesus]. For as in Adam all die, so in Christ all will be made alive" (1 Cor. 15:21–22). The other context, Romans 5, relates to Paul's exposition of the origin of sin on the basis of Genesis 3. Adam's disobedience is set in antithesis with the obedience of Jesus as the last Adam, who reversed the fate of sin and death.

Savior

Of the twenty-four New Testament occurrences of the term Savior, one half can be found in the Pauline tradition, almost all in the Pastorals. There are two occurrences in other Pauline letters (Eph. 5:23; Phil. 3:20). The frequent usage of the term Savior implies that Paul shifted focus from Jesus' earthly ministry to his death, resurrection, and current rule at the right hand of the Father. While for Paul, Jesus' teaching and ministry are not insignificant, with the rest of the New Testament writers, he comes to major in the soteriological significance of Jesus Christ.

The Story of Christ in Paul's Letters

Jesus as the Soon-Coming Lord: 1 and 2 Thessalonians

First Thessalonians is a pastoral letter of exhortation to a Gentile Christian community facing affliction and perhaps persecution. The second letter, whether from Paul himself or from a later disciple, continues to offer encouragement and hope in light of the second coming of Christ. The Thessalonian correspondence has little to say about the earthly story of Jesus; it focuses on the end of the story, namely the *parousia,* the coming of the Lord as eschatological Savior and Judge to rescue his people. Clearly, the story of the church, as it turned away from idols to worship the true God and to wait for the return of his Son from heaven (1 Thess. 1:9–10), is associated with the story of Israel as an elected community (1:4–5; 2:11–12; 5:9). Jesus, like the prophets of the Old Testament, is presented as a model of victorious suffering. Jesus' own suffering on the cross and his subsequent resurrection as vindication from the Father lay the foundation for the future hope of resurrection for the afflicted Christians. On the basis of this hope comes an urgent call to a life of holiness (4:1–9).

Paul clearly is familiar with the major titles of Christ, such as Messiah/Christ and Son of God, but he does not offer a significant exposition of them. His preferred term here is the Lord, for Jesus is seen here in his dual role as the eschatological Judge (especially 2 Thessalonians) and Savior. The Lord Jesus Christ is elevated at the right hand of God in the heavens and will return soon to take up the believers, both those who have died in Christ and those currently living, to be with him eternally.

Though the Thessalonian correspondence does not provide a complete Christology, it is an overture to a Christology that Paul develops more fully in other writings.

Jesus as the Wisdom of God: 1 Corinthians

Both letters to the church at Corinth are christologically pregnant pastoral responses to a charismatic church. Paul's focus in the first letter is on the cross of Christ as the criterion for a balanced spirituality and theology. It is here that we find Paul's only exposition of the Eucharist, which Jesus instituted as a memorial of his death (11:23–26). In chapter 15, Paul records the early Christian creed he had received: Jesus Christ died for our sins, was buried, was raised on the third day, and appeared to numerous witnesses. His resurrection is the basis not only for our resurrection but also for Christian faith in general: If Christ had not been resurrected, our faith would be in vain. Jesus' resurrection is also the pledge of his second coming. In several places, 1 Corinthians also expands on the idea of Christ's preexistence (8:6; 10:4, 9). In sum, this book contains some of the key elements of the christological doctrine developed in subsequent creeds and formulations of the first centuries: Jesus' preexistence, death, resurrection, and second coming.

First Corinthians is a pastoral response to issues of church division. To combat the problem, Paul holds up to the Corinthians a view of Christ as the embodiment of God's wisdom. The Corinthians were boasting about their own wisdom *(logos)*, but Paul underlines the special nature of Christ's wisdom, namely, the cross. Only the crucified Christ, a "stumbling block," qualifies as true wisdom and God's power in weakness (1:23–24). In fact, the cross of Christ is the focus of Paul's preaching and faith (1:17). This wisdom, hidden from human wisdom, is found in Christ (2:1–9). By virtue of the cross, Christ is not only our wisdom but also our righteousness, holiness, and redemption (1:30).

In addition to the motif of wisdom Christology, Paul makes several other interesting allusions in 1 Corinthians, all of which elaborate his Christology: Christ as the rock of the Moses story from which the people drank in the wilderness (10:4); Christ as the last Adam who has reversed the fate of condemnation (15:20–49); and Christ as the Passover lamb (5:7).

Jesus as the Reconciler: 2 Corinthians

When Paul writes his second letter to the church at Corinth, the problem of division is less critical, and Paul has a chance to give an exposition of his gospel and his apostolate. Again, Paul goes back to the Old Testament and compares his mission with the calling of Moses. Recounting the story of Moses' veil in chapter 3 (see Exod. 34:29–35) and the covenant between Israel and Yahweh, Paul argues that in Christ a new spiritual covenant has been made and that he has been appointed as minister of that covenant. Christ, the mediator of this new covenant, is the "glory of God." In the Old Testament, whenever God manifested himself in a special way, he was described as "glory" (2 Cor. 4:6). (See, for example, the dedication of the Solomonic temple in 1 Kings 8.) For Paul, Christ likewise is "the Lord of glory" (1 Cor. 2:8). All who behold Christ are transformed "from glory to glory" into the same image (2 Cor. 3:18). In 2 Corinthians, Paul also calls Christ the image of God (4:4) and relates the light of Christ that shone into his heart on the road to Damascus to the light of God that shone at the creation of the world (4:6).

The focus of this letter, as in much of Paul's theology in general, is the exposition of the role of Christ as the agent of reconciliation. In Christ, God has reconciled the world to himself, the world that because of sin was in enmity with God, so that we may become the righteousness of God; Christ not only bore our sin but was "made sin" for our sakes (5:17–21). This pattern of reconciliation is depicted as the model for overcoming divisions in the church (6:1–9).

Jesus as Our Faithfulness: Galatians

The pastoral issue in Galatians is faith in Christ vis-à-vis the Jewish faith. Though faith in Christ, the Jewish Messiah, is based on the Old Testament, it also surpasses and qualifies it. Religiously and socially, the Christian churches were called to live a life free from the prescriptions of the Mosaic law.

Paul's christological emphasis once again is on the death of Christ (see the strong appeal in 3:1), but Paul's focus is distinctive in light of the pastoral challenge: How do Gentile Christians share in the covenant promises given to Abraham, the father of Israel? Paul is always a contextual theologian. For example, when addressing the Corinthians and their question about resurrection, he drew an analogy between Adam, the first human being, and Christ, because this Gentile audience would more readily connect with this Old Testament figure. Here in Galatians, a reference to Abraham is appropriate because Abraham was the father of Israel and their faith, and the Galatians sought to identify with this Jewish patriarch. Paul's christological emphasis is also shown in the fact that while he is not indifferent to future hope (see 5:5, 21), he says next to nothing about the *parousia* but rather delves into the cross of Christ.

Paul's argument is based on the story of Israel (chaps. 3–4). To prepare his listeners for a reading of Israel's story through the lens of Christ, he asks why Christ died if righteousness could be attained through the law (2:21). Now that Jesus, who was also born "under law" (4:4), has offered himself freely for our sins, salvation is attainable only through faith in him. Paul also reminds his readers that it is only in and through Christ that the original promise of blessing to all nations given to Abraham (Genesis 12 and 15) comes to fulfillment, since Christ has reversed the curse of the law, changing it into blessing (3:13–14).

The juxtaposition of justification by faith with that of works comes to a sharp focus in 2:15–21, especially in 2:16 (NRSV):

> Yet we know that a person is justified not by the works of the law but through the faith of Jesus Christ. And we have come to believe in Christ Jesus, so that we might be justified by the faith of Christ, and not by doing the works of the law, because no one will be justified by the works of the law.

The translation given here is the alternative reading found in the footnote of the NRSV: "the faith of Christ" instead of "faith in Christ," to show that the passage emphasizes that it is by virtue of the faith and faithfulness of Christ that believers are justified (in Greek, *pistos* has both of these meanings: "faith," "faithfulness"). While "faith in Christ" is the medium for receiving salvation, the basis is the covenant-faithfulness of the author of salvation. This interpretation is gaining more and more support among New Testament scholars.

Thus, Paul highlights here the all-important significance of Christ's story for the salvation of not only the people of Israel, to whom the promise of blessing was given in the beginning of their history, but also all nations of the world.

Jesus as Our Righteousness: Romans

Romans is a missionary letter from Paul to the congregation at Rome, whom Paul did not know personally but whose support he was seeking in order to extend his missionary endeavors. To substantiate his appeal, he offers the most detailed exposition of his theology and Christology; this was possible because Paul was not combating an urgent pastoral need in the congregation.

To put Christ's work on the cross in the correct perspective, Paul shows the hopelessness of the human situation—both for Jews and for Gentiles—as a result of sin (chaps. 1–3). In fact, so hopeless is their condition that death is the only expected result (chap. 5). As a response, he offers the cross of Christ as the only basis of justification (3:21–31). Taking once again the story of Abraham as his paradigm, he argues on the basis of Christ's story that even Abraham's faith was oriented to and fulfilled in the coming of Christ (chap. 4). Christ has become the end (the Greek term *telos* also means "goal") of the law and has opened up the doors for the salvation of Gentiles (10:4). Yet the story of Israel is not forgotten; in a masterful way, Paul relates the story of Gentiles and the story of Israel in light of Christ's story (chaps. 9–11).

In chapters 6–8, Paul gives further exposition of the possibility of life based on faith in Christ. Whatever the meaning of the highly disputed chapter 7—whether Paul is recounting his story before or after conversion—it is clear that only on the basis of the faithfulness of Christ have the demands of the law been met. In chapter 8, Paul also develops the importance of the role of the Holy Spirit with regard to salvation and spiritual life. This is one of the main sources for a Christology that recently has come to be known as Spirit Christology. (This will be discussed in part 3.)

The Christ story of Romans is both similar to stories in other major letters of Paul and an expansion on them. As in Galatians, questions about righteousness and the law play a crucial role, but whereas the underlying story of Galatians moves from Abraham to Christ, that of Romans is more universal in scope, beginning with Adam (as in 1 Corinthians 15) and moving to

Christ. In all these stories, however, the death and resurrection serve as the focal point.

Jesus as Humble Servant: Philippians

Often the Christology of Philippians is viewed only through the lens of the Christ hymn in 2:5–11, a liturgical text Paul gleaned from the Christian tradition and applied to his doctrine of Christ. No doubt, it is one of the main passages, if not the main passage, in Paul's writings that talks about Christ's preexistence, incarnation, death, resurrection, and exaltation. But this is not all that Philippians says about Christ.

Philippians is a friendly letter of encouragement written from prison to a church Paul had founded. The main purposes of the letter are to admonish the Philippians to carry on with their lives in a way worthy of the gospel of Christ, to further the proclamation of the gospel, and to thank the Philippians for their gift to him. There is little doctrinal or theological discussion apart from the Christ hymn; still, the book provides a fruitful pastoral exposition of Christology.

In the beginning of the letter, Paul locates the position of Christians in Christ, by virtue of which they are called "saints," not necessarily in the sense of being more pious than others but rather in the sense of being receivers of Christ's holiness (1:1–2). In light of the coming *parousia,* "the day of Christ" (analogous to the preferred Old Testament eschatological expression "the Day of the Lord"), Paul reassures the Philippians of the certainty of their salvation (1:6). Already at the beginning of the letter, the story of these Christians is included in the larger story of Israel and the nations in light of Christ's story:

> Through Christ, God began the work of establishing the Philippians in righteousness, consecrating them to himself as he did Israel of old. But this work will only be completed by God at Christ's parousia. In the meantime, the sanctified Philippians must prepare themselves for that day so that they can stand pure and blameless. The primary actor of this story is God who is Father; the agent of salvation is Jesus Christ who is Lord; and the beneficiaries are Gentiles such as the Philippians who have been granted an elected status formerly reserved for Israel of old.[3]

Paul's own story is linked to that of Christ; Christ is his life and death (1:21). His death and resurrection are part of Christ's (3:9–11), and knowledge of Christ is the highest goal of his life. Therefore, he is ready to forsake everything for Christ's sake (3:7–8).

3. Matera, *New Testament Christology,* 121.

It cannot be mentioned too often that in all his writings, Paul, the theologian, is first and foremost a pastor. Even the Christ hymn in 2:5–11 stands in the middle of a parenetic section in which the apostle urges believers to shape their lives according to the mind of Christ (2:5). Whatever the origin of the hymn and whatever the nuances of translation about which scholarly debate continues, this hymn should be read primarily in its present form and context in Philippians. The text falls into two sections: Verses 6–8 provide the narrative focus on the humility of Christ, while verses 9–11 explain how God vindicated Christ because of his obedience. Christ humbled himself and, unlike the first Adam (Paul does not refer here to Adam by name, but the reference is implied), who wanted to be equal to God, "emptied" himself. For centuries, *kenōsis* Christology (from the Greek term *kenōsis,* "emptying") has maintained that as a result of this emptying, Christ divested himself of divine prerogatives so that he no longer enjoyed divine status. This is probably not what Paul means, since such a meaning would sever the relationship between the preexistent and the incarnate Christ. What Paul means, rather, is that Christ did not take advantage of his divine status but rather was content to be in human form, to the point of surrendering himself to death on the cross. The first point of the text, then, talks about a preexistent being who had divine status and enjoyed equality with God. Nonetheless, he did not take advantage of his divine status but took on the status of a humble servant. This kind of humble attitude is an example to Christians, who are called to consider others higher than themselves (2:1–4).

The second part of the hymn (2:9–11) shows that on the basis of his obedience, Jesus was exalted by God and was given a name above every other name, *kyrios,* the Lord. Allusion to Isaiah 45:22–23, one of the strongest claims for monotheism in the Old Testament ("For I am God, and there is no other. . . . Before me every knee will bow; by me every tongue will swear"), shows that for Paul the resurrected and exalted Christ enjoys the same status as the God of Israel. But it is important to note that this Lord is Jesus: If Lord refers to his status as God after resurrection and exaltation, Jesus, his earthly incarnate name, reminds us that he was Lord even from eternity. The fact that Paul is able to call "Jesus" the Lord means that Jesus is the Lord not only by virtue of his death and resurrection; he was Lord before these events. If that is the case, to avoid adoptionism, one must believe that Jesus shared in the divinity (lordship) of the Godhead before his incarnation, that is, from eternity. Scholarship debates this crucial christological issue, but in my judgment, for Paul the issue was settled.

Jesus as the Embodiment of Fullness: Colossians

According to Colossians, "Christ is all, and is in all" (3:11). Famous is the comment of J. B. Lightfoot, the great New Testament theologian of the nineteenth century: "The doctrine of the Person of Christ is here [in Colossians] stated with greater precision and fullness than in any other of St. Paul's epistles."[4] While for most current New Testament scholars this is an overstatement, most agree that Christology plays a vital role in this prison epistle. The hymnic passage of 1:15–20 especially has received a great deal of attention. It talks about Christ as the one in, through, and for whom all things were created and reconciled. Many scholars wonder if an older liturgical hymn is behind this passage, as in the case of the Christ hymn of Philippians 2. The concern in Paul's mind is that the believers at Colossae were in danger of resorting to human wisdom and traditions (2:6–23) that were less than perfect foundations when compared to the fullness in Christ (2:1–5).

The basis of Christ's story in Colossians is the transfer of believers from "the dominion of darkness" into "the kingdom of the Son he loves" (1:13). In the past, people were enemies of God; now in God's Son they have been reconciled to him (1:21–22). The one who administered the reconciliation is seated at God's right hand and rules over the kingdom of God (1:13; 3:1). While the story of Israel is not explicit in Colossians, there are several hints that Israel's and the church's stories are intertwined. For example, Paul regards the Christians as the true circumcision of Christ (2:11); circumcision (instituted in Genesis 17) was the sign of the covenant between Yahweh and Israel.

The hymnic passage in 1:15–20 has two parts. Verses 15–18a tell us that Christ is the image of the unseen God and the beginning of all creation because all things were created in him. Christ is also the head of the church. Verses 1:18b–20 identify Christ as the origin (the Greek term *archē* also means "beginning") of everything, visible and invisible, and the firstborn from the dead in whom the fullness of God dwells. Through Christ's blood, God reconciled the world, the entire universe, to himself. This hymn, therefore, associates Christ with creation, preservation, redemption, the church, and the entire purpose of the world. Even though scholarship is not unanimous, it also seems that Christ's preexistence is affirmed here; how else could Christ be the origin, instrument, and goal of creation? Still, the word *firstborn* has presented difficulties for christological interpretation because it may be interpreted in a way that makes Christ less than God, in other words, a first creature. This passage, among others, has given rise to unorthodox or heretical interpretations such as Arianism, which will be discussed in a later chapter. One way of dealing with passages such as this is to recognize that the Bible often uses metaphorical language to describe the way God interacts with the world, and we cannot interpret them too literally.

One of the most distinctive christological claims in Colossians is found in 2:6–23, where Paul intends to show the inadequacy of all human wisdom and traditions in light of the fullness of Christ. Paul states that "in Christ the full-

4. J. B. Lightfoot, *Saint Paul's Epistles to the Colossians and Philemon* (London: Macmillan, 1879), 122.

ness of the Deity lives in bodily form" (2:9; see also 1:19); not only in his state of exaltation but also in his incarnation, Christ represented divine fullness.

Therefore, Colossians expands considerably Paul's Christology in that even creation is subsumed under christological categories. In a sense, Paul pushes the christological boundaries beyond the question of individual salvation or even the salvation of Israel and the nations to the final consummation and purpose of everything that exists, unseen powers included. This cosmic orientation of Christology and soteriology is not unusual for Paul, but it is less visible elsewhere, except for Ephesians and Romans 8. It can also be found in the Book of Hebrews (the opening verses).

Jesus as Mystery: Ephesians

Ephesians' origin, authorship, and other background issues have been debated, as has its theology, especially whether it represents authentic Pauline theology or is a later development that goes beyond Paul. The following discussion follows the mainline scholarly judgment and treats the letter as belonging within the sphere of Pauline theology.

The most distinctive feature of the Christology of Ephesians is that it is closely linked to ecclesiology. Paul's view of the church here is that of a new humanity, composed of Jews and Gentiles alike (2:11–22), which is in the process of growing into "the fullness of Christ" (4:13).

The Christ story in Ephesians begins with an expanded story of blessing that can be found in Christ; this blessing is constructed along the lines of the Jewish *berakhah,* a liturgical act in which one praises God for all his goodness and gifts. The blessing Paul is talking about comes "in Christ" (1:3); out of that flow all the various facets of the blessing, such as election (1:4), grace and forgiveness (1:6), and redemption through his blood (in other words, the cross) (1:7). Furthermore, true knowledge and wisdom are found in Christ, as is adoption as God's children (1:9–12). This mystery of salvation has now been disclosed to the elect; for others it is still unknown (1:9–10). So comprehensive is Paul's understanding about Christ and the salvation he accomplished that he uses this unique expression: God's plan of salvation is "summed up" (or gathered) in Christ (1:10), an expression that occurs only one other time in the New Testament (Rom. 13:9). A similar comprehensive term appears in Ephesians 2:14, where Christ is called our "peace"; Christ not only brings peace but *is* peace in his person. This saying perhaps goes back to the Old Testament concept of *shalom,* which means not merely peace but wholeness, happiness, and well-being.

In a remarkable prayer at the end of the first chapter, Paul expands on the role of Christ "in the heavenlies." He talks about Christ being raised from the dead and seated at the right hand of God, "far above all rule and authority, power and dominion, and every title that can be given" both in this age and the age to come. Christ has been put in charge and has authority over everything, including the church (1:20–23). Reference to Christ's dominion includes the cosmic victory of all resisting spiritual powers (see also 2:1–2).

As already mentioned, the integral relationship in Ephesians is between Christology and ecclesiology. In 1:21–22, Paul makes this connection clear. According to this passage, the enthroned Christ is the head of the church, which is his body. As the body of Christ, the church has been filled by Christ, who is filling all things in creation and the universe. Whereas elsewhere Paul talks about the church as the body of Christ in reference to the head (Christ) and members (Christians) and the relationship between the members (Rom. 12:4–5; 1 Cor. 12:26), in Ephesians and Colossians, he refers to its cosmic and corporate dimensions.

In Ephesians, Paul writes more about the mystery of Christ that has been hidden for ages and has now been revealed to Paul and through him to other Christians. This mystery is that the Gentiles have become fellow heirs of the promises of the gospel (3:6). As a result, God has effected in Christ a reconciliation, the eradication of enmity between God and human beings, and also between the two alienated groups of people, namely, the Jews and the Gentiles. These two groups now form a new person in Christ (2:15).

Summing Up Pauline Christology

An examination of the major letters of Paul with regard to his understanding of Christology reveals that in his pastoral responses to existing church and mission needs, he argues from a christological foundation. Each letter, read in its own unique context, sheds light on his emerging understanding of Christ. The main features of Pauline Christology may be summarized as follows:

1. Paul's main focus is on the salvation brought about by Christ; therefore, he focuses on the cross, resurrection, and *parousia* of Christ.
2. Paul believes in the preexistence of Christ.
3. In his later writings, Paul's perspective widens beyond individual salvation and the salvation and union of Jews and Gentiles to encompass cosmic and corporate aspects.
4. For Paul, Christ's person and work represent the origin and goal not only of human life but also of creation, including all the spiritual powers.
5. Paul clearly regards Christ both as a real human being (incarnation), even though he rarely discusses the earthly life of Jesus, and as a divine being.

It was up to the early church to put these various christological perspectives together. This is the topic of part 2.

Part 2

Christ in History

The second part of this book delves into the question of how the christological tradition emerged and developed over time. This survey of history, however, is not meant to be comprehensive but selective. Two main topics from two time periods will be examined in some detail.

The first topic focuses on christological developments during the first five centuries of the church, the time during which the canon was emerging. During this time, the main questions that have to do with the person and work of Jesus Christ were raised and various foundational answers were offered, though these answers were not final in status. Still, all later developments of Christology, those of our time included, need to take stock of the answers offered during the first five centuries.

The second topic is the quest of the historical Jesus, which began in the eighteenth century and eventually, as a result of the Enlightenment and other worldview changes, changed the entire course of interpreting Jesus. The Enlightenment was a watershed for Christian theology—and for the intellectual milieu of the West. On the eve of modernism, nothing was left untouched by the new philosophical and scientific developments. Therefore, to gain perspective on current thinking concerning Jesus Christ, knowledge of this background is absolutely necessary.

4

Early Christological Disputes

What Was at Stake in the Historical Disputes?

Often, beginning students of theology are tempted to ask two legitimate questions: Why should we bother ourselves with an antiquarian discussion of christological issues of the past that seem irrelevant to our current concerns? And what is the point of these finely nuanced disputes—what difference do they make after all? One may also wonder why the church ever entered into disputes surrounding, for example, conceptual distinctions between Christ's divinity and his humanity. Why didn't it just stick with the Bible?

It belongs to the essence of faith and worldviews in general that we often simply accept the tenets of our faith or worldview without much explicit reflection on them. But we also have a built-in need to make sense of what we believe. Therefore, it is most natural that as the church began to establish itself and its distinctive identity apart from Judaism, out of which it arose, Christians began to ask doctrinal questions: Who is this Jesus after all? What is the nature of the salvation he claims to have brought about? How is he different from us, and how is he similar to us?

When questions such as these were asked, Christians naturally went first to the Bible. After all, the Bible was the accepted book of the church. But the New Testament did not yet exist (not until the fourth century were its contents finally ratified), even though Paul's and other Christian leaders' writings began to circulate soon after the death and resurrection of Jesus Christ. Very soon, these writings and written sermons (the Book of Hebrews and

1 Peter, for example, were both originally sermons) were given high regard, but even these writings did not address all the questions, especially those having to do with the exact natures of Christ's divinity and humanity and their relationship.

Thinking about Christ developed in various quarters of the expanding church parallel to the establishment of the New Testament. It is significant to note that the christological developments of the first five centuries—the topic that forms the first section of part 2—do not differ from the biblical Christologies. Though the Christian church gives the New Testament canon a higher status than the Christian tradition of the first five centuries, we need to remind ourselves that those who lived close to New Testament times were in a good position to offer a definitive interpretation of the Christ event.

Among theologians there have been differing assessments concerning the development of classical christological dogma as it has come to be expressed, for example, in creeds. Some consider the dogmatic development an aberration that replaced New Testament Christology with philosophical reflection on the person and natures of Christ. Those with this perspective have rejected the Christology of the patristic period, seeing it as a Hellenization of Christianity in which Greek metaphysical speculation supplanted the biblical historical mode of thought. The great historian of theology Adolf von Harnack expressed this view clearly in his celebrated *What Is Christianity?*[1] He regarded the development of dogma as a deterioration and a deviation from the simple message of Jesus of Nazareth. Many others have concurred.

Contrary to this position is a conception that has been called the dogmatic approach to Christology. According to this view, the development of christological dogma moved from the more functional Christology (what Christ has accomplished for us, i.e., the concerns of salvation) of the New Testament to the more ontological thought (Christ in himself, i.e., the concerns of the person of Christ) of the creeds, and this movement was progress. Theologians of this persuasion believe this kind of development in thinking was both helpful and necessary and therefore welcome the more philosophical approach of the creeds.

Yet another position judges the early councils' doctrine to be a true expression of the reality of Christ but nonetheless finds the development of dogma marked by a gradual narrowing of the questions. For example, while the questions surrounding Christ's divinity and humanity are to be taken seriously, even nowadays, they are not the only questions to be considered, perhaps not even the most crucial ones. Thus, while these early developments were legitimate against their own background, they are neither exhaustive nor final formulations. Each age has to wrestle afresh with these issues and provide its own

1. Adolf von Harnack, *What Is Christianity?* (1900; reprint, Philadelphia: Fortress, 1957).

answers, even though building critically on tradition. This last view seems to be the most coherent one, and a majority of theologians have embraced it.

This brings us once again to the relevance of these questions for our own needs and contexts. Nowadays, we hear so much about the need for theology to be contextual, to relate to the questions that arise in a particular context. We have to understand that, in fact, these early christological disputes were in themselves contextual responses to the culture of the day, the Greek/Hellenistic culture, which was philosophically and conceptually oriented, in contrast to the Hebrew/Judaic culture, which was less philosophical and more holistic in its approach to divine things. Early Christian thinkers attempted to express christological convictions based on the testimony of the Old Testament and emerging Christian writings in thought forms that would be understandable even to educated people of the time.

The questions we bring to Christology today are vastly different from the questions of the early centuries; yet we also keep asking the same questions: Who is this Jesus? How does his humanity make sense in the third millennium? What does it mean to believe in this divine Savior? We also ask questions such as, How do men and women together confess their faith in Christ? If Christ is male, is his maleness exclusive of motherhood and feminism? How does the idea of Christ as the Liberator relate to social injustice? How do we understand creation and the world process in light of Christ being the origin and goal of creation? These questions and many others are still related to those tentative, sometimes conflicting, answers our fathers and mothers in faith proposed.

Was Jesus a Real Human Being?

Ironically enough, one of the main debates concerning Christ in the New Testament was the question of his humanity. In the Johannine community, belief in Christ's humanity became the criterion for true orthodoxy, as is evident in 1 John 4:2–3: "This is how you can recognize the Spirit of God: Every spirit that acknowledges that Jesus Christ has come in the flesh is from God, but every spirit that does not acknowledge Jesus is not from God." It seems that the fact of Jesus' divinity had been settled among Johannine Christians, but the Christians to whom John wrote still struggled with Christ's true humanity and the seeming incompatibility between his divinity and his humanity.

In the second century, the christological debate centered on the question of the divinity of Christ; most early church fathers took it for granted that Christ was human. What required explanation was how he differed from other human beings. In this discussion, the Johannine concept of *Logos* was introduced, and its implications for a more developed Christology were considered.

Two heretical views concerning the specific nature of Christ's humanity were rejected. Both of these views, Ebionitism and Docetism, were attempts to define Jesus' humanity in a way that did not compromise his divinity.

Ebionitism

Ebionites (from the Hebrew term that means "the poor ones") were primarily a Jewish sect during the first two centuries that regarded Jesus as an ordinary human being, the son of Mary and Joseph. These Jewish believers, to whom the monotheism of the Old Testament was the dearest heritage, could not begin to imagine that there was another god besides the God of Israel. Such a belief would naturally lead to polytheism.

Our knowledge of the Ebionites is scattered, and it is not easy to ascertain what they believed. For example, Justin Martyr thought Ebionites regarded Jesus as Christ the Messiah but considered him still a man, born of a virgin. But what kind of Christ would that be? More than likely, most Ebionites saw Jesus as one who surpassed others in wisdom and righteousness but was still more a human being than a god.

According to the early church historian Eusebius from the third century, there were actually two classes of Ebionites. Both groups insisted on the observance of the Mosaic law. The first group held to a natural birth of Jesus, who was characterized by an unusual moral character. The other group accepted the virgin birth but rejected the idea of Jesus' preexistence as the Son of God.

Ebionitism was quickly rejected by Christian theology because it was obvious that regarding Jesus as merely a human being compromised the idea of Jesus as Christ and Savior.

Docetism

The other early view that defined Jesus' humanity in a nonorthodox way, prominent especially during the second and third centuries, was called Docetism. The term comes from the Greek word *dokeō*, "to seem" or "to appear." According to this understanding, Christ was completely divine, but his humanity was merely an appearance. Christ was not a real human being. Consequently, Christ's sufferings were not real.

Docetism was related to a cluster of other philosophical and religious ideas that are often lumped together under the umbrella term Gnosticism (from the Greek term *gnōsis*, "knowledge"). This term is elusive and may denote several things. The most important contribution Gnosticism made with regard to Docetism was the idea of dualism between matter and spirit. It regarded spirit as the higher and purer part of creation, whereas matter represented frailty and even sinfulness. The idea of religion in Gnosticism was an exercise in escaping from the material, visible world into the haven of spirit. It is easy to see how this kind of orientation was linked to Docetism: To make Christ really "flesh" (cf. John 1:14) would compromise his divinity and his "spirituality."

Christian theology denied both Docetism and Ebionitism. Docetism had a divine Savior who had no real connection with humanity. Ebionitism had only a human, moral example.

The first major attempt to express in precise language the New Testament's dual emphasis on Christ as both a human being and a divine figure came to be known as *Logos* Christology, for the simple reason that these early fathers adopted the Johannine concept of *Logos*.

Early *Logos* Christologies

Justin Martyr, one of the most important second-century apologists (Christian thinkers who wanted to offer a reasonable defense of the Christian faith vis-à-vis contemporary culture and philosophy), sought to establish a correlation between Greek philosophy and Judaism. The idea of *logos,* referring to wisdom, learning, philosophy, divine insight, and so on, while originating in Greek culture, was not foreign to Jews. Philo, a contemporary of Jesus who lived in Alexandria in Egypt and was an influential thinker and historian, wrote about Jewish writers who had made a connection between the *logos* and the Old Testament word or wisdom of God. Such a connection is understandable given the important role the word of God plays in the Old Testament. The word is instrumental, for example, in creation (Genesis 1).

Justin creatively made use of contemporary intellectual elements, especially in Stoic and Platonic philosophies, for the purposes of apologetics. Taking John 1:14 as his key text, he argued that the same *logos* that was known by pagan philosophers had now appeared in the person of Jesus of Nazareth. According to Justin, philosophers taught that the reason in every human being participates in the universal *logos*. The Gospel of John teaches that in Jesus Christ the *logos* became flesh. Therefore, whenever people use their reason, Christ, the *Logos*, is already at work. "We have been taught that Christ was the First-begotten of God, and we have indicated . . . that he is the Word of whom all humankind partakes. Those who lived by reason are Christians, even though they have been considered atheists."[2] In Jesus, Christians have full access to the meaning of the *Logos,* while pagans have only partial access to it. According to the early apologists, the divine *Logos* sowed seeds throughout human history; therefore, Christ is known to some extent by non-Chris-

---

2. Justin Martyr, *The First Apology* XLV.

tians. This concept was known as *logos spermatikos* ("seeds of *Logos* sown" in the world). In his *Second Apology,* Justin explained the fullness of the Christian doctrine of Christ:

> Our religion is clearly more sublime than any human teaching in this respect: the Christ who has appeared for us human beings represents the Logos principle in all its fullness. . . . For everything that the philosophers and lawgivers declared or discovered that is true was brought about by investigation and perception, in accordance with that portion of the Logos to which they had access. But because they did not know the whole of the Logos, who is Christ, they often contradicted each other.[3]

The apologists also found in the Old Testament indications of the existence of the *Logos* in human form; an example of this kind of "theophany" (from the Greek terms *theos,* "God," and *phaneō,* "appearance," "manifestation") is the mysterious angel of Yahweh in Genesis 18 who appeared to Abraham and his wife, Sarah.

Origen, a church father from the Eastern Christian church, brought *Logos* Christology to its fullest development. According to his thinking, in the incarnation, the human soul of Christ was united with the *Logos.* On account of the closeness of this union, Christ's human soul shared in the properties of the *Logos.* Origen brought home this understanding with the help of a vivid picture from everyday life:

> If a lump of iron is constantly kept in a fire, it will absorb its heat through all its pores and veins. If the fire is continuous, and the iron is not removed, it becomes totally converted to the other. . . . In the same way, the soul which has been constantly placed in the Logos and Wisdom and God, is God in all that it does, feels, and understands.[4]

As a consequence of this union between the *Logos* and Jesus of Nazareth, Jesus is the true God. Yet to guard the leading theological principle of the Eastern wing of the church, namely, the preeminence of the Father, Origen reminded his followers of the principle of *autotheos,* which simply means that, strictly speaking, God only and alone is God. Origen did so not to lessen the divinity of Christ but to secure the priority of the Father. Origen believed that the Father had begotten the Son by an eternal act; therefore, Christ existed from eternity. In fact, there were two begettings of the Son: one in time (the virgin birth) and one in eternity by the Father. To make his point, Origen appealed to John 1:1, which has no definite article in the Greek expression "the Word *[Logos]* was God" and therefore could be translated "the Word was *a*

3. Justin Martyr, *The Second Apology* X.
4. Origen, *De Principiis* II.vi.6.

God" (or perhaps, "divine"). While Origen's exegetical ground is not convincing to modern interpreters, his *Logos* Christology represents a significant milestone in the development of the christological tradition. *Logos* Christology has been a dominant way of interpreting Christ's incarnation, and it has taken various forms throughout history.

The Unique Status of the Father in Relation to the Son

The study of theology, as with any other academic field, requires mastery of its basic vocabulary. Some terms are used in everyday language (e.g., *person*) but in theology have a different, often strictly defined, meaning. Other terms are coined specifically for the purposes of theological accuracy. One of the latter kind of terms was coined to explain the relationship among the members of the Trinity that assured the supremacy of God the Father. The term is *monarchianism,* which means "sole sovereignty." There are two subcategories of this view, "dynamic" and "modalistic" monarchianism. Both emerged in the late second and early third centuries and stressed the uniqueness and unity of God in light of the Christian confession that Jesus is God. Such views, similar to those of Origen, were eventually rejected by Christian orthodoxy.

The concern for the uniqueness of God the Father is understandable given that Christian theology grew out of Jewish soil. The leading theme of Judaism in the Old Testament was belief in the One God, as expressed in Deuteronomy 6:4 and a host of other passages. While these two monarchianist views were rejected, they express a noteworthy milestone in the struggle of Christian theology to retain its ties to the Jewish faith and to explicate fully the implications of Christ's divinity.

Dynamic Monarchianism

The etymology of dynamic monarchianism explains its meaning: The sole sovereignty of the Father was preserved by the idea that God was dynamically present in Jesus, thus making him higher than any other human being but not yet a God. In other words, God's power (Greek, *dynamis*) made Jesus *almost* God; as a consequence, the Father's uniqueness was secured.

Theodotus, a Byzantine leather merchant, came to Rome, the leading city of Christianity, at the end of the second century. He taught that prior to baptism Jesus was an ordinary man, although a completely virtuous one; at his baptism, the Spirit, or Christ, descended upon him and gave him the ability to perform miracles. Jesus was still an ordinary man, but he was inspired by the Spirit. Some of Theodotus's followers went farther and claimed that Jesus actually became divine at his baptism or after his resurrection, but Theodotus himself did not concur.

In the second half of the third century, Paul of Samosata further developed the idea of dynamic monarchianism by contending that the Word *(Logos)* does not refer to a personal, self-subsistent entity but simply to God's commandment and ordinance: God ordered and accomplished what he willed through the man Jesus. Paul of Samosata did not admit that Jesus was the Word, *Logos*. Instead, the *Logos* was a dynamic power in Jesus' life that made God dynamically present in Jesus. This view was condemned by the Synod of Antioch in 268.

Modalistic Monarchianism

According to modalistic monarchianism, the three Persons of the Trinity are not self-subsistent "persons" but "modes" or "names" of the same God. They are like three "faces" of God, with a different one presented depending on the occasion. Whereas dynamic monarchianism seemed to deny the Trinity, indicating that Jesus is less than God, modalistic monarchianism appeared to affirm the Trinity. Both, however, tried to preserve the oneness of God the Father, though in different ways.

Several early third-century thinkers such as Noetus of Smyrna, Praxeas (perhaps a nickname meaning "busybody"), and Sabellius contended that there is one Godhead that can be designated as Father, Son, or Spirit. The names do not stand for real distinctions but are merely names that are appropriate and applicable at different times. In other words, Father, Son, and Spirit are identical, successive revelations of the same person. This view is sometimes called Sabellianism after one of its early proponents.

A corollary idea follows: The Father suffered along with Christ because he was actually present in and personally identical with the Son. This view is known as *patripassianism* (from two Latin terms meaning "father" and "passion").

Modalistic monarchianism was considered heretical by the church, even though its basic motivation, to preserve the unity of God the Father, was valid. Early Christian theologians soon noticed its main problem: How can three (or two) members of the Trinity appear simultaneously in the act of salvation if they are but three names or modes of one and the same being? The account of Jesus' baptism, during which the Father spoke to his Son and the Spirit descended on the Son, seemed to contradict the idea of modalism.

But even the orthodox position had to struggle with the question, If Christ is divine but is not the Father, are there not two Gods? Tertullian, one of the ablest early Christian theologians, coined much of the trinitarian vocabulary. He sought to clarify this problem with a series of metaphors:

> For the root and the tree are distinctly two things, but correlatively joined; the fountain and the river are also two forms, but indivisible; so likewise the sun

and the ray are two forms, but coherent ones. Everything which proceeds from something else must needs be second to that from which it proceeds, without being on that account separated.[5]

By analogies such as these, Tertullian and others believed they had clarified the New Testament distinction between Father and Son without leading to belief in two gods. But one may seriously ask if this was the case. Metaphors such as the one depicting the Father as the sun and the Son as a ray imply subordinationism, that Christ is inferior to the Father. In fact, Tertullian admitted this: "For the Father is the entire substance, but the Son is a derivation and portion of the whole as He Himself acknowledges: 'My Father is greater than I.'"[6] In fact, these ideas and related problems associated with defining Christ's relation to the Father led to the emergence of a new set of questions.

As soon as Christian theology had combated these two versions of monarchianism, it faced an even more challenging problem named Arianism, after Arius, a priest of Alexandria. Even though historically it is unclear whether Arius himself ever expressed ideas related to Arianism, it is evident that a major debate took place in the third and fourth centuries concerning the way Jesus' divinity and relationship to the Father could be expressed. It was not so much a question of denying Jesus' deity but rather how to express it without diminishing the status of the Father. In many ways, therefore, monarchianism and Arianism approach the same problem and have as their background the same kind of concerns. The issue raised by Arianism was tentatively dealt with at the Council of Nicea in 325, but as with any doctrinal formulation, Nicea also raised new issues and questions.

How to Define Christ's Deity

We do not know for sure what Arius taught and therefore are dependent on the writings of his opponents. According to his opponents, the basic premise of Arius's thinking was that God the Father is absolutely unique and transcendent, and God's essence (the Greek term *ousia* means both "essence" and "substance") cannot be shared by another or transferred to another, not even the Son. Consequently, for Arius, the distinction between Father and Son was one of substance *(ousia);* if they were of the same substance, there would be two gods. Rather than sharing the same "essence" with the Father, the Son is the first and unique creation of God. A saying attributed to Arius emphasizes his main thesis about the origin of Christ: "There was [a time] when he was not." This view was problematic because it meant that Christ

5. Tertullian, *Against Praxeas* chap. 8.
6. Ibid., chap. 9.

was begotten of God in time, not from all eternity. Christ, therefore, was a part of creation and inferior to God even though greater than other creatures.

It is easy to see the concerns and logic of Arianism. On the one hand, it attempted to secure the divinity, or at least the supreme status, of Jesus in regard to other human beings. On the other hand, it did not make Jesus equal to the Father. In a sense, Jesus stood in the middle.

Mainstream Christian theology had to respond to this challenge because it seemed to compromise the basic confession of Christ's deity. The ablest defender of the full deity of Christ was the Eastern father Athanasius. He argued in response to Arius that the view that the Son was a creature, albeit at a higher level, would have a decisive consequence for salvation. First, only God can save, whereas a creature is in need of being saved. Thus, if Jesus was not God incarnate, he was not able to save us. But both the New Testament and church liturgy call Jesus Savior, indicating that he is God. Worship of and prayer to a Jesus who is less than God would also make Christians guilty of blasphemy.

The response of Athanasius provides a model of the way early Christian theology developed. Academic or intellectual concerns were not primary, even though argumentation was carried on at a highly sophisticated level. The soteriological concern, the question of salvation, was the driving force behind theological developments. Christology is a showcase example of this. Early Christian theologians did not sit comfortably in their studies seeking to produce something novel about Christ. They were pastors and preachers whose primary concern was to make sure that people knew how to be saved. The fact that what was confessed in church liturgy was considered doctrinally binding shows the full force of the ancient rule *lex ora lex credendi* ("the principle of prayer is the principle of believing"): What is believed and worshiped becomes the confession of doctrine.

In the spirit of Athanasius's and other mainline theologians' responses to Arius, the Council of Nicea in 325 defined Christ's deity in a way that made Christ equal to God the Father. The text says:

> We believe . . . in one Lord Jesus Christ, the Son of God, begotten of the Father [the only begotten, that is, of the essence of the Father, God of God], Light of Light, very God of very God, begotten, not made, being of one substance *[homoousios]* with the Father; by whom all things were made [both in heaven and on earth]; who for us men, and for our salvation, came down and was incarnate and was made man; he suffered, and the third day he rose again, ascended into heaven; from thence he shall come to judge the quick and the dead.

An appendix at the end listed Arian tenets to be rejected:

> But for those who say: "There was a time when he was not;" and "He was not before he was made;" and "He was made out of nothing," or "He is of another

substance" or "essence," or "The Son of God is created," or "changeable," or "alterable"—they are condemned by the holy catholic and apostolic Church.[7]

The creed said that Christ was not created but was "begotten of the substance of the Father." The key word was the Greek *homoousios,* which created great debate. It means literally "of the same substance" or "of the same essence," indicating that Christ was equal in divinity to the Father. Not all theologians were happy with that definition. Even though, as mentioned above, virtually all confessed Christ's divine nature, the question was how to define it. Especially theologians from the Eastern wing of the church, the Greek church, would have preferred the Greek term *homoiousios.* The difference is one *i,* which makes a difference in meaning: *homoi* means "similar to," whereas *homo* means "the same." In other words, this formulation would not make Christ identical with the Father but similar to the Father. Greek theologians had concerns about the stricter formulation because they believed it was not biblical and could lead to modalism. For Eastern theology, the distinctive "personhood" of the Father and the Son was important in addition to securing the privileged status of the Father. Western theologians objected to the "similar to" interpretation, believing it could be interpreted in a subordinationist way, meaning that the Son is (in this case, slightly) different from the Father and therefore less than the Father.

This difference of opinion between the Eastern and Western wings of the church did not lead to a division or a permanent labeling of either side as heretical, but it did highlight a growing gulf between the Christian East and the Christian West. Even though both traditions at least formally concurred with the Nicean formulation, they began to develop their own distinctive approaches to Christ, namely, the Antiochian and Alexandrian schools. Each school produced a distinctive Christology, which in turn gave rise to distinctive christological heresies. In a way, the heresies that arose took seriously the concerns of each of these schools and pushed the boundaries until the theological consensus came to the conclusion that they had gone too far.

7. Philip Schaff, ed., *The Creeds of Christendom,* 6th ed. (1931; reprint, Grand Rapids: Baker, 1990), 1:28–29.

5

From the Council of Nicea (325) to Chalcedon (451)

Up until the Council of Nicea in 325, the main questions surrounding Christ focused on whether he was divine and how to define precisely his divinity in relation to the Father. After Nicea these questions still loomed in the background, but the focus shifted to the corollary problem: Granted that Christ is divine, how are Christ's two natures—divine and human—related to each other? It is one thing to confess that Christ is human and that he is divine; it is another thing to determine how to hold together these seemingly opposite claims. If a person is fully divine, doesn't that nature by definition render that person not fully human and vice versa?

Two orientations emerged among Christian churches, partly because of cultural and geographical differences and partly because of influences from the surrounding societies and religions. The Eastern church was centered in Alexandria in Egypt, an ancient center for learning. This tradition expressed itself in Greek, and it emphasized soteriological questions. The response of Athanasius to Arius is a good example of this orientation. Eastern theologians focused on the divinity of Christ. The humanity of Christ, of course, was not denied, but for soteriological reasons, theologians did not show much interest in the human side. Their doctrine of salvation was expressed in terms of deification or divinization (from the Greek term *theōsis,* "denoting God"), which means "becoming like God." The Western wing of the church was centered in Antioch and used Latin for its sacred writings. While Western theologians fully embraced the divinity of Christ, they often put more emphasis on Christ's humanity. Their understanding of salvation, consequently, was fashioned primarily as moral obedience and justification by faith on the basis of Christ's obedience to his Father.

Christ's Divinity and Our Deification: The Eastern Tradition

The Eastern Alexandrian school focused on redemption in the sense of human life being taken up into the life of God, or deification. If human nature is to be deified, it must be united with the divine nature. For this to happen, God must become united with human nature in such a manner that the latter shares in the life of God; this is what happened in and through the incarnation.

In considering the incarnation of Christ, Eastern theologians emphasized the idea of the divine *Logos* assuming human nature. They were clear about the distinction between the presence of the *logos* in the world and the specific event of the *Logos* taking on human nature in the incarnation, according to John 1:14. Naturally, such a view raised the question of the relationship between the divinity and the humanity of Christ.

Cyril of Alexandria responded by emphasizing the reality of the union of the two natures in the incarnation. The *Logos* existed "without flesh" before its union with human nature; after that union, one nature existed, for the *Logos* had united human nature to itself. This emphasis on the one nature of Christ distinguished the Alexandrian school from the Antiochian school, as Cyril's exposition shows:

> We do not affirm that the nature of the Logos underwent a change and became flesh, or that it was transformed into a whole or perfect human consisting of flesh and body; rather, we say that the Logos . . . personally united itself to a human nature with a living soul, became a human being, and was called the Son of Man, but not of mere will or favor.[1]

This raised the question, What kind of human nature was assumed? Did Christ's nature encompass all of human nature? A heretical view called Apollinarianism tried to answer these questions in a less than satisfactory way.

Apollinarianism

Apollinarius of Laodicea worried about the increasingly widespread belief that the *Logos* assumed human nature in its entirety. He wondered whether

---

1. See Cyril of Alexandria, *The Epistle of Cyril to Nestorius,* in *Nicene and Post-Nicene Fathers,* series II, vol. XIV, ed. Philip Schaff and Henry Wace (Peabody, Mass.: Hendrickson, 1994).

that conviction would lead to the belief that the *Logos* was contaminated by the weaknesses of human nature. If so, the sinlessness of Christ would be compromised. To avoid this unacceptable view, Apollinarius suggested that if a real human mind in Jesus were replaced by a purely divine mind, then and only then could Christ's sinlessness be maintained. He argued that a purely human mind and soul were replaced by a divine mind and soul, preventing contamination of the divine *Logos* by any sin from a human mind.

As appealing as this idea seems, it renders the human nature of Christ incomplete. Alexandrian theologians soon noticed that the price for protecting Jesus' sinlessness in this way was too high. Apollinarianism compromised Jesus' role as Savior, as Gregory of Nazianzen (a Cappadocian father also called Gregory of Nazianzus) noted: How could human nature be redeemed if only part of it was assumed by the *Logos?*

> The unassumed is the unhealed, however, that which is united to his Godhead is saved. If only half of Adam fell, then Christ assumes and saves only that half of his nature. But if his nature fell in its totality, then it must all be united to the nature of him who was begotten, and thus be saved in its totality. Let them not begrudge us our salvation in its totality, or clothe the savior with nothing more than bones and nerves and something which looks like humanity.[2]

Gregory of Nazianzen built on the Eastern view of Origen and others, according to which the incarnation accomplished a "recapitulation" of human history; the God-man Jesus not only experienced all phases of human life from birth to adulthood to death but also restored the history of humanity by facing Adam's temptation without sinning. Gregory of Nazianzen maintained that if all of human nature was not assumed, taken up in the humanity of Christ, then Jesus' role as Savior was incomplete.

The logic of Eastern Christology was governed by soteriological motives. Christ had to be fully and genuinely divine and fully and genuinely human to serve in the capacity of the Savior. If Christ were less than human, he would not be able to identify with us, and even worse, our human nature would not be taken up into his deified humanity. On the other hand, if Christ were less than divine, he would not possess the power and authority to save us, even if he could sympathize with us. The Eastern church was never able to define in precise theological terms the relationship between the two natures of Christ—and as mentioned earlier, it emphasized his divinity—but it held firmly to the basic christological conviction that would secure salvation.

2. Gregory of Nazianzen, *Letter to Cledonius the Priest Against Apollinarius,* Epistle CI, in *A Select Library of the Nicene and Post-Nicene Fathers,* series II, vol. VII, ed. Philip Schaff and Henry Wace (Grand Rapids: Eerdmans, 1978–79), 440.

The proposal of Apollinarius did not meet acceptance, and other routes were taken to secure the sinlessness of Christ while focusing on his divinity even in the incarnation. That attempt gave rise to another heretical view in the Eastern school known as Eutychianism.

Eutychianism

The thesis of Eutychianism is simple: Christ had two natures before the incarnation but only one nature after it. The background to the emergence of this view was the so-called Nestorian controversy surrounding Christ's two natures (to be discussed in the next section). This controversy led in the first part of the fifth century to the adoption of a view championed mainly by the Western church. According to the adopted view, Christ had two natures that were united without confusion. Many Alexandrians, Cyril for example, were not happy about this conclusion because it seemed to ignore their emphasis on Christ's one nature. Antiochenes accused Cyril and other Alexandrians of heresy for not acknowledging clearly enough the two natures, human and divine, whereas Cyril's supporters thought he did not emphasize strongly enough Christ's one nature. Eutyches, an Eastern archimandrite and politically influential figure, became the Alexandrian spokesperson against the emphasis on two natures. At the Synod of Constantinople in 448, Eutyches said that whereas Christ had two natures before the incarnation, he had but one afterward. However, a precise understanding of his view is difficult to establish. What kind of "one nature" did Christ have after his incarnation? Was Eutyches, for example, Docetist in denying Christ's human nature? Was Christ's humanity swallowed up by his divinity? The synod excommunicated Eutyches and rejected his view. (That synod was followed by a set of ecclesio-political events such as the famous "Robber Synod" in Ephesus in 449 that restored Eutyches and vindicated his orthodoxy.) The final decision concerning Christ's natures came at Chalcedon in 451.

Christ's Humanity and Our Obedience: The Western Tradition

Two Natures of Christ

The Western tradition, centered in Antioch, focused more on moral aspects of the Christian life (e.g., discipleship) than on soteriology. Antiochene theology taught that on account of their disobedience, human beings exist in a state of corruption, from which they are unable to save themselves. If redemption is to take place, it must be on the basis of a new obedience on the part of humanity. Because humanity is unable to break free from the bonds of sin, God is obliged to intervene. This leads to the coming of the Redeemer, who unites humanity and divinity and thus establishes an obedient people of God.

This view defends the two natures of Christ: He was at one and the same time both God and a human being. The Alexandrians criticized this view, saying it denied the unity of Christ. Against this criticism, Antiochenes responded that it was in their interest to uphold Christ's unity while simultaneously recognizing that the one Redeemer possessed both a perfect human nature and a perfect divine nature. Western theologians talked about a "perfect conjunction" between the human and the divine natures of Christ.

In his *On the Incarnation,* Theodore of Mopsuestia, who stressed the fact that the two natures of Christ do not compromise his unity, wrote, "In coming to indwell, the Logos united the assumed [human being] as a whole to itself, and made him to share with it in all the dignity in which the one who indwells, being the Son of God by nature, possesses.[3] Still, Alexandrians remained suspicious, believing that the stress on two natures leads to a doctrine of "two sons": Christ seemed to be not a single person but two persons, one human and one divine. One strand of the Antiochene school did in fact emphasize the two natures so much that it affirmed a view that separated the humanity and the divinity from each other, making them more or less separate entities. This view is known as Nestorianism.

Nestorianism

The label Nestorianism is questionable because we do not know for sure whether Nestorius, patriarch of Constantinople in the first part of the fifth century, actually taught this doctrine. It is possible, however, to lay aside the question of the origin of this view and look merely at the challenge this view presented to orthodoxy.

The controversy surrounding Nestorianism arose over the use of the term *theotokos* ("God-bearing") in regard to Mary. Was Mary, the mother of Jesus, the mother of God? Nestorius, as a spokesperson for a larger group, stated that *theotokos* is appropriate insofar as it is complemented by the term *anthrōpotokos* ("human-bearing"). However, Nestorius's own preference was *Christotokos* ("Christ-bearing").

What was at stake in these technical terminological distinctions? What was the concern of Nestorius and his opponents? Nestorius maintained that it is impossible to believe that God would have a mother; no woman can give birth to God. Instead, what Mary bore was not God but humanity, a sort of instrument of divinity. Nestorius feared that if the term *theotokos* were applied to Mary without qualifications, it would lead to either Arianism, according to which Jesus was not equal to God, or Apollinarianism, which taught that

---

3. Quoted in Alister McGrath, *Christian Theology: An Introduction* (Oxford: Blackwell, 1994), 290.

Jesus' human nature was not real. In the East, however, the term *theotokos* was widely used by Alexandrians. It was often coupled with another ancient concept, *communicatio idiomatum* ("communication of attributes"), that played a significant role in various doctrinal contexts throughout history. With regard to Jesus' two natures, the expression means that what pertains to one nature also pertains to the other. In other words, because we can say that Mary bore the human baby Jesus, we can also at the same time say that Mary bore the divine person Christ.

What, then, made Nestorius's doctrine unorthodox? Here we come to the difficulty of establishing Nestorius's view exactly. Nestorius's opponents, especially the Eastern theologian Cyril of Alexandria, labeled Nestorius's view heretical, suggesting that obviously Nestorius believed that Jesus had two natures joined in a purely moral union but not in a real way (as *communicatio idiomatum* suggests). Cyril's interpretation of Nestorius's view was called Nestorianism: Christ was actually two distinct persons, one divine and the other human. Nestorius repudiated this interpretation of his view, but this interpretation continued until it was rejected at the Council of Ephesus in 431.

Having rejected the view of Nestorius as extreme, theologians refined the doctrine of Jesus' humanity and divinity with the help of the concept *communicatio idiomatum*. If Jesus was fully human and fully divine, then what was true of his humanity was also true of his divinity and vice versa. This principle was also applied to Mary: Jesus Christ is God; Mary gave birth to Jesus; therefore, Mary is the mother of God. Soon, this view became a test of orthodoxy. But it is easy to see that when pressed, this orthodox view gives rise to another problem: Jesus suffered on the cross; Jesus is God; therefore, God suffered on the cross.

The Council of Chalcedon

The Council of Chalcedon (451) attempted to solve the christological debates in a way that could be embraced by both Alexandrians and Antiochenes. The council never reached this noble goal, but it was able to combat the major deviating views. The council reaffirmed the Nicene Creed and rejected Nestorianism and Eutychianism. The text says:

> We, then, following the holy Fathers, all with one consent, teach men to confess one and the same Son, our Lord Jesus Christ, the same perfect in Godhood and also perfect in manhood; truly God and truly man, of a reasonable [rational] soul and body; consubstantial [co-essential] with the Father according to the Godhood, and consubstantial with us according to the Manhood; in all things like unto us, without sin; begotten before all ages of the Father according to the Godhood, and in these latter days, for us and for our salvation, born of

the Virgin Mary, the Mother of God, according to the Manhood; one and the same Christ, Son, Lord, Only-begotten, to be acknowledged in two natures, inconfusedly, unchangeably, indivisibly, inseparably; the distinction of natures being by no means taken away by the union, but rather the property of each nature being preserved, and concurring in one Person and one Subsistence, not parted or divided into two persons, but one and the same Son, and only begotten, God the Word, the Lord Jesus Christ, as the prophets from the beginning [have declared] concerning him, and the Lord Jesus Christ himself has taught us, and the Creed of the holy Fathers has handed down to us.[4]

The main concern of Chalcedon was to steer a middle course between the dangers of Nestorianism, which separated the two natures—thus the use of the words "indivisibly" and "inseparably"—and Eutychianism, which eliminated the distinction between the two natures—thus the use of the words "inconfusedly" and "unchangeably." Although the council was unable to state definitely how the union of the two natures occurred, it was able to say how this union cannot be expressed. The controlling principle of Chalcedon holds that provided that Jesus Christ was both truly divine and truly human, the precise manner in which this is articulated or explored is not of fundamental importance. Maurice Wiles neatly summarizes the aim and achievement of Chalcedon:

> On the one hand was the conviction that a saviour must be fully divine; on the other hand was the conviction that what is not assumed is not healed. Or, to put the matter in other words, the source of salvation must be God; the locus of salvation must be humanity. It is quite clear that these two principles often pulled in opposite directions. The Council of Chalcedon was the church's attempt to resolve, or perhaps rather to agree to live with, that tension. Indeed, to accept both principles as strongly as did the early church is already to accept the Chalcedonian faith.[5]

One could perhaps say that, on the one hand, Chalcedon functioned as a signpost pointing in the right direction, and on the other hand, it was a fence separating orthodoxy and heresy.

---

4. Philip Schaff, ed., *The Creeds of Christendom,* 6th ed. (1931; reprint, Grand Rapids: Baker, 1990), 2:62–63.
5. Quoted in McGrath, *Christian Theology,* 295.

6

Subsequent Developments

Continuing Dissenting Voices to Orthodoxy

The christological developments of the first five centuries are the most decisive ones with regard to the later history of theology. Up until the time of the Enlightenment and the subsequent quest of the historical Jesus—topics to be studied in the next two chapters—the questions raised during the early centuries continued to be debated and the early creeds continued to be affirmed.

Throughout history, Christian theology developed as pressures from the right and the left caused oscillation between seemingly opposing forces. The church at times even tolerated views that appeared to contradict the established view. One example of this process is the issue of *monophysitism*, which means literally "one nature." As shown in the preceding discussion, the Eastern school of Alexandria opted for emphasizing the divinity of Christ, even to the point that many Antiochenes doubted whether Alexandrians had a clear conception of Christ's two natures. The most outspoken defender of the Alexandrian one-nature view, Cyril of Alexandria, at first insisted on Christ's oneness in every respect: one person, one nature *(physis)*, one particular individual. Gradually, however, he admitted that Christ was both human and divine, and one needed to acknowledge both natures. He tried to ease the difficulty of speaking of two natures by stating that even though Christ had two natures, he was only one person. That made possible the full use of the term *communicatio idiomatum,* the "communication of attributes": What pertains to one nature pertains also to the other.

Many Eastern theologians, while paying lip service to the formulation of Chalcedon, with its focus on two natures, did not want to give up their preference for one-nature Christology. In the sixth century, a movement of monophysite churches arose from the Eastern camp and existed as a dissenting voice to Chalcedon. These churches believed in the one nature of Christ; he was divine rather than human. This doctrine remains normative within most Christian churches of the eastern Mediterranean world: Coptic, Armenian, and Syrian churches. Even though dissenters, they are included in the Orthodox church family.

A related problem arose from the debate concerning the natures of Christ: the question of the will(s) of Christ. Macarius of Antioch firmly declared that he would never say Christ had "two natural [independent] wills" even if he "were to be torn limb from limb and cast into the sea."[1] Monothelitism (from two Greek terms meaning "one will"), the belief that Christ had only one will rather than two, soon encountered serious opposition. First, it seemed to contradict the Bible, for in Gethsemane Christ prayed, "Not my will but thine be done," obviously implying that Christ made a distinction between his two wills. Furthermore, monothelitism seemed to go against the doctrine of salvation, as Gregory of Nazianzen noted in his famous axiom, "That which has not been assumed cannot be healed."[2] If Christ did not have a real human will, then the human will, which obviously is the root of all sin and rebellion against God, has not been saved. "If he did not assume a human will, that in us which suffered first has not been healed."[3] As a consequence, in 681, the Third Council of Constantinople declared that Christ had two wills. Nevertheless, monophysites never agreed with that declaration.

Christological Orientations of the Reformation Period

Almost one thousand years later, during the time of the Reformation, the classical questions of Christ's humanity and divinity were again debated. The precise meaning of the often used catchword *communicatio idiomatum,* "communication of attributes," was examined as once again theologians asked, Can the human Jesus take on the attributes of God and remain human? Can God take on human attributes and remain divine?

Martin Luther took seriously the communication of attributes, so much so that he accepted that God suffered and died on the cross. The logic was sim-

1. Quoted in Jaroslav Pelikan, *The Spirit of Eastern Christendom* (Chicago: University of Chicago Press, 1974), 70.
2. Gregory of Nazianzen, *Letter to Cledonius the Priest Against Apollinarius,* Epistle CI, in *A Select Library of the Nicene and Post-Nicene Fathers,* series II, vol. VII, ed. Philip Schaff and Henry Wace (Grand Rapids: Eerdmans, 1978–79), 440.
3. Ibid.

ple: If Christ was both human and divine, the person who died on the cross was both the human Jesus and the divine God. In Luther's words, "Since the divinity and humanity are one person in Christ, the Scriptures ascribe to the deity, because of this personal union, all that happens to the humanity, and vice versa. . . . It is correct to talk about God's death."[4] This view has sometimes been called *theopassianism*, meaning that God suffered in a genuine way. (This is not quite the same as *patripassianism*, which means that God as the Father suffered.) Luther firmly believed that the incarnation did not involve an abandonment of divine attributes; the divine nature was present throughout the earthly life of Jesus. Luther also followed a logical syllogism that can be stated as: God is the creator of the world; Jesus Christ is God; therefore, Jesus Christ is the creator. On the basis of this application, one can say that Jesus, lying in the manger, is the creator of the world.

Leaders of the Reformed tradition (John Calvin, Ulrich Zwingli, and others) strongly disagreed with Luther. Zwingli insisted that "strictly speaking, the suffering appertains only to the humanity."[5] Calvin did not reject the idea of the communication of attributes, but he was more reserved about its application. He said that God could not really suffer and experience crucifixion: "Surely God does not have blood, does not suffer, cannot be touched with human hands."[6]

Lutherans and the Reformed could not agree on this issue. Yet neither side was labeled heretical, even though Lutherans accused the Reformed of Nestorianism, while the Reformed accused Lutherans of monophysitism. It is important to note that these two parties had different motives. For Lutherans, the key issue was God's self-revelation in the shame of the cross. The Reformed believed the sovereignty of God in free grace was more crucial. In a way, the two sides were not arguing about the same point, which often happens in theological debates.

There were differing orientations not only between various camps of Reformation churches but also between the representatives of a single tradition. A good example is the seventeenth-century debate among Lutheran theologians about Christ's act of emptying himself in the incarnation (Philippians 2:7 talks about Christ "emptying himself" [Greek, *kenōsis*]). All Lutheran theologians agreed that the Gospels make no reference to Christ making use of all his divine attributes on earth, but they differed on how to explain this. Two camps emerged. The one argued that Christ used his divine powers in

---

4. Quoted in "The Formula of Concord," article 8, in *The Book of Concord*, ed. Theodore G. Tappert (Philadelphia: Fortress, 1959), 599.

5. Ulrich Zwingli, *On the Lord's Supper*, The Library of Christian Classics, vol. 24 (Philadelphia: Westminster, 1953), 213.

6. John Calvin, *Institutes of the Christian Religion*, ed. John T. McNeill (Philadelphia: Westminster, 1960), 2.14.2.

secret, the other that he abstained from using them altogether (this was called *kenōsis* Christology, which later developed in many directions). Both parties believed that Christ possessed divine attributes; the question concerned their use.

Luther's Theology of the Cross

One lasting contribution to Christology made during the Reformation is Martin Luther's theology of the cross. This view has recently been revived by many, most notably the Reformed theologian Jürgen Moltmann, whose *Crucified God* is one of the most creative theological interpretations of the cross of Christ.

Love was the controlling principle of Luther's Christology, and he made a distinction between two kinds of love: God's love and human love. Luther outlined his theology of love and the cross in an early academic presentation, the Heidelberg Disputation (1518). The difference between the two kinds of love—*amor Dei,* "God's love," and *amor hominis,* "human love"—comes to light in the last thesis of the Disputation: "The love of God does not find, but creates, that which is pleasing to it. . . . Rather than seeking its own good, the love of God flows forth and bestows good."[7] Human love is oriented toward something inherently good, and self-love defines the content and the object of the love. Men and women love something that they believe they can enjoy. God's love is the opposite of human love: It is directed toward something that does not yet exist in order to create something new. Luther sometimes called God's love *amor cruces,* the "love of the cross": "This is the love of the cross, born of the cross, which turns in the direction where it does not find good which it may enjoy, but where it may confer good upon the bad and needy person."[8] God's love is born out of the cross of Christ and is manifested through God's gracious works in the world. With divine love, the movement is downward, whereas with human love, it is upward. In other words, God loves those who do not deserve to be loved, whereas humans by nature love those from whom they can expect something good.

Focusing on Christ's cross, Luther argued that God works in the world in a way that seems to be the opposite of his own being. He appears to hide himself under shame, weakness, and helplessness. Christ's earthly path, from being a miracle worker and esteemed teacher to the shame of the cross, reveals that God's revelation of himself is unintelligible to the natural mind. The natural mind imagines the works of God to be beautiful, fine, and attractive, but

7. Martin Luther, "Heidelberg Disputation," article 28, in *Luther's Works, American Edition,* ed. Jaroslav Pelikan (St. Louis: Concordia, 1955–67), 31:57.
8. Ibid.

according to Luther, the opposite is the case. He described the works of God with biblical imagery, citing Scripture: "He had no form or comeliness" (Isa. 53:2 RSV); "The LORD kills and brings to life; he brings down to Sheol [hell] and raises up" (1 Sam. 2:6 RSV). In other words, God makes us "nothing" *(nihil)* and "stupid" in order to reveal his real love to us.

The life of Jesus, according to Luther, also testifies to the paradoxical nature of God's dealings with the world, what he called God's "alien work" in contrast to God's "proper work." Luther sometimes called these two facets the work of God's left hand and the work of his right hand. God's alien work involves putting down, killing, taking away hope, leading to desperation, and so on. God's proper work is the opposite: forgiving, giving mercy, taking up, saving, encouraging, and so on. In doing his alien work, the work of his left hand, God turns out to be the devil. In other words, for Luther, God appears to be acting in a way Satan does. The dying Christ has to cry, "My God, my God, why have you forsaken me?" (Mark 15:34). Luther argued that sometimes God uses even Satan for his alien work.

Luther also made the famous distinction between two kinds of theologies, "theology of glory" and "theology of the cross." In Exodus 33:18–34:9, Moses asks God to show his face, and God responds, "But . . . you cannot see my face; for man shall not see me and live" (33:20 RSV). Instead, God lets Moses see his back. On the basis of this event, Luther differentiated between God's visible properties, such as humanity, weakness, and stupidity, and God's invisible properties, such as virtue, divinity, wisdom, justice, and goodness. The theology of glory wants to see in Christ the admirable characteristics of God, whereas the theology of the cross looks at the shameful aspects of the cross that hide God's real nature. According to Luther, only theologians of the cross receive insight into who God really is.

To further highlight the saving significance of the revelation of God in Christ, Luther called Christ the "greatest sinner" and even the "only sinner." In his person, Christ "absorbs" all our sins and becomes sin for our sake.

Once Again: What Was Really at Stake in the Early Christological Debates?

To conclude this survey of the christological debates and their implications for the following centuries, we may ask once again, What was really at stake in these finely nuanced yet often emotional debates? Can we as students of Christology in the third millennium appreciate the concerns and see the relevance of those struggles first with regard to their own contexts and then perhaps with regard to ours as well?

By now it should be clear that the driving force of the debates was not academic precision, though that was not ignored. Soteriological questions, the concern to secure salvation, was the leading motif; thinking on Christ was done in the midst of the liturgical life and prayer of the church. William N. Placher expresses this in a fine way. He first admits that it is sometimes tempting to dismiss the christological debates as quibbles over details, and then he continues:

> But by and large Christians avoided definitions until they felt their salvation stood under threat. For Ignatius of Antioch, going off to face suffering and death in the confidence that Christ had taken that road before him, it was not quibbling to reject the Docetist view that Christ had only seemed to suffer and die. Athanasius thought that Arianism implied that Christ might change and turn evil; he did not consider that point trivial. Apollinarius' view that Christ had not had a human mind posed a real threat to people who hoped for the transformation of their humanity because it had been united with divinity, and who did not want to leave their minds behind. Pious believers praying to Mary, the bearer of God, found Nestorianism deeply disturbing.

Placher then admits that, nevertheless, some aspects of the debate remain an insoluble mystery. But "that is no excuse for not trying to understand what one can understand, particularly when challenges to faith raise hard questions and demand clarification. In such a context, the christological discussions represent a great accomplishment."[9]

As christological debates were carried on, three principles guided the endeavor. And even though the questions we ask today are often different from those of our forefathers, each of these principles also concerns us:

1. Is this understanding compatible with the Bible? Even though Christians continued to debate which books belonged to the New Testament canon, they recognized the general authority of the sacred writings.
2. Is this teaching in harmony with the liturgy and prayer of the church? Academic theologians currently have a great deal of freedom to pursue their own, often idiosyncratic, questions, but when theologians are pastors who teach the people of God, it is left to congregations either to receive or to reject new theories. Often the worship of God has been a guide to a doctrine.
3. Is this view helpful in terms of salvation? What we believe about Christ not only has to be in accordance with the Bible and church life but also has to make sense in view of our need for salvation. More often than not, soteriological needs have helped to combat unorthodox teachings.

9. William C. Placher, *A History of Christian Theology: An Introduction* (Philadelphia: Westminster, 1983), 85.

7

A New Christological Style

The Age of Independent Reason

In 1774, the French philosopher and author Voltaire climbed with his friend to a nearby hill to see the sunrise. It is told that having taken off his hat, Voltaire knelt down and cried, "I believe! I believe in you! Powerful God I believe! As for monsieur Son and madame His mother, that's a different story."[1] As ironic as this statement is, it reflects the new emerging worldview of the Enlightenment in the late seventeenth and eighteenth centuries. Belief in God was still possible, not because of divine revelation in the Bible but on the basis of "natural religion." When it came to Christology and related church doctrines such as Mariology, however, these thinkers did not find much that was credible.

Immanuel Kant, a contemporary of Voltaire, expressed the mentality of the new perspective on the world in a less radical yet equally pointed way as he explained the essence of "Enlightenment" (from the German *Aufklärung*, meaning literally "clearing up"):

> *Aufklärung* is our release from our self-imposed tutelage—that is, a state of inability to make use of our own understanding without direction from someone else. This tutelage is self-imposed when its cause lies not in our own reason, but

1. Quoted in William C. Placher, *A History of Christian Theology: An Introduction* (Philadelphia: Westminster, 1983), 237.

in a lack of courage to use it without direction from someone else. . . . "Have courage to use your own reason!"—that is the motto of *Aufklärung*.[2]

The heyday of the Enlightenment was the eighteenth century, but its repercussions are still being felt at the beginning of the third millennium. Though much of the naivete and unfounded optimism of the Enlightenment was eventually left behind, this new outlook left nothing untouched. The Enlightenment is often called the Age of Reason, a label emphasizing the ability of human reason to understand the mysteries of the world. This term is ambiguous, for many earlier times in history, especially the Middle Ages, were just as much times of reason. In fact, the great scholastic systems of Christian doctrine written by Thomas Aquinas and others are grand examples of the use of reason in explicating Christian faith. The main difference was the *independent* use of reason free from church authorities, divine revelation, and other people's tutelage. That was the essence of the Enlightenment.

Enlightenment thinkers had a specific conception of rationality and knowledge. They believed that science had developed valid and ever cumulative methods of acquiring knowledge about the world and human beings. By replacing ancient superstitions, traditional religious convictions, and authorities, whether secular or ecclesiastical, the new methods of science promised to reveal the mysteries of the world and to better the conditions of ignorance, poverty, and perhaps even wars.

The Enlightenment and other related philosophical developments encouraged people to question inherited beliefs, even those regarded as divinely sanctioned and that had been taken for granted in the past. John Locke, the most influential English philosopher of his day, argued that "reason must be our best judge and guide in every thing."[3] Locke distinguished among that which we can prove by reason, that which we can prove to be contrary to reason, and mysteries above reason that our rational powers cannot determine one way or the other. If something is contrary to reason, we must reject it no matter what religious authority it claims. In the mid-1600s, the French philosopher René Descartes argued that we can achieve certain knowledge only if we begin by doubting everything, even our own existence. Only if we examine all our beliefs critically can we be sure that we do not take for granted an unexamined belief that is unfounded. Even though belief in God remained untouched by Descartes's method of skepticism, others took his method and applied it to theology too, with dramatic results.

    2. Cited in Alister E. McGrath, *The Making of Modern German Christology 1750–1990* (Grand Rapids: Zondervan, 1987), 14.
    3. John Locke, *An Essay Concerning Human Understanding* 4.19.4 (London: George Routledge Sons, 1909), 595.

Protestant theology was more open to the influence of Enlightenment thinking than was Catholic theology. This is understandable in light of the fact that Protestantism involved a desire to get rid of collective decision making in favor of individual freedom to decode Scripture for oneself. Protestantism has always been less institutionally governed and more open to individual initiatives, and it has produced many varied denominational and ecclesiastical forms.

As a result of this radical transformation of the intellectual climate, science finally had the freedom it needed to pursue its own questions. In medieval times, even the results of scientific inquiry had to be surrendered to the scrutiny of religious and political authorities. Galileo Galilei, himself a devoted believer in God, encountered the resistance of his own colleagues as he tried to be open to his scientific observations. Until this time, philosophy had served the cause of religion and had been regarded as the handmaiden of theology, the queen of sciences. Now, the handmaiden claimed independence from her master and repudiated any demand for her subordination. Kant's *Critique of Pure Reason* (1781) found no way for a rational philosophy to defend belief in God or other metaphysical claims. Kant, himself a believer in God, not on the basis of rational reasons but on the basis of moral necessity (as his other main work *The Critique of Practical Reason* [1788] argued), did not set out to further atheism but to open up windows into a philosophically independent inquiry into the conditions of knowledge.

Biblical criticism was a natural result of this new openness to the independent use of human reason. Whereas in the past the biblical text had been taken as a trustworthy historical account, now it faced mounting doubts and denials. The Bible had to be studied as a historical document according to the same methods and principles applied to the study of any other historical work. It was not left to the Holy Spirit but to the human spirit and human reason to judge whether the text was convincing.

Much of what had been comfortably endorsed in earlier approaches to religion had to be reevaluated. Locke's *Reasonableness of Christianity* (1695) argued for a religion that could be defined within the limits of reason and common sense. When Locke looked at the Bible, he found a simple faith and the call to a moral life, with nothing much contrary to reason. In Locke's reading of the Bible, Jesus exposed the errors of polytheism and idolatry, established a clear and rational morality, and reformed the worship of his time, freeing it from superstition. While Locke found in the Bible encouragement for moral excellence and the promise of forgiveness in light of the weakness of human nature, he did not find mention of the doctrine of the Trinity or many other traditional doctrines. Therefore, Locke concluded that later doctrinal developments (such as the Trinity) should not be the focus of Christianity; rather, it should focus on morality and commonsense, or natural, religion. In 1730,

M. Tindal, in his book *Christianity as Old as Creation, or, the Gospel, a Republication of the Religion of Nature,* put Christianity on par with natural or "rational religion" and argued that there was no need for divine revelation.

The Critique of Traditional Christologies

The Enlightenment found no place for the miracle stories of the evangelists or those in the rest of the New Testament.[4] David Hume's *Essay on Miracles* (1748) was seen by many as a repudiation of the possibility of miracles: They cannot be proven on the basis of evidence because there are no contemporary analogues. How could one, for example, convince a doubter of the certainty of Jesus' resurrection when there are no means of providing historical or scientific evidence? Hermann S. Reimarus and Gotthold E. Lessing, the pioneers of the quest of the historical Jesus, reminded their contemporaries of the simple fact that human testimony to a past event cannot be regarded as convincing. The great French thinker Denis Diderot went so far as to claim that even if the entire population of Paris were to assure him that a dead man had just been raised from the dead, he would not believe a word of it.

Traditional theology and Christology had operated with the concept of original sin going back at least to St. Augustine in the fourth century. In the wake of the Enlightenment, the idea of human nature corrupted by sin was vigorously opposed. The famous French pedagogue and philosopher Jean-Jacques Rousseau found this idea not only most pessimistic but also foreign to his idea of Romanticism, in which the idea of the beauty and harmony of nature, including human nature, was the leading motif.

When one begins to criticize individual doctrines of the Christian church, such as the divinity of Christ, the possibility of miracles, and original sin, one opens the door to a full-scale reevaluation of Christian theology and its basic convictions. This in fact happened during the Enlightenment, and this endeavor has often been called "doctrinal criticism." The seventeenth-century historian of theology J. F. W. Jerusalem noticed that several traditional dogmas, such as the two natures of Christ and the existence of the Trinity, were not found in the New Testament but were later products of the church based on the Greek concept of the *logos*. These doctrinal aberrations, therefore, should not be regarded as binding or legitimate but should be abandoned. Such was necessary to correct the basic mistakes in the history of dogma. Similarly, according to Jerusalem's contemporary G. S. Steinbart, the Augustinian doctrine of original sin, the concept of the satisfaction of sin, and the

4. This section is heavily indebted to the excellent survey in Alister E. McGrath, *The Making of Modern German Christology 1750–1990,* 2d ed. (Grand Rapids: Zondervan, 1994), 23–28.

doctrine of the imputation of righteousness were all nothing more than intrusions of arbitrary assumptions into Christianity.

The Agenda for the Quest of the Historical Jesus

As a result of the changes on the intellectual, academic, and religious scene, a radically new approach to the study of Christology arose in the eighteenth century. It was called the quest of the historical Jesus. The basic thesis of this quest was simple: There was a serious discrepancy between the real Jesus of history and the New Testament interpretation of Jesus as a superhuman redeemer.

The idea of a superhuman redeemer was unacceptable to Enlightenment thinkers, whereas the idea of an ethical teacher was not. These theologians believed that with the help of new methods of historical-critical research, it was possible to go behind the "husk" of the New Testament interpretation and find the "kernel" of the true history of Jesus. This meant focusing on the earthly life of Jesus, especially his role as teacher, and at the same time downplaying the role of his death and resurrection. Both the idea of atonement and the possibility of resurrection were utterly impossible according to Enlightenment thinking.

The Enlightenment brought to light the supposed conflict between faith and history. What one believed on the basis of the New Testament interpretations of faith in Christ and salvation was not in harmony with what one knew on the basis of historical research. To a more detailed look at this quest we now turn.

8

The Beginning of the Quest
of the Historical Jesus

The Jesus of History as He Really Was

The phrase "quest of the historical Jesus" was coined at the turn of the twentieth century by Albert Schweitzer, the great New Testament scholar whose book *The Quest of the Historical Jesus: A Critical Study of Its Progress from Reimarus to Wrede*[1] was the first full-scale assessment of the results of this endeavor and also the end point of its first phase. The subtitle in the German defines the quest as "A History of Research into the Life of Jesus," better suggesting the goal of the quest, namely, to write a biography of Jesus. The underlying idea of the quest was to discover the truth about Jesus as he really was, free from the faith interpretations of the church and theology. Those involved anticipated that scientific research into the origins of Jesus would show that the Jesus of history was different from the Christ of Scripture, the creeds, and Christian piety.

The period covered in Schweitzer's book is commonly called the original quest of the historical Jesus; it culminated and terminated with Schweitzer's own critique and constructive proposal. In the 1950s, a new quest arose, pioneered by Ernst Käsemann, which was followed by a third quest that began in the 1980s.

1. Albert Schweitzer, *The Quest of the Historical Jesus: A Critical Study of Its Progress from Reimarus to Wrede,* 3d ed. (London: H. & C. Black, 1954).

In the play *Nathan the Wise,* written by the German playwright and philosopher Gotthold E. Lessing, the Moslem emperor Saladin asks the Jew Nathan which religion is the true religion.[2] In reply, Nathan tells a story of a father who loved all three of his sons equally and gave each of them a valuable ring at his death. The sons knew that one of the rings was magical and made its wearer beloved by God and other people. The sons consulted a judge and were advised to live as if each of the rings were the magical one. The lesson of Lessing's play is simple: Each religion is of equal value. No one faith contains the ultimate truth; all religions point in the same direction. For Lessing, Christianity had a great deal to contribute to humanity's religious search, even if there were serious historical inaccuracies in the Gospel stories about Jesus. In opposition to the older dogmatic consensus concerning the special status of Jesus among founders of religions, Lessing's view leaned toward relativity and pluralism. This was the direction the Enlightenment had to take in its denial of supernatural divine revelation. But in addition to being skeptical about the possibility of divine revelation, these thinkers also raised serious doubts about the possibility of gaining the kind of historical data that would lead from a consideration of the Jesus of history to faith in Christ, the divine-human being.

Jesus of History and Christ of Faith

Lessing has become famous for this skeptical attitude concerning the epistemological value of history (*epistemology* is the branch of philosophy that inquires into the conditions of human knowledge): How can history ever provide access to the kind of knowledge necessary for religion or philosophy? There is a serious gap between "historical" and "rational truth," in the famous words of Lessing:

> If no historical truth can be demonstrated, then nothing can be demonstrated by means of historical truth. That is: accidental truths of history can never become the proof of necessary truths of reason. . . . That, then, is the ugly broad ditch which I cannot get across, however often and however earnestly I have tried to make the leap.[3]

This "ugly broad ditch" means that the Gospel accounts place Jesus in the past, but we are not able to verify those accounts. Therefore, who can tell us whether they are reliable? If we trust the eyewitness reports of the evangelists, then our faith rests on the authority of others. For Lessing, because miracles

2. Gotthold E. Lessing, *Lessing's Theological Writings,* trans. Henry Chadwick (Stanford: Stanford University Press, 1957).

3. Gotthold E. Lessing, "On the Proof of the Spirit and Power," in *Lessing's Theological Writings,* 53–55.

were not happening in his own day, he could not believe that they had happened in Jesus' day. In the spirit of the Enlightenment, he asked, "How is it to be expected of me that the same inconceivable truths which sixteen to eighteen hundred years ago people believed on the strongest inducement should be believed by me on an infinitely less inducement?"[4]

But the ugly broad ditch is more than just the inaccessibility of historically reliable information. There is also the more existentialist question concerning the value and meaning of those past events for people living hundreds of years after they occurred: "If on historical grounds I have no objection to the statement that this Christ himself rose from the dead, must I therefore accept that this risen Christ was the Son of God?"[5] This question shows a valid insight into the difference between historical facts and the interpretation of those facts.

Lessing appealed to the writings of a contemporary advocate of the quest of the historical Jesus, Hermann S. Reimarus, professor of Oriental languages at the University of Hamburg. Reimarus, who died in 1768, had wanted to popularize his ideas during his lifetime, but his article "On the Intentions of Jesus and his Disciples," which was part of a larger writing collection titled *Apology or Defence of the Rational Worshipper of God*, had been withheld from publication because of its radical nature. By 1778, Lessing had published extracts of Reimarus's work under the title *Fragments from an Unnamed Author*. He had found the work in the library at Wolfenbüttel; thus, these writings are also known as the "Wolfenbüttel Fragments."

In these posthumously published fragments, Reimarus argued that miracles were impossible; therefore, those portions of the Bible were not credible to modern readers. Even worse, if Jesus or his disciples claimed authority on the basis of miracles, they were to be regarded as fraudulent. Having come to this conclusion, he aimed to combat both Christianity and Judaism on the basis of rationalist criticism of the Bible.

For Reimarus, Jesus was a pious Jew who had dedicated his life to calling Israel to repentance in order to establish the kingdom of God on earth. Jesus had no intention of introducing a new teaching, certainly not "Christian doctrines" or ceremonies. But as time went on, Jesus became more and more fanatical, obsessed with the idea that he could free people from the Roman occupation. Jesus saw himself as a Jewish apocalyptic visionary but not as a divine figure. The disciples of Jesus invented the idea of "spiritual redemption." Finally, Jesus' hopes were misguided, and he died disillusioned with the God who had forsaken him. Such was Reimarus's interpretation of the death of the Messiah. After the disastrous fate of Jesus, the disciples, determining that there would be no general persecution, emerged from hiding and proclaimed the resurrection of the dead Jesus. The disciples also invented the idea

4. Ibid., 53.
5. Ibid., 54.

that soon this resurrected Jesus would return from heaven to establish his es-chatological kingdom. Thus, in Reimarus's interpretation, both Jesus and his followers were wrong: Jesus, because he wrongly believed that God had authorized him to be the deliverer of his people, and the disciples, because they encouraged false expectations of the coming kingdom.

The attack on the historicity of the resurrection was especially scandalous. Similarly scandalous was the radical claim of a dichotomy between the intentions of Jesus and those of the apostolic church (that Jesus never wanted to be the kind of supernatural Savior his disciples interpreted him to be). Understandably, these claims elicited a wave of responses defending the orthodox faith of the church. But Reimarus's questions could not be silenced. Lessing, as the publisher of these ideas, did not give unqualified support to Reimarus's theses, but he did defend the right to ask the questions. According to Lessing, as he expressed in his main work, *The Education of the Human Race* (1780), Jesus was one of the great educators of the human race, being "the first reliable, practical teacher of the immortality of the soul."[6]

The "Lives of Jesus"

In the aftermath of Lessing and Reimarus, two types of literature abounded, both of which tried to approach the life of Jesus from a distinctive perspective: the rationalist lives of Jesus and the more conservative lives of Jesus. The rationalist lives of Jesus sought to provide natural explanations for unusual events and thus to continue the Enlightenment agenda of advancing independent human reason as the guide to religion. These rationalist lives of Jesus attempted to offer a reasonable explanation of Jesus' person and actions. H. E. G. Paulus, in his *Life of Jesus as the Basis for a Pure History of Early Christianity* (1828), argued that what was truly miraculous about Jesus was his holy disposition. Individual miracle stories were capable of rational explanation. Jesus did not walk on the water but was standing on the shore. The five thousand were fed by those who had brought extra provisions, and so on.

The most famous life of Jesus interpretation is Friedrich E. D. Schleiermacher's lectures on *The Life of Jesus* (1820). Schleiermacher, the "father of modern theology," regarded John's Gospel as a historical outline into which could be inserted material from the other Gospels. His perspective on the meaning of Jesus' life was that of "religious experience." As the "father of liberalism," Schleiermacher set the tone for the liberal agenda. Whereas Kant had located religion in the ethical realm, and most Enlightenment advocates had insisted on the rational nature of religion, Schleiermacher located religion in human

---

6. Quoted in William C. Placher, *A History of Christian Theology: An Introduction* (Philadelphia: Westminster, 1983), 250.

experience and feelings (it has to be noted that the German term *Gefühl* is broader than the English term *feeling;* it also denotes "intuitive," "pre-reflexive," and has to do with piety). Here one can see the pervasive influence exerted on Schleiermacher by pietism, the renewal movement that sought to revitalize Christian life and save it from "dry head knowledge."

For Schleiermacher's theology in general and his Christology in particular, religious experience is primary; theology is secondary. Doctrinal formulas are historical and bound to a particular time and context and thus can never be absolute. All theology should be centered on the Christ experience: "Christianity is a monotheistic faith . . . and is essentially distinguished from other such faiths by the fact that in it everything is related to the redemption accomplished by Jesus of Nazareth."[7] What is redemption according to Schleiermacher? It is stimulation and elevation of the natural human God-consciousness through the "entrance of the living influence of Christ," who had "an absolutely powerful God-consciousness."[8] Christology is to be inferred from the present impact of Jesus of Nazareth on the believers within the church. To describe Jesus' influence on believers, Schleiermacher used two terms that highlight the dignity of Jesus. These terms are impossible to translate into English in the sense that he used them: *Urbildlichkeit,* which denotes Jesus' ideality, and *Vorbildlichkeit,* which refers to his power to reproduce it in others.

Not surprisingly, Schleiermacher rejected two-nature Christology, believing it belonged to the area of speculative metaphysics. The only way to talk about the divinity of Christ is to refer to his absolute God-consciousness. Apart from that, Jesus is like us, though with a higher degree of God-consciousness.

In contrast to the rationalist authors, those with more conservative leanings, who were afraid of the collapse of the entire foundation of Christian faith, attempted to produce traditional harmonizations of the Gospels as evidence of the historical reliability of the Bible. These more conservative students of Christology also produced a number of meditative and spiritual lives of Jesus. J. J. Hess's popular three-volume *History of the Three Last Years of the Life of Jesus,* finished in 1772, highlighted the significance of Jesus' suffering for Christian piety, while F. V. Reinhard's *Essay on the Plan Developed by the Founder of Christianity for the Benefit of Humanity* (1781) focused on the ethical contribution of Jesus' teaching.

The purpose of the quest of the historical Jesus was, then, to inquire into who Jesus of Nazareth was apart from later ecclesiastical and theological interpretations. While this project never reached its goal, it was one of the catalysts for later movements such as classical liberalism, the next topic, and shaped research into the person of Jesus Christ in various ways.

7. Friedrich E. D. Schleiermacher, *The Christian Faith,* 2d ed. (Edinburgh: T & T Clark, 1928), 52.
8. Ibid., 385.

9

The Liberal Picture of Christ

The Agenda of Classical Liberalism

The term *liberalism* is widely used in everyday language; for example, it is used in politics or to describe the lifestyles of certain individuals or groups. In theology, the term *liberalism,* especially when joined with the term *classical,* refers to the rise of the post-Enlightenment orientation that sought to reconstruct Christian belief in light of modern knowledge. Naturally, this tendency arose out of the basic convictions of the Enlightenment and could never have emerged without it. To be relevant, liberalism wanted to adapt itself to the new scientific and philosophical mind-set. Like the Enlightenment, it championed the freedom of the individual thinker, Christian theologians included, to criticize and reformulate beliefs free of authorities.

In regard to Christianity, liberal theologians focused on its ethical dimension rather than on metaphysical doctrines of Christ's two natures or preexistence. They sought foundations other than the absolute authority of the Bible; they regarded the results of the rapidly developing critical-historical method of Bible study as more reliable foundations. Classical liberalism also operated with the concepts of "husk" and "kernel": The plain history of Jesus was the kernel that needed to be uncovered from the husk of interpretations of Jesus by the early church.

Along with confidence in the human ability to find that kernel, there was a drift toward God's immanence at the expense of God's transcendence. Whereas older orthodoxy posited a radical discontinuity between the natural and the supernatural, between God and human beings, liberalism suggested continuity. This also meant continuity between religions. Another major difference between liberalism and orthodoxy was liberalism's dynamism: Religious truths, rather than being conceived of as fixed doctrines to be believed, were viewed as developmental and evolutionary in nature. That is, doctrines were interpretations of reality created by the persons perceiving them. When it came to the doctrine of revelation, which in orthodoxy had focused on the words of Christ, liberalism focused instead on the person of Christ and encounters with him. The Bible is not the "pure" Word of God but rather an interpretation of the religious experiences of the authors. This led Friedrich Schleiermacher and others to look at the human being as the means of receiving knowledge about God in opposition to the older approach in which the human being and the world were interpreted from the viewpoint of God.

The following features describe classical liberalism's distinctive outlook regarding Christ:

1. Liberalism opposed the dogmatic Christ of the early creeds and was suspicious of the Christologies of Paul and John, which were too heavily interpretative and neglected actual history.
2. The main aim was to reconstruct the life of Jesus from the Synoptics in the form of a biography.
3. The best way to write a biography of Jesus was through a psychological description of Jesus' inner life and inner development to his full consciousness.
4. Liberalism emphasized the humanity of Christ and downplayed the classical view of his divinity.
5. Liberalism clearly opted for "low Christology" rather than the high view of creeds and classical orthodoxy that saw Jesus as a divine figure.
6. When it came to the Gospels, priority was given to Mark because it was believed to be the most historical and the least theological. In addition, the collected sayings of Jesus, the theoretical "Q" source,[1] was regarded as most reliable.

The Life of Jesus Critically Examined

Having read Schleiermacher's main christological work, *The Life of Jesus,* D. F. Strauss subjected it to a sharp criticism in his work *The Christ of Faith*

1. Q source (from German *Quelle,* "spring" or "well") is shorthand for a hypothetical source that contained primarily sayings of Jesus. The Gospel writers may have used this source when writing the Gospels.

and the Jesus of History (1865). Strauss was suspicious of Schleiermacher's method; Schleiermacher held to some supernaturalist views yet at the same time wanted to write a rationalist life of Jesus. Strauss was also critical of his own highly acclaimed teacher, one of the true giants of philosophy, G. W. F. Hegel. In his analysis of religion, Hegel had come to the conclusion that incarnation, the idea of divine-human union, was a necessary idea and could be justified rationally. Strauss concurred with his teacher but asked the question, Must the idea of incarnation necessarily be realized in one specific individual? Why not the entire human race or a group of human beings? To respond to this question and to clarify the task of research into the life of Jesus, he set himself the ambitious task of offering a critical study that took stock of earlier work in the field and suggested his own corrective. The title of the book clearly reveals its purpose: *The Life of Jesus Critically Examined* (1836).

Strauss accepted a basic historical framework for the life of Jesus as depicted in the Gospels: childhood in Nazareth, baptism by John the Baptist, public ministry of teaching, clash with the religious leaders, and finally death on the cross. However, he maintained that this outline went back to the creative imagination of the early church in its desire to interpret Jesus' life as a fulfillment of Old Testament prophecy. Messianic expectation demanded that the Messiah perform miracles and act like a new Moses and a Davidic king. Once Jesus acquired the reputation of being the Messiah, Christ, his followers created myths about him. Strauss firmly believed that the pious devotion of the early church had turned the historical Jesus into a divine figure.

To get at the historical basis of Jesus' life, Strauss conducted a thorough historical-critical investigation of the Gospels. He contended that the Gospel writers shared the mythical worldview of their culture. But in contrast to Hermann S. Reimarus, who regarded the evangelists as fraudulent, Strauss maintained that the mythical language had to be accepted as a natural mode of primitive people. His reflections on the much disputed term *myth* are his lasting contribution to biblical studies and theology. In the nineteenth century, *myth* came into prominence as a category to describe the miraculous in the Gospels, first with regard to the virgin birth and the resurrection of Jesus. Strauss extended the use of myth to cover all miraculous events in the Gospels. He also expanded the focus of myth from a miracle to the *story* of a miracle. Myths were means of expressing a conviction with the help of a story. For example, the story about the resurrection helped express the conviction that Jesus lives. Clearly, myths were not history; myths could be regarded as "true" stories in that they were not meant to be lies (in other words, they communicated a message, albeit not always what the text literally said) but were not historically accurate.

According to Strauss, the Gospel accounts are basically reliable if not historically accurate. However, the factual kernel at the heart of the mythical husk is of no significance since Christian proclamation is primarily philosophical in nature, not directly connected with history. Here Strauss agreed with the basic approach of his teacher Hegel, who advocated the concept of "universal truth" (truth that is valid always and everywhere, even apart from specific historical contexts). Strauss thought that whether the resurrection happened was not important; what was important was that belief in the resurrection communicated an expression of the cultural consciousness of a primitive people.

Consequently, Strauss criticized both the rationalists and the orthodox. The orthodox, who freely accepted the supernaturalism of the biblical canon, demanded belief in the incredible, especially miracles, which was not acceptable to modern people. The rationalists, on the other hand, wanted to interpret the Bible within the confines of naturalism and therefore distorted the text beyond credible limits in an attempt to find a natural explanation for miracles and other beliefs. Yet Strauss acknowledged that the church cannot believe in a Christ who is only one among us. The concept of myth helped Strauss avoid these two extremes. With the help of myth, he was able to appropriate the truths expressed in the early preaching of the evangelists. For example, the incarnation could be reinterpreted as credible to modern men and women by applying the truth that the Gospels present in mythical form not to Jesus alone but to the human race as a whole. In other words, incarnation is not limited to one particular person such as Jesus of Nazareth. Rather, incarnation means the presence of God(-consciousness) in humanity in general. Jesus may just be a special "concentrated" expression of that presence.

Toward the end of his life, Strauss published still another book, *The Old and New Faith* (1872), which conveyed that Jesus has no special relevance for Christianity; what matters is a purely humanistic ethic. This work soon brought Strauss's influence to an end.

Jesus and the Kingdom of God

For another noted representative of liberalism, Albrecht Ritschl, the emerging conflict between theology and science arose out of a failure to distinguish between "scientific" and "religious" types of knowledge. The former strives for pure theoretical, disinterested knowledge, in other words, ascertaining the way things are. The latter consists of value judgments about reality and attempts to determine the way things ought to be. Whenever this distinction is blurred, Ritschl argued, problems arise. But if the area of theology is thus defined, what is the source and norm of theology? Predictably, Ritschl was nervous about the continuing use of metaphysics. According to Ritschl, it is not the Bible, which in the past was regarded as the Word of God, that should be the source of theology but rather the "apostolic circle of ideas" (the original message of Jesus as it was received by the first disciples before later theological interpretations), in which the teaching of the kingdom of God is the center. He based this determination on the simple fact that in his and other liberals' interpretations of the life of Jesus, the center of Jesus' preaching is the kingdom of God.

The term "kingdom of God," however, is ambiguous and could have several meanings, for example, an eschatological transformation of the world. But this kind of end-time view of the kingdom of God was foreign to the naturalist orientation of classical liberalism. In their understanding, Jesus' teaching about the kingdom of God was entirely ethical in nature. Jesus proclaimed a kingdom centered on the unity of humanity organized according to love. Out of this preaching came the main affirmation concerning the Father of Jesus: God is love. According to liberal thinkers, theology is not interested in metaphysical speculations about who God is, certainly not about the attributes of God or the doctrine of the Trinity—topics on which the classical writers had spent so much ink—but about the "effects" of God, how God relates to us. In fact, Ritschl was more interested in the kingdom of God centered around the primacy of love than in God himself.

Not surprisingly, Ritschl denied the classical views of the divinity and humanity of Christ and reformulated them radically; he regarded the classical view of the two natures as "scientific" rather than "religious" and therefore misplaced. The truly religious estimate of Jesus is interested in his historical conduct, "for in this does he exercise influence upon us."[2] The only meaning of "divinity" is the unique "vocation" given to Jesus by God and its influence on us in effecting our salvation. Jesus perfectly fulfilled the ideal of the kingdom of God in love and emphasized the moral influence of his life.

In his main work, the three-volume *Christian Doctrine of Justification and Reconciliation,* Ritschl took as the starting point for Christology the "moral effects of the life, passion, death and resurrection of Christ towards the founding of the Church."[3] However, in contradiction to his main view of theology, he allowed the preexistence of Jesus some room. Jesus "preexisted" in the sense that he and his work are eternally known and willed by God. What, according to Ritschl's later work, was new about Jesus? "Jesus was conscious of a new and hitherto unknown relation to God."[4]

Adolf von Harnack, church historian from the University of Berlin, left his mark on the recent history of theology with his widely acclaimed book *What Is Christianity?* originally published in 1900. In that work, he responded to the basic, simple question of what Christianity was originally,

---

2. Albrecht Ritschl, *The Christian Doctrine of Justification and Reconciliation,* vol. 3 (Edinburgh: T & T Clark, 1900), 413.
3. Ibid., 3.
4. Ibid., 386.

that is, in the mind of Jesus apart from later theological developments. Harnack argued that Jesus desired no other belief in his person than what was contained in keeping his commandments. His consciousness of himself as the Son of God was nothing but the practical consequence of knowing God as the divine Father.

Harnack came to the conclusion that there were three basic principles in Jesus' teaching: the (ethical) kingdom of God, the Fatherhood of God, and the infinite value of the human soul. In Harnack's view, Jesus' preaching was concerned exclusively with the individual and summoned a call to repentance. All Christian dogmas, especially trinitarian and christological doctrines, were later Hellenizations of the simple gospel of Christ. In this sense, he talked about the "deterioration of dogma"; he regarded the development of dogma as a sort of chronic illness. The notion of dogma owed nothing to Jesus but was a result of the transition of the gospel from a Jewish to a Hellenistic milieu.

The most famous statement of Harnack, often quoted and often misinterpreted, stated, "The Gospel, as Jesus proclaimed it, has to do with the Father only and not with the Son (though Jesus) was its personal realization and its strength, and this he is felt to be still."[5] This does not mean that Jesus was not conscious of his calling but rather that the entire thrust of Jesus' message and life was to serve the kingdom of his Father.

Central to Harnack's project was the rejection of classical Christologies and the rejection of the claim that exegetes can reach the historical Jesus, the image of the ethical kingdom. In line with liberalism, he dismissed apocalyptic elements in the Gospels and saw doctrines as secondary, for the gospel is nothing other than Jesus Christ himself. The gospel is not a doctrine about Jesus but is the person of Jesus.

Classical liberalism brought the quest to its logical end. Those involved in a naturalistic inquiry into the life and psychology of Jesus of Nazareth were naive in that they hoped to go behind the interpretations of Jesus' followers. Several scholars, mainly in the area of New Testament studies, trained in the spirit of liberalism, however, soon began to doubt the possibility of what liberalism attempted and raised a series of questions that the movement could not address. To this topic we turn next.

5. Adolf von Harnack, *What Is Christianity?* (1900; reprint, New York: Harper, 1957), 144.

10

The Collapse of the Original Quest

The Eschatological Message of Jesus

Soon after the heyday of Adolf von Harnack's proposal (that the essence of Christianity is the ethical teaching of Jesus about the Father and the kingdom of God), doubts arose about the propriety of the methodology and aim of the original quest. The aim of classical liberalism to construct an authentic, psychological life of Jesus as an ethical teacher and a model of righteousness came to an end with the rise of various types of criticism. The decisive beginning of the growing skepticism was marked by Albrecht Ritschl's son-in-law, Johannes Weiss, in his work *Jesus' Proclamation of the Kingdom of God,* published in 1892. The basic thesis of Weiss was that, as unappealing as the idea of apocalypticism and the coming end of the world was to modern readers of the Bible, there was no denying the thoroughly eschatological nature of Jesus' preaching. Late Jewish apocalypticism and the expectation of the imminent end of the world and the coming of the Messiah and the kingdom of God are radically otherworldly: "The kingdom of God, as Jesus conceived it, is a radically otherworldly entity which stands in diametric opposition to this world."[1]

If eschatology is removed from his preaching, Jesus of Nazareth is turned into a liberal teacher who has little to do with Jesus of Nazareth. In other

---

1. Johannes Weiss, *Jesus' Proclamation of the Kingdom of God* (1892; reprint, London: SCM, 1971), 114.

words, Weiss sought to wake up the proponents of the original quest to the painful realization that, though they wanted to paint a reliable picture of the Jesus of history, they had let the Enlightenment outlook so permeate their approach that they were unable to see the reality of Jesus. In decisive strokes, Weiss portrayed the apocalypticism and eschatology of Jesus' message in six theses:

1. The kingdom Jesus preached was transcendent and supramundane rather than an ethical teaching.
2. The kingdom belonged to the future and was not (only) part of today.
3. Jesus did not regard himself as the founder of the kingdom but waited for God to bring it.
4. The kingdom was much larger than the small circle of his followers and could not be identified with the band of the disciples.
5. The kingdom was not expected to grow gradually but would entail a radical cosmic transformation.
6. The kingdom's ethic was not continuous with liberalism's expectations but was mainly negative and world-denying.

Weiss also maintained, in contrast to liberalism, that Jesus expected to become the Son of Man, even though eventually he came to realize that this would occur only after his death.

Albert Schweitzer took up the basic theses of Weiss and brought them to their logical conclusion. He emphasized even more the eschatological nature of Jesus' message. For Schweitzer, liberalism's portrait of Jesus was a false modernization. Still, he believed that it might be possible to reach the historical Jesus, but it required total attention to the preaching of Jesus as it is displayed in the Gospels. Eschatological conceptions lay at the very heart of Jesus' teaching. Jesus did not send the Twelve to teach the people about ethical life but to warn them of the coming end and judgment; the disciples were to go from one city to another hastily and to call for repentance (Matthew 10 and par.). They were "men of violence" (Matt. 11:12 RSV) who would provoke the messianic tribulation that would herald the kingdom; the Twelve were not expected to come back from their mission trip until the end. When the end did not come, Jesus decided to offer his own life as a ransom for many (Mark 10:45), as a way of helping to usher in the kingdom.

Out of these accounts emerged a portrait of Jesus as a remote and strange figure: "He comes to us as one unknown."[2] Jesus expected to be the Son of Man, the Messiah coming on the clouds as a judge; he truly believed that this

2. Albert Schweitzer, *The Quest of the Historical Jesus,* 3d ed. (London: A & C Black, 1954), 401.

was to be his vocation. Initially, he revealed this messianic secret only to the inner circle of his disciples. According to Schweitzer, Judas told the secret to the high priest, who used it as the ground for Jesus' execution.

In the preaching of this apocalyptic visionary from Nazareth, the value of the kingdom is infinite; everything has to be forsaken for its sake. The kingdom would be totally new, not—as older liberals thought—a continuation of the ongoing ethical betterment of the world. The kingdom Jesus preached was supernatural; it would entail cosmic disturbances.

This is what Jesus taught and expected, but—unfortunately, says Schweitzer—he was, of course, wrong! The end did not come! He was mistaken in his hopes. What then is the significance and value of the life of Jesus for us? Schweitzer responded that the value of Jesus comes through knowing him in a mystical encounter: Jesus still "comes" to us as we follow him in discipleship. Through this encounter we gain inspiration to live authentic lives and to put into practice the noble teachings and life example of Jesus.

Gospel Criticism and the Impossibility of Writing a Life of Jesus

Weiss and Schweitzer were not the only critics of the original quest. Several other theologians began to question the possibility of writing a life about Jesus for the simple reason that our sources, the Gospels, do not allow it. They are not meant to be sources for a historical construct of the life of Jesus.

Traditionally, the Gospel of Matthew was regarded as the primary source for the life of Jesus; it was the first Gospel in the New Testament and seemed to be a good candidate for the one the other evangelists used when compiling their own narratives about Jesus. In 1776, however, following the ground-breaking insights of J. J. Griesbach's *Synopsis of the Gospels of Matthew, Mark, and Luke* and the emergence of the concept of the Synoptic Gospels, the Markan priority slowly began to be established. The liberal scholars came to the conclusion that Mark was in fact the most reliable guide to the history of Jesus because it seemed to be the least theological. But then a decisive blow to this assumption came from the Markan specialist William Wrede, whose *Messianic Secret in the Gospels,* published in 1901, showed that even the Gospel of Mark was a product of theological interpretation. Mark had interpreted the story of Jesus in light of the idea of the "messianic secret" (or "messianic mystery" from the German *Messiasgeheimnis*): Jesus did not reveal his messiahship to the people and even forbade others to do so. According to Wrede, the church explained Jesus' reservation about sharing his messiahship by devising stories that Jesus had secretly revealed his messiahship to the disciples and had forbidden them to broadcast it. In other words, Wrede argued that even Mark's Gospel, rather than being a historical source for the life of Jesus, was instead a collection of his disciples' interpretations. Therefore, the details of

Jesus' life were unavailable. This conclusion threw into question the rationale for the search for a historically accurate life of Jesus.

Martin Kähler, a systematic theologian, rejected the quest of the historical Jesus as historically fruitless and theologically bankrupt. In 1892, he subjected the original quest to harsh criticism in his highly polemical work *The So-called Historical Jesus and the Historical Biblical Christ.* He argued that given the limitations of the sources, it is impossible to construct a life of Jesus, and even if sources were available, no historian could reach what alone interests believers: the suprahistorical Savior. Critical-historical study can lead to only an Ebionite or an Arian Jesus, not to a suprahistorical Jesus, the object of faith. In Kähler's opinion, liberal Christology had drawn a false analogy between Jesus and humankind. The difference between the two is one not only of degree but also of kind. Therefore, liberalism's Jesus of history lacks the soteriological significance of the Christ of faith. Kähler also reminded his contemporaries of the fact that the New Testament proclamation of Christ does not presuppose a distinction between "the memory of the days of his flesh and the confession of his eternal significance."[3] Kähler feared that liberal study made faith dependent on human research; instead, he insisted that the Christ who influenced the course of history is the Christ who is preached, the Christ of faith. Ironically, Kähler's proposal appealed not only to conservatives who believed that their faith was grounded in history but also to radical thinkers such as Paul Tillich (whose views will be examined in part 3).

Another decisive criticism of the liberal quest of the historical Jesus came from the so-called History of Religions School, whose ablest proponent was Ernst Troeltsch. This approach, which reached its heyday between 1880 and 1920, sought to understand Jesus Christ in the context of the religious and cultural settings of the surrounding nations. It emphasized the continuity between the Bible and the ancient Near Eastern cultures and the discontinuity between the Bible and modern times. Weiss and Wrede shared many of the assumptions of this school.

Troeltsch was a radical champion of historical research and discredited supernaturalism in favor of history. In his view, Christology had to be based on solid historical research, and this research discredited the dogmatic approach to Christianity. In the spirit of his school, Troeltsch thought that everything human beings produce is historical, the result of historical development, including religion. Christianity is a historical phenomenon, an outcome of social and national conditions.

Troeltsch is often regarded as the first pluralist. For him, religion was participation in the divine presence and union between the human spirit and the absolute Spirit; this union was a sort of metaphysical reality within the psyche, a "transcendental subjectivity" that is available to all people every-

3. Quoted in Alister E. McGrath, *The Making of Modern German Christology 1750–1990,* 2d ed. (Grand Rapids: Zondervan, 1994), 114.

where. Troeltsch's understanding of general revelation was based on this insight, namely, that all people in all religions have the capacity to experience God. Of course, for him, this revelation was historical, not absolute. Therefore, both the Old Testament and the New Testament were phases in revelatory history. Jesus was not God but a mediator—psychologically and morally but not ontologically (in the sense of being of the same essence with God)—between God and human beings. Jesus had significance in that he mediated God's presence, though he was not unique in this regard.

Troeltsch believed that each religion has its own particular nature. Therefore, other religions cannot be brought closer to Christianity. Even though Christianity is the highest religion because it is the most universal and is not directly tied to a particular culture or society, its adherents do not have the right to "convert" others to Jesus Christ. Each religion has its own specific idea about how to experience God, and religions are valid in their own ways in their particular contexts. Troeltsch, therefore, rejected the idea of an absolute revelation in Jesus; he also rejected the idea of an incarnation in history. In the modernized version of Christianity, there was also no place for sin, miracles, or redemption.

The History of Religions School, with its idea of the continuity between the Bible and its surrounding religions, was both a critique and a continuation of the agenda of classical liberalism. On the one hand, it was critical of the naivete and idealism of liberalism's desire to paint a historically reliable picture of Jesus. On the other hand, the History of Religions School shared with liberalism the idea of continuity between the divine and the human, though with different emphases. Subsequent developments in the study of Christology emphasized exactly the opposite: discontinuity between humanity and God/Christ and the inability of humans to know anything about the divine unless the transcendent God reveals himself in Christ. This was the emphasis of neo-orthodoxy and Karl Barth, who will be studied in part 3.

The death blow to the original quest, however, did not end the search for the historical Jesus. It was revived in the middle of the twentieth century, though with a vastly different agenda.

Recent Developments of the Quest

The New Quest

In the 1950s, the new quest of the historical Jesus was taken up by Ernst Käsemann, a student of Rudolf Bultmann who wanted to revise the agenda of the original quest. Käsemann believed that writing a biography of Jesus, as the original quest had hoped to do, was not possible, nor could he agree with Bultmann and others that the historical details of Jesus' earthly life were secondary to faith in Christ (a view opposite to that of the original quest). Nevertheless, Käsemann believed that the main content of Jesus' public life could be reconstructed; available sources give a clear enough picture of Jesus' life and teaching.

Once again the importance of history to *kērygma,* the apostolic proclamation of salvation through Jesus Christ, was fully acknowledged. Even though the evangelists were theologians, they believed they had access to reliable historical information. On the basis of this conviction, one could assume continuity between the preaching about Jesus and information about Jesus. Moreover, the preaching about Jesus is the only source for the history of Jesus. Käsemann's colleague Gerhard Ebeling similarly contended that if it were shown that Christology had no basis in the historical Jesus but rather was a misinterpretation of Jesus, the entire idea of Christology would be ruined. In other words, to confess Christ, we have to know something about the Jesus of history.

The Third Quest

Yet to be seen is the future of the third quest and whether it has a common agenda other than the conviction that more can be known about Jesus than was discovered or admitted in the earlier quests. Even though it is not easy to present common "results" of this latest phase of the quest, it can be said that most participants share the conviction that Jesus was not the Jesus of liberal Protestantism nor of the new quest. Rather, he was a historical figure whose life and actions were rooted in first-century Judaism with its particular religious, social, economic, and political conditions.

Three main varieties of the third quest have been distinguished: the radical, the conservative, and the "new perspective." The most radical approach to the study of Jesus is exemplified by the Jesus Seminar in the United States. It seeks to examine the layers of tradition in both the New Testament and extra-canonical accounts of Jesus' words in order to find a valid base for determining who Jesus really was. The Jesus Seminar has become famous for its series of red letter editions of Jesus' words such as *The Parables of Jesus,* published in 1988. Utilizing various colors, this particular scholarly consensus communicates its opinion concerning which words of Jesus most likely came from Jesus himself (red color).

The conservative tradition is represented by the British scholar C. F. D. Moule and his *Origin of Christology.*[4] Moule is critical of the idea of an evolutionary process, in the manner of the History of Religions School, that connects belief in Christ as a divine figure with conceptions from the surrounding mythical and mystery religions. Instead, Moule believes that the development process through which the Jesus of history became the confessed Christ of

---

4. C. F. D. Moule, *Origin of Christology* (Cambridge: Cambridge University Press, 1977).

faith goes back to Jesus himself, and that process was legitimate. In this regard, Moule shows evidence that the titles Son of Man, Son of God, Christ, and Lord relate to the historical Jesus and are not foreign to him. In other words, these New Testament titles are not later interpretations of Jesus but are firmly rooted in Jesus' own life and words. The same principle applies to the Pauline developments of Christology.

The most distinctive orientation of the third quest, what has been called the "new perspective," seeks to place Jesus in the context of the religious, social, economic, and political world of Judaism. It asks questions such as, Why did Jesus instigate such opposition from the political and religious establishment of the Jews? Several Jewish scholars, including Martin Buber and J. C. G. Montefiore, have joined the quest here. Similarly, several non-Jewish scholars, such as John K. Riches with his work *Jesus and the Transformation of Judaism,*[5] have tried to examine the Jewish background and conditions of the Jesus event.

Of special interest to the third quest is the relationship between Jesus and politics, especially his relationship with the revolutionary movements of his time. For example, it has been suggested that Jesus sympathized with the goals of the Zealot movement, an aggressive nationalist movement, but these sympathies were downplayed by the evangelists. This proposal, however, has met with rejection by the majority of scholars.

The topic of miracles, which has been discussed since the beginning of the original quest of the historical Jesus, has been a subject of lively debate in recent decades. The most radical position has maintained that the miracle stories point to the fact that Jesus was a magician and that the Gospels deliberately tried to obscure the truth. A British theologian who teaches in the United States, Colin Brown, has responded to this claim and to the related suspicion that miracle stories are only the intrusion of later tradition developed under the Hellenistic idea of "divine men," who were supposed to perform miracles. According to Brown, the Gospels present two conflicting types of theology, that of the evangelists and that of the Jewish authorities. According to the evangelists' theology, Jesus, the Christ, was anointed and empowered by the Spirit in accordance with the Old Testament expectations. By contrast, the theology of the Jewish authorities, based on the Old Testament Law, interpreted Jesus' miracles and claims in light of the warnings concerning false prophets (especially Deuteronomy 13, which warns of false prophets who perform miracles and therefore lead people astray). The miracles of Jesus are thus understood in different ways depending on whether one believes the evangelists or the Jewish authorities. For Jesus' followers, the miracles were

5. John K. Riches, *Jesus and the Transformation of Judaism* (1980; reprint, New York: Seabury Press, 1982).

signs pointing to the coming of the kingdom of God in the person and work of Christ.

It is one of the ironies of history—and theological scholarship—that as soon as everyone thought the quest of the historical Jesus was a chapter in history—interesting in itself but shown to be impossible—a new wave of inquiry emerged in the 1950s. This was followed by the unprecedented enthusiasm of yet another wave, the third quest. While there are radical, irreconcilable differences between these various stages—and one almost questions the wisdom of connecting them terminologically—they share the desire of questioning much of two thousand years of ecclesiastical and theological formulations of Christology. The third quest is alive and well, and one hopes that those involved will begin to dialogue more widely with systematic theology.

Part 3

Christ in the Contemporary World: Western Christologies

The third part of this book is devoted to introducing various christological interpretations that arose during the twentieth century based on the historical and biblical developments studied above. The twentieth century produced more christological interpretations than any other century in the history of Christian theology. And the continual appearance of new monographs and articles on the topic has created a situation in which no one can keep up with all the developments. For a basic survey such as this, however, a discussion of selected approaches is sufficient.

The approach taken here in regard to the mosaic of recent Western Christologies is as follows: Ten theologians who have written extensively on Christology will be studied. These theologians were selected with a view to theological, ecclesiastical, and ecumenical representativeness. Three theologians from the first part of the twentieth century, namely, Karl Barth, Rudolf Bultmann, and Paul Tillich, were selected because they embody the various routes taken after the quest of the historical Jesus and pave the way for most later figures. The rest of the theologians chosen for this survey represent the major Christian traditions: Eastern Orthodox (John Zizioulas), Roman Catholic (Karl Rahner), various traditional Protestant churches (Reformed: Jürgen Moltmann; Lutheran: Wolfhart Pannenberg), and newer Protestant churches

(Anabaptist: Norman Kraus; Baptist: Stanley Grenz). John Hick, while representing a mainstream tradition (Anglican), has questioned much of mainstream theology with his pluralism. The only major Christian tradition not represented in this survey is Pentecostalism, for the simple reason that a specifically Pentecostal Christologist has yet to appear.

A qualifying comment, however, is in order: Even though the survey is representative with regard to ecclesiastical and ecumenical variety, that is not the main point. Each theologian selected for a closer scrutiny represents his own tradition in a unique way. Certainly, Pannenberg is a Lutheran theologian, but his wide ecumenical attitude and self-critical treatment of the Lutheran tradition hardly make him a typical Lutheran theologian. The same principle applies to other theologians. For example, Zizioulas is as much the expositor as the critic of his own tradition, Eastern Orthodoxy. Furthermore, Grenz was chosen not because he is a Baptist but because he represents a theological movement often called evangelicalism. This transdenominational approach has distinctive convictions as different from, say, the liberalism of Tillich as from the existentialism of Bultmann.

11

Karl Barth

Dialectical Christology

The Theology of the "Holy Other"

Karl Barth—who has been hailed as the church father for the twentieth century and undoubtedly one of the most significant voices of modern Christian theology—targeted his criticism toward liberal teachers under whose tutelage he had received his theological training. He believed the main problem with liberalism was that it blurred the radical boundary between God and humanity and made religion a matter of this world:

> To speak about God meant to speak about humanity, no doubt in elevated tone, but . . . about human faith and works. Without doubt human beings were magnified at the expense of God—the God who is sovereign Other standing over against humanity. . . . This God who is the free partner in a history which he himself inaugurated and in a dialogue ruled by him—this divine God was in danger of being reduced to a pious notion: the mythical expression and symbol of human excitation oscillating between its own psychic heights or depths, whose truth could only be that of a monologue and its own graspable content.[1]

1. Karl Barth, "The Humanity of God," in *Karl Barth: Theologian of Freedom,* ed. Clifford Green (London: Collins, 1979), 48.

111

Barth condemned liberal theology for focusing too much on humanity and thus replacing the traditional starting point of theology "from above" with an approach "from below." The background to Barth's break with liberal theology came mainly from two sources. First, the liberal theology he had been taught was useless in his weekly task of preaching to a small Swiss country church. Consequently, he devoted his time to a careful, painstaking study of Scripture; later on, as he was writing his monumental thirteen-part *Church Dogmatics* (1932–67), he included in his theological discussion detailed and extensive exegesis of the biblical text. To one key verse alone, John 1:14, he devoted more than forty pages! Second, he was appalled by his liberal teachers' sympathies with Germany's war leaders in 1914 and concluded that this was another result of liberalism's failure to make distinctions between this-worldly and transcendent agendas.

The starting point for Barth's theological fame was his commentary *The Epistle to the Romans,* first published in 1918 and completely revised four years later. In that work he presented the outline of what has been called "neo-orthodoxy," "dialectical theology," or "theology of crisis." This theology continued the basic convictions of classical orthodoxy as presented in the creeds and patristic and other theologies before the Enlightenment such as the divinity of Christ and divine revelation; therefore, it was contrary to liberalism. At the same time, it was *neo-,* "new," a modification of orthodox beliefs such as the doctrine of election and the Bible as God's Word. It was characterized by a sharp dialectic between the otherness of God and humankind, the impossibility of humanity's knowing anything about God apart from God's self-revelation, and so on. In this dialectical theology, God and world were set in antithesis, as were revelation and religions. Christianity is not a religion that represents humanity's independent search for God; rather, Christianity is the self-revelation of God in Jesus Christ. Such a theology was called a theology of crisis because it depicted humanity as utterly desperate apart from the sovereign election and redemption of God in Christ. Barth's theology, written during the two major crises of the modern world, World Wars I and II, reflected the uncertainties of those turbulent times.

For Barth, God is totally Other. There is no contact point between humankind and God apart from that which God has created, that is, the person of Jesus Christ. God stands over and against humanity and everything human in an infinite qualitative distinction and is never identical to anything that we name or worship as God. Barth describes this wholly other God as the perfection of divine love and divine freedom. The freedom of God's love means that God's love is not necessary unless he freely chooses to love. The same can be said of God's freedom; it is totally free. God's unlimited love and freedom meet in Jesus Christ, who establishes the covenant of love that serves as the basis for our salvation.

With Rudolf Bultmann, Albert Schweitzer, Johannes Weiss, and others, Barth argued for the strong eschatological orientation of the New Testament and the preaching of Jesus. In his opinion, Christianity that is not "totally and utterly eschatology, has totally and utterly nothing to do with Christ."[2]

Christ in the Trinity

To say that Barth's theology is completely Christocentric is not meant to downplay the equally thoroughgoing trinitarian orientation of his system. In fact, Barth's theology is authentically structured around the principle of the Trinity. The entire panorama of the history of salvation is seen from the standpoint of the Trinity. Therefore, his starting point is not the brief history of Jesus in the incarnation but his history in eternity, with the preexistent Christ as the Second Person of the Trinity.

For Barth, the Trinity is that which makes the doctrine of God distinctively Christian. "The doctrine of the Trinity is what basically distinguishes the Christian doctrine of God as Christian, and therefore what already distinguishes the Christian concept of revelation as Christian, in contrast to all other possible doctrines of God or concepts of revelation."[3] The doctrine of the Trinity is the only possible Christian answer to the question, Who is the self-revealing God of the Bible? God's revelation is God himself. God is who he reveals himself to be. Consequently, Jesus Christ is identical with God. "The reality of Jesus Christ is that God Himself in person is actively present in the flesh. God Himself in person is the Subject of a real human being and acting."[4]

Whereas classical theology freely used the term *person* with reference to the three members of the Trinity, Barth does not. He thinks the modern term *person* differs so much from the earlier usage that it confuses. The modern use of the term *person* implies the existence of three different members of the Trinity with their own wills and minds. Barth prefers the term "mode of Being" (from German *Seinsweise*). God has only one personality and therefore to talk about three persons is contrary to this principle. Barth notes that if Christ were a distinct person, he could not possibly act as God's *self*-revelation.

The Ambiguous Nature of the Humanity of Christ

Barth has no difficulty accepting the divinity of Jesus Christ. To him, the more challenging aspect of the person of Christ is the meaning and value of

2. Quoted in Alister E. McGrath, *The Making of Modern German Christology 1750–1990,* 2d ed. (Grand Rapids: Zondervan, 1994), 128.
3. Karl Barth, *Church Dogmatics,* vol. 1, part 1 (Edinburgh: T & T Clark, 1975), 301.
4. Karl Barth, *Church Dogmatics,* vol. 1, part 2 (Edinburgh: T & T Clark, 1956), 151.

Christ's humanity. Barth notes that the New Testament always assumes the genuine humanity of Jesus, who is qualitatively different from all other humans. Before he became flesh, Jesus was the Son of God and was by nature God. Because he is God, however, he is human in a different way from all other humans. Jesus Christ as God can act in an absolute way and also in a finite way. He assumed a worldly form without giving up his divine form. Barth assures us that God does not cease to be God in the incarnation. Jesus is authentically human only as the Son of God. The Son did not give up being God by becoming man, but at the same time, as man he was not omnipotent and eternal but limited in time and space. The incarnation shows us that for God it is just as natural to be lowly as to be exalted.

Moreover, Jesus did not simply assume the place of humankind in general. First of all, he took upon himself the Jewish flesh of the time and, even more, sinful humanity. By doing so Christ made himself the target of the divine judgment that was to be ours. With reference to the familiar story of the prodigal son in the Gospel of Luke, Barth talks about the journey of the Son "into the far country." Christ as the obedient Son became servant of all. Barth always reminds us that even though there is no doubt about the full and authentic humanity of Jesus Christ, the New Testament portrays this genuinely human being as the one who is qualitatively different from all other humans.

In considering the humanity of Christ, Barth owes much to the thinking of Søren Kierkegaard, the highly original Danish thinker. Kierkegaard maintained that the real contemporaries of Jesus were not Jesus' contemporaries in history but modern believers. For Kierkegaard, there was nothing special in being an eyewitness; after all, most people missed Jesus' significance even though they saw the miracles and heard his extraordinary wisdom in teaching. This is what Kierkegaard called the "divine incognito," the fact that the deity of Christ was thoroughly hidden in the humanity. Kierkegaard also taught Barth that "truth is subjectivity," and he contrasted the "objective" approach to God and Jesus Christ with the "subjective." In the objective approach, God and Christ are treated as objects, facts to be grasped intellectually and scientifically. In the subjective approach, they are treated existentially, and the relation of the knower to the known is passionate, not that of an outside observer. For Kierkegaard, Christian faith and knowledge of Christ are a matter of inward appropriation. "If Christianity were a doctrine, then the relation to it would not be one of faith, since there is only an intellectual relation to a doctrine."[5]

In a sense, we have to say that, for Barth, the fact of Christ's human nature is not a problem, nor is there anything significant in it. He agrees with other

5. Søren Kierkegaard, *Concluding Unscientific Postscript to the "Philosophical Fragments,"* ed. and trans. Howard V. Hong and Edna H. Hong (Princeton, N.J.: Princeton University Press, 1977), 326.

neo-orthodox thinkers and with Bultmann that it is difficult to find any historically valid information about the Jesus of history and that even if it were accessible, it would not be of great help. To the one who wants to place one's faith
in Christ, the details of Christ's earthly life are not significant. After all, the
human life of Jesus, what he did and taught, is not the main focus of God's revelation. On the contrary, for Barth, the information we obtain about Jesus
through the use of the historical method serves more to conceal than to reveal
his deity. In a famous exchange of letters with Adolf von Harnack, his teacher,
he went so far as to argue that the meager results of historical inquiry into Jesus
could paradoxically serve a good purpose by demolishing a place where faith
might be tempted to seek false support. This is in accord with Barth's view of
revelation: The words and events of the Bible in themselves are not revelatory
unless God manifests himself in an encounter event with the person reading or
listening to the Word. Barth is not bothered at all by the "ugly ditch" of Gotthold Lessing, the problem of the historical and existential distance of modern
times from the times of the Gospel stories. For him, what happened to Christ
has an abiding, once-for-all significance for humankind. How do we know that?
How can we be sure that an event that occurred centuries ago has such a meaning? Again, Barth appears to be a fideist. He bluntly says that we must accept
the significance of Christ's death and resurrection from the testimony of the
church and ultimately from the biblical witness.

Barth is opposed to the attempts of certain apologists to argue on the basis
of Jesus' miracles and extraordinary life that Christ was truly divine. He
thinks that even if the entire biography of Jesus, based on the most reliable
historical information, could be written, that endeavor would hide the real
deity of Christ rather than make it evident. This happened in Jesus' lifetime:
The more miracles he did, the more opposition he encountered. "Flesh and
blood" could never reveal to Peter, one of the closest disciples of Christ, his
true messiahship.

The Mediator

Barth's theology is Christ-centered; Barth saw this as the emphasis of the
Bible:

> When Holy Scripture speaks of God, it concentrates our attention and
> thoughts upon one single point. . . . And if we look closer, and ask: who and
> what is at this point upon which our attention and thoughts are concentrated,
> which we are to recognize as God? . . . Then from its beginning to its end the
> Bible directs us to the name of Jesus Christ.[6]

6. Karl Barth, *Church Dogmatics,* vol. 2, part 2 (Edinburgh: T & T Clark, 1957), 52–54.

The Catholic interpreter of Barth, Hans Urs von Balthasar, described Barth's theology as an intellectual hourglass "where God and man meet in the center through Jesus Christ. There is no other point of encounter between the top and bottom portions of the glass."[7] Another interpreter of Barth, Alister E. McGrath, says, "Every theological proposition in the *Church Dogmatics* may be regarded as christological, in the sense that it has its point of departure in Jesus Christ."[8]

The role of Christ as the mediator between the transcendent God and humankind comes to focus in Christ's dual role as the agent of revelation and of reconciliation. By virtue of the incarnation, God and humanity are united. In his divinity, Jesus represents God to humankind; in his humanity, Jesus represents humankind to God. By virtue of the incarnation, human beings can be made participants in the covenant to which God has obliged himself. In this covenant, God acts on behalf of humankind through and in Christ.

Revelation is possible only by virtue of Christ's mediation. Thomas Aquinas and other medieval theologians had assumed with their "analogy of being" conception that knowledge of God is an innate capacity within human experience or human nature; in other words, they assumed an analogy between creation and the Creator. Barth repudiates this idea and suggests the principle of an "analogy of faith": Knowledge of God and faith are possible only because God graciously gives them in Jesus Christ, who is both God and human. One either has them or does not. Every attempt to prove knowledge of God and/or faith is almost idolatry. This view is "fideism" (from the Latin word meaning "faith"), a reliance on faith rather than reason in the pursuit of religious truth. Faith requires a blind leap of faith.

Jesus Christ is the final and ultimate revelation of God and the focus of revelation. The Word of God appears in three related forms: in the person of Christ; in the written Word, the Scripture; and in the Word preached. The Bible in itself is not God's Word but rather becomes such to the extent that God causes it to be his Word in an encounter between God and a human being. The Word of God is an event rather than a communication of doctrines. The Bible is a witness, for it points beyond itself to another, to Jesus Christ. The event of Jesus Christ in human history makes possible the miracle of knowledge of God. In the process of revelation, Jesus Christ reveals himself, not information about himself. Therefore, the final authority of Scripture lies in the person of Christ.

For Barth, Jesus stands between God and humankind as the mediator who brings redemption and salvation. He became man to plead our case. Through his passion and death, he reestablished the covenant between God and hu-

7. Hans Urs von Balthasar, *The Theology of Karl Barth* (New York: Holt, Rinehart & Winston, 1971), 170.
8. McGrath, *The Making of Modern German Christology*, 131.

manity that had been broken, not only by the first human pair but by all of us. As the Son of God, he had the authority to make this substitution and to permit his death.

An Electing God and Elected Man

> Of Jesus Christ we know nothing more surely and definitely than this—that in free obedience to His Father He elected to be man, and as man, to do the will of God. If God elects us too, then it is in and with this election of Jesus Christ. . . . It is in him that the eternal election becomes immediately and directly the promise of our own election as it is enacted in time.[9]

The Christ-centeredness of Barth's theology also comes into sharp focus in the way Barth conceives of election, one of the guiding principles of his theology in general and his Christology in particular. In contrast to the traditional Reformed position, according to which God has elected some for salvation and others for perdition (double predestination), Barth maintains that all God's elective actions are centered on Christ and Christ only. The election of God does not apply to individuals. Barth regards John Calvin's Reformed doctrine of election as too static and a misrepresentation of the Bible. The passages in the Bible that talk about election (Romans 9 and Ephesians 1 being the most important ones) have to be read christologically. When doing so, one formulates a doctrine of election and predestination in light of God's work of revelation and atonement. By sending his Son to be the incarnate God-man, God revealed his will to save men and women, not to reject them. The incarnation is proof that God is for humanity, not against it.

The only person to be elected by God is the person of Jesus Christ. This is Barth's major modification of the traditional view of election. The eternal will of God is realized in the election of Jesus Christ from eternity. There is no other will of God, no other unchangeable "decree" (a technical term in classical theology that denotes God's predetermined will to elect) apart from or beyond Jesus Christ and his election. God is not bound to a deterministic, unchangeable decree; rather, like a king with "holy mutability," he is absolutely free to fulfill his purpose of saving all.

Jesus Christ, as the focus of God's election, acts not only as an individual but also as the representative of humanity. In him, the entire human race has been chosen for salvation. But Barth goes further. Jesus Christ is not only the elected man but also at the same time the electing God. This is Barth's version of double predestination: Jesus Christ acts in his dual role as the elected man

---

9. Barth, *Church Dogmatics* 2.2:105–6.

and electing God. Therefore, Barth completely alters the classical concept of double predestination according to which some are chosen for salvation while others are chosen for condemnation.

As the representative of the entire human race, Christ has freely chosen not only to become a man but to become a man for us; he chose the "reprobation, perdition, and death"[10] that was ours. Voluntarily, he chose to be rejected by humanity and crucified on the cross. Thus, God elected Christ to bear completely the pain and cost of redemption. God chose to accept the cross and the lot of fallen humanity. Furthermore, God elected Christ to take from us the judgment. Christ was rejected in order that we might not be rejected. The negative side of predestination, which was to be ours, was directed toward Christ.

Rather than speaking about double predestination with regard to individuals, Barth instead uses the term "universal election." All human beings are included in the election of Jesus Christ by God. Because Christ was condemned on the cross for our sins, no other condemnation follows. Not all are living as elected, however, and it is the task of the elected community, the church, to proclaim that a person "belongs eternally to Jesus Christ and is not rejected, but elected by God in Jesus Christ" and "that the rejection which he deserves on account of his perverse choice is borne and cancelled by Jesus Christ; and that he is appointed to eternal life with God on the basis of the righteous, divine decision."[11]

Some people, therefore, know that they are elected, while others have not yet realized it. The former are already living in light of being elected, the others as if they were not. What this means in terms of the doctrine of salvation is a disputed issue in Barthian studies and a debate we cannot enter here. It is clear, however, that Barth is either a universalist (the view according to which all will be saved) or at least has strong universalist leanings. An assessment of Barth's view by another neo-orthodox theologian, Emil Brunner, leaves little doubt about the main orientation of Barth's doctrine of election in Christ:

> What does this statement, "that Jesus is the only really rejected person," mean for the situation of humanity? Evidently this: that there is no possibility of condemnation. . . . The decision has already been made in Jesus Christ—for all of humanity. Whether they know it or not, believe it or not, is not so important. They are like people who seem to be perishing in a stormy sea. But in the reality they are not in a sea in which one can drown, but in shallow waters, in which it is impossible to drown. Only they do not know it.[12]

10. Ibid., 2.2:163.
11. Ibid., 2.2:306.
12. Emil Brunner, *The Christian Doctrine of God* (London: Lutterworth Press, 1949), 348–49.

12

Rudolf Bultmann

Mythological Christology

A New Approach to the Study of the Gospels and Jesus

What makes the figure and thinking of Rudolf Bultmann so fascinating is that he drew from many different sources, especially neo-orthodoxy, existentialism, particularly Martin Heidegger, and liberalism, even though he saw himself as a critic of that movement. A contemporary of Karl Barth, Bultmann was both indebted to and critical of his ideas. Also of interest is the fact that he was not a systematic theologian, as are the other Christologists discussed in this section, but rather a New Testament scholar. Nevertheless, the importance of his ideas for systematic theology has been significant. One of his main contributions to theology was his refusal to separate biblical exegesis from constructive theology.

Bultmann had to deal with the aftermath of the collapse of the liberal quest of the historical Jesus, but he did so in light of a rapidly developing New Testament methodology. Bultmann was one of the main architects of a new approach to Gospel study, namely, form criticism. The basic idea of form criticism is that the frameworks of the Gospel stories were created by the authors for their own specific purposes, and thus the Gospels are less helpful for historical investigation than for theological interpretation. Bultmann wanted to analyze in detail the traditions that lie behind the Gospels as they were shaped by the Christian communities. He came to the conclusion that what the Gospels tell about Jesus and his life relates more to the *Sitz im Leben,* life situation, of the early church than to the historical life of Jesus. For example, many sayings attributed to Jesus were instead the theological interpretations of his followers.

Bultmann also continued the long tradition of the History of Religions School, which argues that many leading ideas of the New Testament go back to non-Jewish sources. In other words, New Testament ideas can be attributed to the contemporary religions and mythologies of the surrounding nations, such as Egyptian mysticism, Hellenistic philosophies, various mystery religions, and so on. The title "Lord" that is applied to Jesus in the New Testament is an example of this kind of borrowed material.

On the basis of form criticism and his disappointment with the original quest of the historical Jesus, Bultmann sympathized with Martin Kähler, who doubted the possibility of acquiring historically valid information about the life of Jesus and went further to claim that even if we could, such information would not help us with regard to faith in Christ. For Bultmann, however, this lack of knowledge concerning the Jesus of history was not a detriment to Christian faith. Rather than the history of Jesus, it is the *kērygma* of the New Testament that is central to faith. In Bultmann's view, that is the approach of the New Testament itself: The New Testament is not concerned about the facts of Jesus' life but the confession of faith. Faith is not knowledge of historical facts but a personal commitment to Christ.

A crucial terminological distinction that Bultmann also borrowed from Kähler involved two views of history that can best be illustrated using the original German terms *Historie* and *Geschichte*. *Historie* means the events of the past as they are; *Geschichte* refers to the meaning and relevance of past events for our lives today. With regard to, say, the resurrection of Jesus, according to Bultmann, it was "historical" in the sense of *Geschichte* in the disciples' minds and hearts, but it did not take place in real *Historie*.

Jesus through the Lens of Mythology

Bultmann took up the concept of myth developed by D. F. Strauss a century earlier and made it a major tool for New Testament interpretation. What makes understanding his view problematic is that Bultmann never defined *myth* consistently and used the category quite loosely. Yet his overall orientation to the study of Christ in the New Testament can be outlined quite reliably, even if his concept of myth is a bit ambiguous.

Bultmann's conception of myth is much wider than that of his predecessor. Myth is not simply a miracle or a story about a miracle (as for Strauss) but rather the way in which reality as a whole is conceived. Myth is a prescientific way of conceptualizing reality. It is a primitive means of objectifying the forces that impinge upon and determine human existence and thus conveys insights concerning it. Calling a story a myth does not imply that the story is untrue; rather, it is a way of putting transcendent reality in this-worldly terms.

Of course, this definition of myth implies a kind of supremacy of modern times over the biblical culture, with its "primitive" and "underdeveloped" worldview. In fact, Bultmann makes this clear in his often-quoted saying, "It is impossible to use electric light and the wireless and to avail ourselves of modern medical and surgical discoveries, and at the same time to believe in the New Testament world of demons and spirits."[1] Bultmann thought it odd that the ancients conceived of the cosmos as a three-storied structure, with continuous traffic between earth and heaven. Their tendency to attribute illnesses and mental disorders to the activity of demons also belonged to this primitive outlook.

But the crucial thing to note with regard to the study of the New Testament is that even though this kind of mythical worldview has long been left behind, it cannot and should not be ignored or eliminated when approaching the biblical narrative about Jesus. With Albert Schweitzer, Bultmann affirmed the thoroughly eschatological orientation of Jesus' message. He was critical of liberal approaches that attempted to eliminate apocalypticism and other mythological elements. The most important myth is eschatological: the imminent end of the world through divine intervention, leading to judgment or reward.

There was in Bultmann's work, as James D. G. Dunn has aptly noted, a hidden apologetic motif; he wanted to communicate the narrative of Jesus to modern men and women in a way that would make sense apart from those mythical elements. Yet in this apologetic, Bultmann was a child of his own times, the era of the first part of the twentieth century:

> It is obvious that he [Bultmann] shared in an uncritical way the presumption of pre-Einsteinian physics that the cosmos was a closed continuum of cause and effect which would sooner or later yield up all its secrets to the all-conquering march of scientific inquiry. But his designation of the ancient world view as mythical was not simply a reflection of the modern disparaging the primitive. It was also a way of removing the mythical from the realm of the scientific and objective. If the Gospel miracles are not scientific descriptions of maladies or cures, then they are about something else, a something else *not* vulnerable to objective analysis or scientific reductionism. Bultmann's endeavor was therefore aimed at expounding this "something else."[2]

1. Rudolf Bultmann, "The New Testament and Mythology," in *Kerygma and Myth,* ed. H. W. Bartsch (London: SPCK, 1953), 5 (Bultmann's article first appeared in 1941).

2. J. D. G. Dunn, "Myth," in *Dictionary of Jesus and the Gospels,* ed. Joel B. Green and Scot McKnight (Downers Grove, Ill.: InterVarsity, 1992), 567.

This takes us to the most famous concept of Bultmann, the project of "demythologization" (an anglicized form of the German *Entmythologisierung,* "stripping off myths"). "Demythologization" does not mean stripping away the mythical expression of the gospel in the spirit of liberalism as if that would provide a "pure" look into what happened and who Jesus was. No, that would leave the gospel open once again to scientific scrutiny. Worse still, that would miss the nature and function of the myth and do injustice to the literary quality of the Gospels. "Demythologizing is rather a matter of experiencing again the gospel and of re-expressing that encounter in the conceptuality of today, though never in such a way that the gospel becomes a mere object."[3] Unlike liberalism, the Bultmannian approach does not mean a removal of but rather a reinterpretation of myths. By removing myths, Bultmann argues, we do away with the central New Testament message.

The purpose of demythologization is to reinterpret a myth existentially. An example here is the end-time myth as preached by Jesus. Even though the world did not come to its end, the myth is still "true" in that it refers to the here and now of human existence, the fact that human beings must face the reality of their own death and are therefore forced to make existential decisions. Similarly, the "judgment" is not about something future but about the present event of our own judgment of ourselves.

For Bultmann, with the help of demythologization, the message of the New Testament can be made intelligible to a modern person. This kind of demythologization already happens in John's Gospel, which teaches that the end has already come, that eternal life is already here, even though the world continues to run its course. Understandably, Bultmann valued John's and Paul's writings as the most important sections of the New Testament because they were not interested in Jesus' earthly life as much as in the significance and meaning of his life for us. Christ encounters us in the *kērygma* and nowhere else, and there is no going beyond the *kērygma* to historical knowledge of Jesus.

In that sense, the concept of myth was not negative for Bultmann, as it is for most people. Most people think that because there is a conflict between history and myth, myth expresses something negative, something that did not happen. Of course, there is this element of "not happening in real history" in Bultmann's conception of myth. For example, Jesus' miracles did not happen literally, and Jesus' resurrection was not a literal resuscitation of a dead person. But still it is a gross misunderstanding of Bultmann's program of demythologization to regard it as negative. If history as a scientific discipline is by definition limited to the area of the observable and the measurable, then something else is needed to talk about that which goes beyond the observable. It is the same principle (though with a different agenda) that the language philosopher Ludwig Witt-

3. Ibid.

genstein, a contemporary of Bultmann, noted when he said that something about which we cannot talk (since it goes beyond the limits of scientific language) is perhaps more important than that about which we can.

Myth is Bultmann's category for talking about things that cannot be dealt with in the confines of the language of history and scientific observations. Myth, then, goes beyond the limitations of science and history. Myth helps us listen to the otherwise outdated, unintelligible language of the Gospels and the rest of the Bible. For example, it is inconceivable for historical research to talk about miracles, yet the Gospel narratives contain many miracles. Doing away with them, as did liberalism and the orientation of the Enlightenment, creates a gross misinterpretation of who Jesus was and what he believed. Myth is able to deal with that kind of material, which is essential to the Gospels.

As Dunn notes, the agenda of demythologization, with all its inherent problems and weaknesses, also contains the legitimate "missionary" desire to communicate the gospel from one culture to another:

> Bultmann's program of demythologizing also retains some validity, at least to the extent that it highlights the problem of translating from one culture and world of meaning to another. Translation of the Gospels is not simply a matter of finding the English (or whatever) words and idioms most nearly equivalent to the original Greek. It is also a matter (in pulpit and study group and classroom) of translating what was not simply expressed but also experienced within one way of conceptualizing reality into the expressions of contemporary experience (including religious experience).[4]

Human Existence and Faith in Christ

As a creative, independent thinker, Bultmann borrowed from various sources for his emerging theology and Christology. Existentialist philosophy, especially in the form developed by Martin Heidegger, provided important contributions that Bultmann believed helped him to communicate the Christian faith in a way that was understandable to modern men and women. Soon he adjusted his doctrine of Christ to the spirit of existentialism so much as to say that what existentialism is all about reflects the heart of the New Testament. Bultmann himself made the connection to existentialism, especially to Heidegger, clear: "The work of existential philosophy, which I came to know through my discussion with Martin Heidegger, has become of decisive significance for me. I found in it the conceptuality in which it is possible to speak adequately of human existence and therefore also of the existence of the believer."[5]

4. Ibid., 568.
5. Rudolf Bultmann, "Autobiographical Reflections," in *Existence and Faith: Short Writings of Rudolf Bultmann,* ed. Schubert M. Ogden (Cleveland: Word, 1960), 288.

Existentialism focuses on an analysis of human existence. In opposition to an "objectivized" view of existence, which views human beings as part of nature, existentialism approaches the specifically human existence in terms of historicity, in terms of concepts that focus on each human as an individual who determines his or her own existence through personal decisions. For Heidegger, existence is never focused on the general or the universal but always on the individual and the personal. It is shaped by the decisions individuals make. Heidegger made a conceptual distinction between human "existence" (meaningful human life with self-chosen purpose) and the "extant" (merely existing) of all other beings.

According to Heidegger, there are two kinds of existence, an "authentic existence" in which people accept the challenge of "being thrown" into the world and yet make sense of their lives, and an "inauthentic existence" that consists of the loss of the distinction between self and the world. For existentialism, a human being is both subject and object, not just an object. At the same time, each human being is a possibility rather than a predetermined actuality. If one takes hold of one's potential, the result is an authentic existence.

Bultmann made creative use of the basic concepts of existentialism in constructing his Christology and its meaning for modern men and women. In his view, the New Testament recognizes two modes of human existence. The first one is "unbelieving and unredeemed," what he also calls inauthentic existence; it is characterized by the delusion of self-sufficiency and adhesion to the visible and transitory world. The other mode of existence is "believing and redeemed," in other words, authentic. In this mode, humans know that the goal or the purpose for which humanity was created is not reached by their own efforts but by committing their lives to faith in Christ. This reveals the main difference between the secular existentialism of Heidegger and the Christian version of Bultmann: For Heidegger, authentic existence is the result of human efforts; for Bultmann, it is dependent on Christ.

As a Lutheran theologian, Bultmann offered an existentialist interpretation of the standard Lutheran concept of justification. His aim was to destroy "every longing for security" based on good works or what he calls "objectifying knowledge" (knowledge that is purportedly indisputable or factual) and to highlight the fact that humans are "in a vacuum." It is only through a total commitment of faith that humans can live, for faith is the gift of God and God's grace. Humans can possess this faith only by listening to the New Testament *kērygma*.[6]

Bultmann did not have a problem accepting the crucifixion as a historical event, but he did not see it as the act of the Son of God, who would make an atonement for sins. More importantly, he did not believe in the literal resur-

6. Rudolf Bultmann, *Jesus Christ and Mythology* (New York: Charles Scribner's Sons, 1958), 84.

rection of Jesus from the dead. Nevertheless, the death and resurrection of Jesus Christ were existentially significant events to him.

The neo-orthodox influences on Bultmann are seen in his understanding of the revelation of God in Christ. Unlike classical theology, which maintains that the definitive self-revelation of God in Christ is found in the Bible, the Word of God, Bultmann believed that the historical Jesus himself is the focus of God's revelation. God's revelation lies in the present encounter of an individual with preaching concerning Christ. Like Barth, Bultmann thought that the Bible is not the Word of God but has the potential of becoming such if and when, in reading it and listening to preaching based on it, people encounter God. What is defining is that in Jesus God acted redemptively; how that occurred and how much or little people know of it was of no interest to Bultmann, because faith in Christ is not dependent on history. As he said, "The message of Jesus is a presupposition for the theology of the New Testament rather than a part of that theology itself."[7]

7. Rudolf Bultmann, *Theology of the New Testament*, vol. 1 (New York: Charles Scribner's Sons, 1951), 3.

13

Paul Tillich

Existentialist Christology

The Method of Correlation

Paul Tillich saw himself as an apostle to the intellectuals: "My whole theological work has been directed to the interpretation of religious symbols in such a way that the secular man—and we are all secular—can understand and be moved by them."[1] Unlike Karl Barth, he strove for correlation, if not synthesis, between modern secular philosophy and Christian theology. For Tillich, the task of theology was to be "apologetic," not in the sense of apologizing for its existence or specific task but in the sense of presenting the case for Christian faith in such a way that modern men and women can understand it and relate it to their needs.

It is not easy to classify Tillich because he was a highly original and creative thinker. He had neo-orthodox leanings; he was trained by the last liberals; he was strongly influenced by existentialist philosophies. The label that might do the most justice to Tillich is "neo-liberalism." Some thinkers such as Tillich shared much of neo-orthodoxy's criticism of classical liberalism, but they wondered if Barth and others were too harsh and one-sided. Perhaps neo-orthodoxy had become too preoccupied with the idea of God's transcendence

1. Quoted in D. MacKenzie Brown, ed., *Ultimate Concern: Tillich in Dialogue* (New York: Harper & Row, 1956), 88–89.

because of its fear that liberalism had brought God down from heaven to the level of humanity. Tillich stood eminent among those thinkers of the mid-twentieth century who did not want to return to neo-orthodoxy, let alone orthodoxy, but wanted to revise and update the classical liberal agenda while at the same time taking notice of advancements in philosophy, the social sciences, and science. Tillich ultimately chose existentialism as his main dialogue partner, even though he disassociated himself from many basic tenets of existentialist philosophers such as Jean-Paul Sartre and Martin Heidegger, who were either atheists or agnostics.

The method of his theological work may best be described as "correlation." The basic idea is simple: Theology should have a mutual working relationship with philosophy in that philosophy asks the relevant questions, and theology provides the answers from the perspective of Christian faith. Tillich elaborated on the method of correlation in terms of the correlation between the question and the answer. Concerning his method, Tillich stated, "Philosophy formulates the questions implied in human existence, and theology formulates the answers implied in divine self-manifestation under the guidance of the questions implied in human existence."[2] The structure of his main theological work, the three-volume *Systematic Theology*, follows this path: First, there is a question related to the intellectual and cultural context, and that is followed by a theological answer. It is understandable that for Tillich reason does not resist revelation but rather asks for it; revelation means the reintegration of reason.

Tillich was extremely critical both of fundamentalism, which wanted to reestablish the ancient doctrines simply on the basis of their implied authority, and of the kerygmatic theology of neo-orthodoxy, which refused to look for any historical or cultural support for its claims. These two approaches, which Tillich labeled "supernaturalistic," ignore the questions of modern men and women. But the naturalistic or humanistic approaches of liberalism do not succeed much better because in them "everything was said by man, nothing to man."[3] The apologetic theology of his own approach presupposed common ground between the Christian message and the contemporary culture. Philosophy played a crucial role in his approach to theology. Tillich argued that the God of Abraham, Isaac, and Jacob and the God of the philosophers is the same God.

The Ground of Being

Tillich's great debt to existentialism is evident in his characterization of the conditions necessary for carrying out the theological task:

2. Paul Tillich, *Systematic Theology*, vol. 1 (Chicago: University of Chicago Press, 1951), 61.
3. Ibid., 65.

Theology, when dealing with our ultimate concern, presupposed in every sentence the structure of being, its categories, laws and concepts. Theology, therefore, cannot escape the question of being any more easily than can philosophy. The attempt of biblicism to avoid non-biblical, ontological terms is doomed to failure as surely as are the corresponding philosophical attempts.[4]

With existentialists, Tillich wanted to highlight the special nature of human existence in ontology (ontology is that branch of philosophy that inquires into the nature and possibility of being or existence): A human being is a "microcosm," different from all other forms of life. The structure of being underlying human existence is difference from the rest of creation. The gateway to Tillich's doctrine of God and Jesus Christ is the ontological question, that is, what it means to say that something is, that it exists.

To get into Tillich's views, we need to take a more focused look at his distinctive terminology. Tillich was not the most systematic thinker, and his definitions are not always watertight. In a way, he followed Rudolf Bultmann in attempting to extract the existential significance of New Testament Christology and soteriology. Instead of using the term *myth* as Bultmann did, Tillich preferred the term *symbol*. Therefore, for Tillich, the fall, for example, is a symbol. Unfortunately, Tillich's use of *symbol* is not consistent, and it is difficult to define it more precisely.

If the question of being is the basic question of philosophy and theology, its counterpart is the question of non-being. This question is present in everything finite. For Tillich, the question of non-being raises the question of a power of being that overcomes the threat of non-being and sustains life. This has to be the "Being Itself" or the "Ground of Being." Without this Ground of Being, everything finite would fall back to non-being or nothingness.

Two terms are absolutely crucial for Tillich's analysis: *essence* and *existence*. These two terms define the entire structure of reality, and they apply to all being. According to Tillich, the term *essence* denotes the potential, unactualized perfection of a thing as it does not yet exist. The term *existence* refers to the actual being that is "fallen" from its essence, in a sense cut off from perfection. In Tillich's thinking, existence is always finite and fallen. It is also limited and distorted by the condition of being cut off from its true being, its essence.

For God to be the Ground of Being that underlies and sustains the being of all others, he cannot be on the same level as we are. It is from this point that Tillich's most controversial and often misinterpreted statement derives: "God does not exist. He is being itself beyond essence and existence. Therefore to argue that God exists is to deny him."[5]

4. Ibid., 21.
5. Ibid., 205.

There has to be a Ground of Being that makes being itself possible. But to give existence to something is to make it a mode of finite being, the condition of fallenness or estrangement. Therefore, if God exists, there is a need for a "God above God." For Tillich, the god who is being itself or the Ground of Being is superior to the supposedly finite God of traditional Christian theism.

New Being

We could probably make a correlation that Tillich did not make himself but that might be helpful both in understanding the force of this distinction for his thinking and in approaching his idea of Christology. Tillich's term *essence* corresponds more or less to Martin Heidegger's concept of authentic existence (which was also utilized by Rudolf Bultmann in his Christian version of existentialism), and Tillich's term *existence* is roughly analogous to Heidegger's inauthentic existence. But according to Tillich, the only kind of existence we know is inauthentic, fallen from the perfect state of essence. It is here that the parallelism to Heidegger begins to fall apart. How did we get from essence to existence? The way Tillich responds to this question takes us to the heart of his Christology, to the idea of Christ as the "New Being," the "restorative principle" of Tillich's theology.

In the third part of his *Systematic Theology,* significantly titled "Existence and the Christ," Tillich analyzes the situation of human existential alienation and the quest for salvation. He offers a reinterpretation of the fall: It is a universal transition from essence to existence. For Tillich, of course, this is not a literal, factual event, but it is "real" in its effects. In a sense, Tillich makes the fall almost necessary; as soon as there is "actualized creation," the exercise of free will, humans lose the state of "dreaming innocence" (essential being in union with God) and enter into estranged existence.

This predicament calls for the coming of someone who is able to break through the estrangement and overcome the distinction between essence and existence. This is where Tillich's system introduces Christ. As the New Being, Christ is the answer for human beings who find themselves under the fallen conditions of existence.

For Tillich, the event on which Christianity is based has two aspects: the fact of Jesus of Nazareth and the reception of this fact by those who receive him as the Christ. The factual, historical Jesus is not the foundation of faith apart from his reception as the Christ. In the spirit of existentialism, neo-orthodoxy, and the Bultmannian approach, Tillich maintains that the history of Jesus and his life are unimportant; regardless of how much critical scholarship eradicates the credibility of the Gospel stories, Tillich's trust in the New Being remains unaffected. All that Tillich is ready to affirm about Jesus is that his was a "personal life." Whatever the details of the life of Jesus of Nazareth, the New Being was and is active in this man.

The symbol "Christ" for Tillich is the one "who brings the new state of things." The meaning of Jesus Christ lies in the fact that he is the manifestation of the New Being, who subjects himself to the conditions of existence and by doing so conquers existential estrangement. Tillich says that it is "the Christ who brings the New Being, who saves men from the old being, that is from existential estrangement and its destructive consequences." In the personal life of Jesus of Nazareth, "essential manhood" has manifested itself.[6]

For Tillich, then, Jesus was not God become man, as the classical orthodox confessions state, but "essential man appearing in a personal life under the conditions of existential estrangement."[7] The subjection of the Christ to estranged existence is symbolized in the cross, and his conquest is symbolized in the resurrection.

Jesus Christ was not divine and did not have a divine nature but rather manifested in and through his humanity an entirely new order of being—essential humanity. In Jesus, humanity became "essentialized" within existence. This was a great paradox, a reversal of the necessary human fallenness. This Christology can properly be called "degree" Christology: Jesus was not different from us in substance but in degree.

Not surprisingly, Tillich maintains that Christology is the function of soteriology. In other words, the question of salvation creates the christological question. That gives Tillich the freedom needed to deal with the details of Jesus' life and even to maintain that as the New Being Jesus Christ need not be "god" in the traditional sense of the term.

If Jesus is not God, as the orthodox position maintains, what then about the revelatory role of Jesus of Nazareth in Tillich's system? Traditionally, Christology has been connected with the revelation of God in one way or another. In his doctrine of revelation, Tillich rejected the concept of revealed words or propositions. He went with the mainline neo-orthodox view in which revelation is never the communication of information but rather an event and experience that can happen through many different media, including nature, history, people, and speech. Anything can become a bearer of revelation. The Bible, then, is not the Word of God. Tillich argues that the traditional view, which identifies the Word with the Bible, added to the confusion about revelation. The Bible only participates in revelation. Tillich makes a distinction between "actual revelation," meaning all events and experiences that manifest the power of being wherever and whenever they happen, and "final revelation," meaning ultimate, unsurpassable revelation, which is

6. Paul Tillich, *Systematic Theology*, vol. 2 (Chicago: University of Chicago Press, 1957), 150.
    7. Ibid., 95.

found in Jesus Christ. Thus, in Christ, the New Being, there is a final revelation of God, but that revelation can never be equated with the testimonies of the Bible. Perhaps the best way to characterize Tillich's view of revelation is to say that the role of Jesus of Nazareth is to illuminate the mystery of being and to point to the possibility of overcoming the state of estrangement. Other sources of illumination are available too. In this way, Tillich sympathizes with the classical liberal thought that sees Jesus as one among others who have enlightened the human situation. Significantly, Tillich refers to Christ with the definite article *the* to underline the fact that *Christ* is not so much a personal name as it is a function or role: the Christ.

Is the Fall a Necessary Event?

One may ask whether Tillich makes the fall necessary in that as soon as one moves from essence to existence, one by definition falls into a limited, estranged, ruptured existence. It has been suggested that Tillich "ontologizes sin." In other words, he makes it an ontological necessity. This interpretation is supported by Tillich's assertion that "man is caught between the desire to actualize his freedom and the demand to preserve his dreaming innocence. In the power of his finite freedom, he decides for actualization."[8]

Tillich identifies the fall with "actualized creation," with the coming to existence of the potential essence. This transition coincides with the exercise of free will and leads to a fall from the state of "dreaming innocence," a term borrowed from Søren Kierkegaard. The state of dreaming innocence is union with God. Leaving that state—a necessary result of human existence with freedom of the will—means anxiety, despair, guilt, and tension.

However, it has to be noted that Tillich does not understand the fall as an event in the history of either the race or the individual but as a symbol for the universal human situation. Tillich tries to soften the necessary nature of the fall by saying that it has the nature of an irrational leap for which humans are responsible. This may be Tillich's way of talking about original sin, as though there may be an event or influence beyond the immediate responsibility of the individual.

The role of Jesus as the Savior is highlighted against the ontological analysis of the human situation. Because God himself cannot appear under the conditions of estranged existence, there is the need for and possibility of the coming of the New Being. The New Being must come from God but need not nor can be God. This leads to the inevitable conclusion that Jesus was a human being, though a very special one in that he was able to overcome the essence-existence dualism, who achieved a union with God open to every

8. Ibid., 35.

other human being. Jesus as the New Being is the one who gives us "courage to be."

What then is salvation for Tillich? He reminds us that the Greek and Latin terms for salvation (*sōtēria* and *salus*, respectively) primarily mean "healing." It is through the New Being that we come to grips with the healing power that gives us the courage to be in the face of the threat of non-being. Salvation, healing, involves participation in God's participation in and victory over the split between essence and existence. It is also participation in the New Being's conquest of humanity's estrangement from God, the world, and itself. Salvation also means receiving God's acceptance and reconciliation. This hopefully leads to transformation in personality and community. Three foundational terms of classical soteriology—regeneration, justification, and sanctification—are restated by Tillich as "participation, acceptance, and transformation."[9]

In the final analysis, how do we assess Tillich's contribution to Christology? Several questions and criticisms have been presented with regard to his highly distinctive approach to Jesus:

> How can Tillich avoid falling into the ancient christological heresies such as adoptionism, docetism, Nestorianism and Monophysitism? Although these viewpoints are totally incompatible, Tillich has managed to combine them without transcending them. His view of Jesus is adoptionistic: Jesus was nothing more than a man who achieved something. His view of Christ is docetic: "Christ" is not identical with the man Jesus and needed not even be Jesus at all, for the humanity and particularity of Jesus seem unnecessary to Christ. Tillich's overall picture of Jesus as the Christ appears Nestorian in that the theologian divides the two. Yet at the same time it smacks of the Monophysite heresy, for Tillich makes Christ something purely spiritual and not tied to the historical personality of the man Jesus.[10]

Obviously, Tillich's idiosyncratic approach to Christology invites considerations such as these in light of the orthodox christological formulation. His theology is thoroughly characterized by the tension and challenge he set for himself at the beginning of his systematic theology: "Theology moves back and forth between two poles, the eternal truth of its foundation and the temporal situation in which the eternal truth must be received."[11] The meaning of the "eternal truth" about God and Christ in his thinking remains open, and many would argue that he majored in the temporal pole of the dialectic.

9. Ibid., 165.
10. Stanley J. Grenz and Roger E. Olson, *Twentieth-Century Theology: God and World in a Transitional Age* (Downers Grove, Ill.: InterVarsity, 1992), 129.
11. Tillich, *Systematic Theology*, 1:3.

14

John Zizioulas

Communion Christology

Being as Communion

John Zizioulas, the Bishop of Pergamon, Greece, is the most significant Eastern Orthodox theologian of our day. Like Bishop Kallistos (born Timothy Ware of England), Zizioulas has built bridges between the East and the West and has introduced the distinctive theological heritage of Orthodoxy to the West. Zizioulas is, however, not only a faithful interpreter and teacher of his own tradition but also a self-critical constructive theologian who is not afraid to correct Eastern theology in light of ecumenical influences. Because his whole life work has been done in the West, his ideas have been accessible to the Western guild of theologians. However, most if not all general introductions to theology ignore the contributions of Zizioulas's theology and the Eastern tradition.

Zizioulas's most distinctive idea that permeates his theology and his view of Christ is that of *koinōnia,* communion. The title of his main book reflects the basic orientation of his thought: *Being as Communion.*[1] His theology in general and his Christology in particular are based on an ontology of personhood acquired from a consideration of the being of the Triune God.

---

1. John Zizioulas, *Being as Communion: Studies in Personhood and the Church* (Crestwood, N.Y.: St. Vladimir's Seminary Press, 1985).

Zizioulas opposes any kind of individualism that is destructive to community. There is no true being without communion; nothing exists as an "individual" in itself. Even God exists in communion. And there is no way to the knowledge of God apart from communion, relationship: "The being of God could be known only through personal relationships and personal love. Being means life, and life means communion."[2]

Zizioulas criticizes the ancient Greek ontology in which God first is God (his substance) and then exists as Trinity, as three persons. His idea is, rather, that of the Greek fathers who claimed that God's personhood consists of the community of three persons. Outside the Trinity there is no God. In other words, God's being coincides with God's personhood.

The main concept of Zizioulas is "person" (the subtitle for his main book is *Studies in Personhood and the Church*). No individual apart from others can ever be a person, not even Christ. On the other hand, "person is no longer an adjunct to a being, a category we add to" a person;[3] rather, person is itself the essence of being. (Here Zizioulas's use of *essence* takes up the ancient trinitarian and christological language of *hypostasis,* from the Greek term meaning "essence" or "substance.")

Zizioulas draws an analogy between the being of God and the being of human beings. What is most characteristic of God is his being in relation. As the Trinity, the three persons of the Godhead interrelate with one another. They have an intra-trinitarian love relationship. With this same love, the Triune God relates to human beings and the world and embraces them in divine-human *koinōnia.* Zizioulas's basic argument thus runs as follows:

> From the fact that a human being is a member of the Church, he becomes an "image of God," he exists as God Himself exists, he takes on God's "way of being." This way of being . . . is a way of *relationship* with the world, with other people and with God, an event of *communion,* and that is why it cannot be realized as the achievement of an *individual,* but only as an *ecclesial* fact.[4]

In fact, Zizioulas insists that communion is not just another way of describing being, whether individual or ecclesial, but that it belongs to the *ontology* of being. Thus, we should speak of an actual "ontology of communion." This concept, interestingly, parallels the way the Roman Catholic Church defined its view of community at the Second Vatican Council (1962–65). *Lumen Gentium* (#9) of Vatican II, the main ecclesiological document, says that God "has, however, willed to make men holy and save them,

2. Ibid., 16.
3. Ibid., 39.
4. Ibid., 15, emphasis added.

not as individuals without any bond or link between them, but rather to make them into a people who might acknowledge him and serve him in holiness."

Zizioulas is first and foremost a theologian of the church. Even when he deals with other topics, there is always an ecclesial element. This is understandable in view of his focus on communion. He has never produced a separate study on Christology, even though christological themes are visible especially in his book *Being as Communion*. Therefore, an analysis of Zizioulas's Christology has to be based mainly on his writings about the church.

"Person" and "Individual"

Zizioulas makes a distinction between "biological" and "ecclesial" being: The former refers to a human being apart from communion with God and others, while the latter denotes a person living in *koinōnia*. As a result of the fall, the human being exists "biologically," in individualism, in a perverted existence. The human being as an individual affirms himself or herself against God and other human beings. The ultimate consequence of this is death. Sin for Zizioulas means turning away from personal communion with God and other fellow humans to communion with only the creaturely world. This kind of "individual" can never be a "person" in the true sense of the term.

The individual, however, can move from biological to ecclesial being, being in communion with God and other people, by virtue of joining the church communion through baptism and faith. In contrast to the merely biological existence in which humans exist as disconnected individuals, in the church humans are made persons, persons in communion. Through baptism and faith, biological existence gives way to existence in *koinōnia*.

This distinction between person and individual is the foundational principle underlying all of Zizioulas's theology and Christology. In Christ and in his church, the way of existence as an individual is overcome. To be a person means that one is "ecstatic" (from two Greek terms meaning "out" and "stand") with "a movement toward communion." In other words, no person is a person in his or her individuality but in referring to something outside his or her self. For Zizioulas, this reference point is communion. The movement toward communion gives true human freedom because the human being is able to transcend himself or herself. It is only in communion with others (including God) that an individual becomes a person and can fulfill his or her destiny.

Being in communion does not, however, mean downplaying the distinctive personhood of each individual. "The person cannot exist without communion; but every form of communion which denies or suppresses the person is inadmissible."[5]

5. Ibid., 18.

Christ: Person and Communion

Foundational to Zizioulas's Christology is the thesis that, on the one hand, God exists only as person in communion within trinitarian persons, and on the other hand, that Christ is the person par excellence. Christ is not merely an individual but rather a person, since his identity is constituted by a twofold relationship: his relationship as Son to the Father and his relationship as head to his body.

Zizioulas is an Orthodox theologian and therefore joins the ancient christological tradition of the creeds and patristics in affirming the doctrine of the two natures of Christ. But his appropriation of the two natures is connected to his basic conviction about communion and personhood. The significance of the two natures of Christ is that in Christ human personhood has become historical reality. According to Zizioulas, the patristic opposition to the two-nature view of Nestorianism was motivated by a desire to make sure that the being of Jesus of Nazareth is identical with the personhood of the Son of God. Likewise, the virgin birth of Jesus is significant in that it ensures that the person of Christ is one and is identified with the essence of the Son in the Trinity, the true communion.

The divine nature of Christ consists of his being, as the divine Son, the Second Person of the Trinity. Deity is nothing external, an additional quality added to his human nature. Just as the divine Son does not stand alone but in an intra-trinitarian love relationship, so also Jesus Christ, the incarnate Son, does not stand merely by himself; he is not an "individual." Both in Jesus' own self-understanding and in the Christology of the early church, Christ is a corporate personality who incorporates many into himself.

In Zizioulas's interpretation, the Christology of the church fathers "looks towards a single goal of purely existential significance, the goal of giving man the assurance that the quest for the . . . authentic person . . . is not mythical or nostalgic but is a *historical reality.*" Jesus Christ is not Savior of the world because he is the bearer of the revelation of God but because "he realizes in history *the very reality of the person*" and makes it the basis of personhood for all men and women.[6]

If the basic need of human beings is to be freed from individualism and depersonalism, then salvation must "consist in an ontological deindividualization that actualizes their personhood." This could also be expressed by saying that "salvific grace can consist only in transforming perverted creaturely existence—perverted insofar as it individualizes human beings—into creaturely existence expressing their being as persons and their communal nature."[7] This happened paradigmatically in the incarnation of the Son of God;

6. Ibid., 54, italics in text.
7. Miroslav Volf, *After Our Likeness: The Church as the Image of the Trinity* (Grand Rapids: Eerdmans, 1998), 83.

in the personhood of Christ, this alienating individualism was overcome. Christology is the proclamation to humankind that their individualized natures can be "assumed" into the personhood of Christ and so freed from individualism in a true personhood and communion.

This is, in other words, "ecclesial" being. In the church, in the ecclesial mode of being, a person is able to transcend exclusivism, as does the personhood of Christ, who is himself communion. When a human being lives on the biological level, there is a necessary exclusivism: The family has priority in love over strangers, the husband lays exclusive claim to the love of his wife, and so on. This is true of "natural," biological existence. In ecclesial being, these biological limits are transcended. Even Christ as true person is constituted ecclesially, for he exists only in communion with his Father and the church.

In the tradition of Eastern soteriology, which freely speaks of divinization or deification as the goal of salvation, Zizioulas maintains that every human being is constituted in Christ into a person by becoming "Christ" on the basis of the same filial relationship that constitutes Christ as the Son of the Father. In Christ a human being is united with God.

Christ as the Truth

Zizioulas takes literally John 14:6, which names Jesus as the truth. Christology is the sole starting point for a Christian understanding of truth. But how should theology understand Christ as truth? Once again, Zizioulas builds on his idea of person and communion. The manner in which Christ is the way, the truth, and the life is communion. Christ, the incarnate Christ, is the truth, "for He represents the ultimate, unceasing will of the ecstatic love of God, who intends to lead created being into communion with His own life, to know Him and itself within this communion-event."[8] So for Zizioulas, because Jesus Christ is truth, communion with the truth (Christ) is salvation. Salvation is not about knowing Christ but about being in communion with Christ.

Consequently, truth is not primarily a cognitive act but rather an event of love between persons; being in truth means being in communion. The question of truth is primarily about personal life and less about cognitive understanding. It is not enough to say "I know Christ" unless as a person I live in communion, in love with Christ.

This has bearing on Zizioulas's understanding of Christ as the revelation of God. Christ is not truth in the traditional sense of revelation from God but rather as a person who exemplifies God's will for communion and love. He

---

8. Zizioulas, *Being as Communion*, 97–98.

does not tell us about God but draws us into communion with him. Consequently, for Zizioulas, God's Word is not truth in the sense of cognitive statements but in the sense of life and communion. One is not to approach God's Word intellectually, as if he or she could "understand" it. Rather, one is to experience God's Word communally "as the sacramental intimation of God's life."[9] This view does not necessarily exclude a cognitive dimension but does emphasize the priority of communal, personal, loving experience.

Christ and the Spirit

A pronounced difference exists between Eastern and Western theologies. One of the most visible differences is the strong pneumatological orientation in the East. Christ is highly honored, but the role of the Spirit is highlighted in a distinctive way. Eastern theology is sometimes called "Spirit-sensitive" theology, since all theological foci are influenced by the Spirit, including Christology.

For Zizioulas, as an Eastern theologian, it is important to work for a proper synthesis between Christology and pneumatology as the basis for ecclesiology. He reminds us of the obvious fact that in the New Testament Easter (the work of Christ) and Pentecost (the outpouring of the Spirit) belong together. We see the mutual relationship between the Son and the Spirit in that just as the Son came down to earth and accomplished his work through the Spirit, so also the Spirit came into the world, sent by the Son (John 15:26). The work of the Spirit is not subordinate to the work of the Son, nor is Pentecost a continuation of the incarnation but rather its sequel, its result.

Zizioulas rightly notes that the New Testament shows a mutuality between Son and Spirit rather than a priority of either one. On the one hand, the Spirit is given by Christ (John 7:39); on the other hand, there is no Christ until the Spirit is at work either at his baptism (Mark) or at his birth (Matthew and Luke). Both of these views can coexist in one and the same canon. In the Eastern liturgy, this mutuality of the Son and the Spirit is exemplified in the way two crucial soteriological events are kept together: Baptism, which symbolizes one's identification in Christ's death and resurrection, and confirmation, the occasion for the anointing with the Spirit, happen at the same time. In contrast, in the West they are separated. In fact, in some churches, confirmation takes place many years after baptism.

In other words, employing Zizioulas's distinctive vocabulary, Christ becomes a historical person only in the Spirit (Matt. 1:18–20; Luke 1:35). Zizioulas is even ready to say that "Christ *exists only pneumatologically.*" In line with Eastern trinitarian sensitivity, he adds that to speak of Christ means to

9. Ibid., 114.

speak at the same time of the Father and the Holy Spirit. This same principle applies also to the church communion, the main focus of Zizioulas's theology: "Thus the mystery of the Church has its birth in the entire economy of the Trinity and in a pneumatologically constituted Christology."[10]

In line with his communion theology, Zizioulas contends that there are two kinds of Christologies. First, we can understand Christ as an individual, and second, we can understand him as a "corporate personality" in his relationship with his body, the church.[11] In his terminology, in the former case we speak of Christ as "individual," in the latter as "person." The role of the Spirit comes to the fore here: "Here the Holy Spirit is not one who *aids* us in bridging the distance between Christ and ourselves, but he is the person of the Trinity who actually realizes in history that which we call Christ. . . . In this case, our Christology is *essentially* conditioned by pneumatology, not just secondarily as in the first case; in fact it is *constituted* pneumatologically."[12] One could also express this idea by saying that the corporate personality of Christ comes into being pneumatologically. Therefore, it is significant that since the time of Paul, the Spirit has been associated with the notion of *koinōnia*. Pneumatology creates for Christology the dimension of communion.

Even though Zizioulas himself has been on the forefront of developing a proper synthesis between Christology and Pneumatology, Christ and Spirit, he is also the first one to acknowledge that not only in the West but also in the East there is still a great deal of work to be done, and a proper balance is difficult to find.

10. Ibid., 112.
11. Ibid., 130.
12. Ibid., 110–11, italics in text.

15

Karl Rahner

Transcendental Christology

Transcendental Experience and Human Openness to Holy Mystery

If John Zizioulas is the present leading Eastern Orthodox theologian, then the late Karl Rahner is the main figure in recent Roman Catholic theology. No other twentieth-century Catholic theologian exercised such a universal influence, not only within the confines of the largest church in the world—about one-half of all Christians belong to the Roman Catholic Church—but also ecumenically. Rahner's contribution to the Second Vatican Council (1962–65), the formative council that decisively set the Roman Catholic Church on the path of *aggiornamento,* renewal and modernization, has been unsurpassed.

Rahner set himself the ambitious task of holding together two seemingly contradictory premises: the universal saving action of God and the necessity of supernatural revelation and faith in Christ. For these two premises to hold, revelation and faith must occur at a universal, transcendental level. Rahner's basic thesis is that God reveals Godself to every person in the very experience of that person's own finite, yet absolutely open-ended, transcendence. God is the Holy Mystery, and it is only in reference to God that the subjectivity of human beings finds a proper ground.

Rahner's theology is not easy to read and understand. His terminology is quite idiosyncratic, and he did not write for a wide audience. His main theological concern was to respond to the challenge of modern Western culture's hesitance to believe in a transcendent God and its tendency, at least since the time of the Enlightenment and liberalism, to talk about God mainly in immanental terms. Rahner wanted to find a balance as an antidote for this malaise. To do so, he introduced the term *transcendental*.

Rahner used the term *transcendental* in several interrelated expressions, such as "transcendental method" and "transcendental experience." Transcendental method is a philosophical tool used to show that by definition a human being is "spirit," open to receive revelation from God. Human beings transcend the limits of "nature" and are oriented toward the Holy Mystery that Christian theology calls God. Transcendental experiences (whenever a human being acknowledges that human life is more than just what one sees in everyday life) reveal evidence for this openness to revelation and that the grace of God in Christ is nothing foreign to the structure of the human being but belongs to its core. In Rahner's technical vocabulary, the natural transcendental nature of humanity is called *potentia oboedientalis*. For him:

> not only are humans always by nature open to God *(potentia oboedientalis)*, they are also always supernaturally elevated by God in that transcendental openness so that such elevation becomes an actual experience of God in every human life. God actually communicates himself to every human person in a gracious offer of free grace, so that God's presence becomes an existential, a constitutive element, in every person's humanity.[1]

The human person, therefore, is "the event of a free, unmerited and forgiving, and absolute self-communication of God."[2] God's self-communication means that God makes his own self the innermost constitutive element of the human person; this is the mystery of the Spirit for Rahner: "God communicates himself in the Holy Spirit to every person as the innermost center of his existence."[3] In other words, in everyday common events, the human person "encounters" the Holy Mystery, God, as part of knowing the world.

What about the need for special revelation in Rahner's theology? His answer is that "categorical revelation," specific revelation in history through events, words, and symbols, is needed to fulfill the "transcendental," implicit, unthematic revelation about God. These two are distinct yet interdependent. Categorical revelation discloses the inner reality of God—the personal character of God and his free relationship with spiritual creatures—that cannot be

1. Stanley J. Grenz and Roger E. Olson, *Twentieth-Century Theology: God and the World in a Transitional Age* (Downers Grove, Ill.: InterVarsity, 1992), 245.

2. Karl Rahner, *Foundations of Christian Faith* (New York: Seabury, 1978), 116.

3. Ibid., 139; see also John R. Sachs, "'Do Not Stifle the Spirit': Karl Rahner, the Legacy of Vatican II, and Its Urgency for Theology Today," *Catholic Theological Society Proceedings* 51 (1996): 21.

discovered through transcendental revelation alone. Therefore, universal, transcendental experience of God in the Spirit does not remove the necessity of historical, special revelation.

> This Spirit is always, everywhere, and from the outset the entelechy, the determining principle, of the history of revelation and salvation; and its communication and acceptance, by its very nature, never takes place in a merely abstract, transcendental form. It always comes about through the mediation of history.[4]

For Rahner, God is the absolute mystery, the absolute person. God is present in human experience of everyday events and happenings, but at the same time, God cannot be known as anything other than indefinable, holy mystery. God cannot be treated as the object of human knowledge, but he is the horizon of our knowing God.

Absolute Savior

Given Rahner's view of humanity and God, it will not come as a surprise that he names his Christology "transcendental." His main christological task is to inquire into the possibility of an absolute God-man, an absolute Savior. In fact, on the basis of his transcendental reflection on the openness of humanity to receive revelation of God, the idea of a God-man within history is not a foreign idea.

The core of Christology for Rahner is the role of Jesus in his mediation of the "new and unsurpassable closeness of God" to humanity.[5] In his person, Christ is the historical presence of God's disclosure to humans. This was validated for Rahner in Christ's resurrection. Before the cross and resurrection, Jesus claimed to be the bearer of this disclosure; his resurrection from the dead validated his claims. It is in this sense that Christ is the absolute Savior.

If Christ is the absolute Savior, it follows that he must be divine. Only a divine Savior is able to mediate in his own person the self-disclosure of God. Christ's divinity is also accentuated by the larger soteriological vision of Rahner. He maintained that salvation encompasses not only our "divinization" but also the beginning of the process of the divinization of the whole world. For this to happen, nothing less than a Savior who is divine is needed, for how could a less-than-fully divine figure communicate to us and the world the saving grace of God?

When we talk about the self-communication of God or even the grace of God, we need to keep in mind that Rahner always thinks in terms of God

4. Karl Rahner, "Jesus Christ in the Non-Christian Religions," *Theological Investigations* 17 (New York: Crossroad, 1981), 46.
5. Rahner, *Foundations of Christian Faith*, 279.

communicating his real presence, not only information about himself. Grace is God's real presence in humanity and the world.

As a Catholic theologian, Rahner also affirmed the full humanity of Christ. In fact, even though this affirmation seems to contradict his insistence on the full deity of the absolute Savior, the idea of Christ's humanity is a central tenet of his system. Rahner adamantly opposed any notion of Docetism, the view that Jesus was not a real human being but only appeared to be human. Jesus' full humanity comes to focus, for example, in the fact that he was not totally infallible. His divine consciousness never took over the less-than-perfect human consciousness. Rahner lamented the fact that classical orthodoxy often misconceived the two-nature view of Christ in a way that compromised the true humanity, making it a "crypto-monophysite," almost one-nature, view. Jesus' human intellect and human freedom especially were down-played, resulting in a mythological notion of Jesus as partly divine, partly human. Rahner's focus on the humanity of Jesus is also understandable given that he was critical of the Bultmannian mythological and nonhistorical approach to Jesus that neglects the history of Jesus and approaches Christ from the perspective of faith alone. Rahner's main approach to Christology is from below, though not exclusively. In this, he wanted to correct the one-sided from above approach of classical orthodoxy. Nevertheless, Rahner's Christology is still "high" in that he also strongly affirmed the full divinity of Christ.

But how was Rahner able to substantiate his insistence on this full union of divinity and humanity? He proposed new perspectives with reference to his transcendental analysis of humanity by which he attempted to overcome the problems inherent in the classical two-nature Christologies of the creeds.

Human beings, while finite, are also able to transcend themselves as "spirit." For Rahner, this is also a crucial christological affirmation. It was God who willed this transcendental nature of humanity to make room for a genuine self-expression of God in the form of humanity. If God is the aim of humanity, unless humanity is able to participate in God, humanity remains less than perfect. Salvation for Rahner is participation in the divine life to which the entire structure of the human being is naturally oriented, over and above that which human nature is able to ascend to on its own. To use Rahner's own expression, humanity is the "cipher of God" by virtue of being created by God for potential participation in God.

> Theologically, in view of the Incarnation, one must say that our human God-openness is intended by God as the potential for divine self-expression. In other words, the human person is the creature that is incomplete without Incarnation. God is the mystery of humanity, and humanity is the cipher of God. Humanity is the question; God is the answer. Just as the question participates in

the answer and the answer participates in the question while transcending it, so God and humanity belong essentially together. God has decided it will be so.[6]

From this it becomes clear that incarnation also means an assumption of part of creation, the human nature, into the inner life of God. We could say that for Rahner incarnation in itself is salvific. Here Rahner borrows core christological and soteriological ideas of the Christian East, even though he rarely if ever makes this connection explicit.

In a sense, incarnation would have been a necessary event even if sin had never entered the world. God's offer of grace naturally leads to the appearance of a God-man because salvation comes not only in Christ's works but also in his person; in his person is the self-communication of God's presence to humanity and the opportunity for human participation in the divine nature. Incarnation can be seen as the ultimate goal of the movement of creation itself. God is gradually taking hold of the world and bringing it to himself. Jesus Christ is the high moment of this convergence—creature and Creator coming together.

Anonymous Christians and the Normativity of Christ

From the very beginning of his theological career, Rahner tackled the challenge of how to understand the universal will of God as presented in 1 Timothy 2:4 (God "wants all men to be saved and to come to a knowledge of the truth") in relation to the equally foundational biblical perspective that Christ is the truth (John 14:6) and that there is no other name in which salvation may be found (Acts 4:12). As a Catholic theologian and one of the main architects of the definitive formulations of Vatican II, he firmly believed that, on the one hand, salvation is available to all people who sincerely follow the precepts of their conscience and the light given to them by their conscience and religion, and, on the other hand, that salvation always comes from Christ, whether to those who are included in the church or to those outside the church. Even those outside the boundaries of the church who are included in the saving will of God in Christ do not attain to salvation by virtue of their own merits but by virtue of the extension of God's grace in Christ to them. To make these basic Catholic convictions understandable theologically, he affirmed the view of "anonymous Christians," a view that has often been misunderstood because it has been discussed apart from the theological system of Rahner.

Rahner's approach to the question of salvation in religions, which in recent theology has been labeled the question of the theology of religions, was based

6. Grenz and Olson, *Twentieth-Century Theology,* 252.

on christological and pneumatological foundations. It is the Spirit of God who enables the human reception of divine grace and the self's experience of existential transcendence. Transcendental experience of the Spirit is oriented toward explicit awareness of something beyond. For Rahner, this orientation is expressed in the religious traditions of the world and reaches its apex in the final self-revelation of God in Christ. Other religions have "individual moments" of this kind, which makes them windows into the mystery of God, even if in a less-than-final way. Because of sin and human depravity, every such event of revelation remains partial and intermixed with error. The value of religions lies in the mediation of these revelatory experiences, even when they contain imperfect features.

In that sense, all religious traditions potentially express truth about God's self-communication in Christ through the Spirit and therefore are part of the history of revelation. This does not mean, of course, that all religions express equally valid expressions of divine self-revelation: There is error in any religion. Through Christ's death and resurrection, God's gracious self-communication in the Spirit was manifested in history: The "world is drawn to its spiritual fulfillment by the Spirit of God, who directs the whole history of the world in all its length and breadth towards its proper goal."[7]

Rahner built on the view of Yves Congar—an influential Catholic colleague—of the "mystical body of Christ," according to which there is a state of being (natural, not-yet-Christian state) in which a person can respond positively to the grace of God even before hearing the gospel. A person in this state qualifies as an "anonymous Christian" insofar as this acceptance of grace is "present in an implicit form whereby [the] person undertakes and lives the duty of each day in the quiet sincerity of patience, in devotion to his material duties and the demands made upon him by the person under his care."[8] According to Rahner, Christ is present and efficacious in non-Christian believers (and therefore in non-Christian religions) through his Spirit. Furthermore, anonymous Christians are justified by God's grace and possess the Holy Spirit.

Joseph Wong adequately summarizes Rahner's pneumatological theology of religions:

> Wherever persons surrender themselves to God or the ultimate reality, under whatever name, and dedicate themselves to the cause of justice, peace, fraternity, and solidarity with other people, they have implicitly accepted Christ and, to some degree, entered into this Christic existence. Just as it was through the

---

7. Karl Rahner, "The One Christ and the Universality of Salvation," *Theological Investigations* 16 (New York: Crossroad, 1983), 203.

8. Karl Rahner, "Anonymous Christians," *Theological Investigations* 6 (Baltimore: Helicon, 1969), 394.

Spirit that Christ established this new sphere of existence, in the same way, any-one who enters into this Christic existence of love and freedom is acting under the guidance of the Spirit of Christ.[9]

In line with the Catholic standpoint, rather than believing that the anon-ymous Christians thesis undermined the validity of the church or its mission, Rahner argued that the individual should be brought to the fullness of faith by the church as it obediently carries out its evangelistic mandate.

---

9. Joseph H. Wong, "Anonymous Christians: Karl Rahner's Pneuma-Christocentrism and an East-West Dialogue," *Theological Studies* 55 (1994): 630. Wong references Rahner, "Obser-vations on the Problem of the 'Anonymous Christian,'" *Theological Investigations* 10 (New York: Seabury, 1976), 291.

16

Jürgen Moltmann

Messianic Christology

A Realistic Theology of the Future

Among Jürgen Moltmann's numerous publications, two books focus explicitly on Christology: *The Crucified God* and his main christological work titled *The Way of Jesus Christ*. Christological discussions are not limited to these two works, however. For example, in his *Theology of Hope,* the first major work that made him internationally famous, the eschatological promise given in the resurrection of Christ creates a "dialectical hope" that is shaped and conditioned by the death of Christ and the resurrection of Christ and of us. Also, in his main ecclesiological work, *The Church in the Power of the Spirit,* Christology plays an important role as part of his trinitarian outlook on the topic of the church; he names the church "The Church of Jesus Christ" in chapter 3.[1]

The leading motif of Moltmann's theology that carries over into all topics is the prominence of eschatology. Moltmann and his one-time colleague

1. Jürgen Moltmann, *The Crucified God: The Cross of Christ as the Foundation and Criticism of Christian Theology* (1972; reprint, New York: Harper & Row, 1974); *The Way of Jesus Christ: Christology in Messianic Dimensions* (London: SCM, 1990); *Theology of Hope: On the Ground and the Implications of a Christian Eschatology* (1964; reprint, London: SCM, 1967); and *The Church in the Power of the Spirit: A Contribution to Messianic Ecclesiology,* trans. Margaret Kohl (New York: Harper & Row, 1977).

Wolfhart Pannenberg became famous in the 1960s as the ablest proponents of the emerging "theology of hope." This theology of hope conceives of God as the power of the future that comes from the eschaton to meet the church and the world.

Moltmann's eschatology is integrally related to Christology in that Christian faith is grounded in hope for the future based on the cross and resurrection of Jesus Christ. As such, it is a realistic hope grounded in history and experience. Moltmann notes that in the past, eschatology served as a useless appendix to theology. After all topics of theology had been dealt with, the doctrine of the last things was added to finish the work. In Moltmann's work, eschatology is the leading theme: His theology is centered on the eschatological kingdom of glory in which God will be "all in all." Moltmann's eschatology, however, like his Christology, is not escapist but firmly anchored in the renewal and restoration of this world. He often reminds us that the idea of liberation, God's promise for the future, is not for another world only but also for the new creation of this world.

Moltmann describes his theology as biblically founded, eschatologically oriented, and politically responsible. His trinitarian and—lately—pneumatological orientation should be added to the list to give a more comprehensive picture of the mature Moltmann.

Moltmann's creative theology draws from various sources: his wide ecumenical contacts, the influence of Eastern Orthodox spirituality and theology, extensive travel in the third world that exposed him especially to the liberation theologies of Latin American and Asia, and so on. Moltmann's voice has also been heard outside the confines of the Western academy, and a growing number of two-thirds world theologians have interacted with his proposals.

The Trinitarian History of God Based on the Cross of Christ

Moltmann is a thoroughly trinitarian theologian. His doctrine of the Trinity takes a distinctive form, however, owing to its christological point of view focused on the cross of Christ. One of Moltmann's most well-known statements is the claim that what happened on the cross was an event between God and God. The cross had effects, not only on humanity but also on God and his identity. God was not the same after the cross. In other words, the Trinity is historical and takes different forms throughout history.

Clearly, Moltmann distinguishes himself from classical orthodoxy, which tends to look at God from the perspective of God's immutability: Nothing in the world, not even the death of Christ on the cross, can change God in any way.

To understand what Moltmann means by this idea that the cross of Christ effected change in God, one has to refer to his idea of divine "self-limitation." The background to this idea is a reciprocal relationship between God and the world: God is dependent on the world, and the world is dependent on God (though the latter holds in a more absolute sense). Historical events such as the cross, resurrection, and sending of the Spirit actually constitute God's being.

According to Moltmann's view of creation, in order for God to create a world distinct from himself, the infinite God had to make room beforehand for finitude in himself. To redeem the world that had turned its back on God, God had to enter into the godlessness of sin and death. "By entering into the Godforsakenness of sin and death (which is Nothingness), God overcomes it and makes it part of his eternal life: 'If I make my bed in hell, thou art there' (Ps. 139:8b)."[2] By his own free choice, God includes in his infinite being the finite. He chooses to make himself vulnerable, but such a choice does not grow out of necessity, thus making God less than omnipotent. On the other hand, it does not leave him untouched.

Moltmann developed a doctrine of the Trinity firmly anchored in the happenings of the world and culminating in the cross of Christ. This is not a speculative, abstract theology of the Trinity but a historically based concrete form of conceiving of the divine mystery: "If one conceives of the Trinity as an event of love in the suffering and death of Jesus—and that is something which faith must do—then the Trinity is no self-contained group in heaven, but an eschatological process open for men on earth, which stems from the cross of Christ."[3]

The Way of Jesus Christ

In his main christological work, *The Way of Jesus Christ,* Moltmann returns to the topic that has occupied him from the beginning of his career. Characteristic of the Christology of the book, he showed an interest in the Old Testament background of the Christian doctrine of Christ. He maintains that in order for Christian theology to gain a proper perspective on Jesus Christ, theologians must take the Jewish framework into account. This view has implications for the current ministry and mission of the Christian church: It should actively continue building bridges to Judaism and carry on dialogue with the messianism of the Old Testament faith.

2. Jürgen Moltmann, *God in Creation: A New Theology of Creation and the Spirit of God* (San Francisco: Harper & Row, 1985), 91.
3. Moltmann, *Crucified God,* 249.

The most distinctive contribution of *The Way of Jesus Christ* is that it depicts Jesus Christ on a journey from his earthly ministry to his *parousia*. In this work, the eschatological perspective on Jesus is even more prevalent: Jesus Christ is "on his way" to the messianic future. Moltmann considers Christ-in-his-becoming. This main christological work is divided, not according to a model of the divinity-humanity of Jesus, but into five stages: his earthly mission, cross, resurrection, present cosmic rule, and *parousia*. At the same time, there is a strong emphasis on Jesus' earthly life.

Moltmann's Christology in *The Way of Jesus Christ* is moving in the direction in which his more recent pneumatological work, *The Spirit of Life*,[4] continues, a direction that might be called a Spirit Christology. Spirit Christology, as the name indicates, approaches the person and ministry of Jesus Christ from the perspective of the Holy Spirit.

In trying to find a proper historical precedent for his approach to Christology, one that also speaks to current problems such as political injustice and ecological threat, he critiques and reappropriates the ancient patristic, particularly Eastern, view of Christ.

Moltmann finds the "cosmological" Christology of the patristic era, with all its flaws (for example, the problem of the two-nature view that makes the divinity of Christ impassible), ecologically fruitful: Its emphasis on the importance of the physical aspects of humanity and the creation lends to an ecological interpretation. It corresponds to the cosmocentric worldview and opens up horizons for a Christology that transcends the limitations of the individual Christian life and the church, the typical foci of Christologies. The basic question for the church fathers is the same one theology still struggles with, namely, the contrast between the transience of the finite and the eternity of the divine. The way patristic Christology tried to solve the problem was to speak of God become human in order to divinize human nature and creation.

Moltmann is much more critical of Enlightenment Christology with its alien agenda, especially its anthropocentric worldview. It resulted in a series of Jesusologies that project the ideals of their culturally conditioned creators. It created an attitude that encourages dominion over nature because it lacks a cosmological orientation of salvation. It also so focused on the human historical Jesus that it excluded metaphysics.

Theology of the Cross

Since Martin Luther and his groundbreaking theology of the cross, as opposed to the theology of glory, no one else has focused on the topic with such

4. Jürgen Moltmann, *The Spirit of Life: A Universal Affirmation* (Minneapolis: Fortress, 1992).

intensity and creativity as Moltmann. His interest in the suffering of Christ was intensified by his experiences as a war prisoner following World War II. Yet after his first main work, *Theology of Hope,* many thought of Moltmann as mainly a theologian of the resurrection. In fact, there is no denying that the resurrection played and continues to play a significant role in his theology, for that is the ground for the "radical hope" of Christian faith. The way Moltmann conceives of the meaning of the resurrection is in its cosmic eschatological framework. In contrast to much recent theology that tends to reduce the meaning of the resurrection, Moltmann has untiringly emphasized that the resurrection of Christ alone grounds the eschatological hope of a new heaven and a new earth.

Because the hope of resurrection goes back to the decisive victory of God in Christ over death, it encompasses and includes the hope of God's righteousness within history, yet it also transcends history. Interestingly enough, in contrast to Pannenberg, Moltmann refuses to subject the event of the resurrection to the scrutiny of historical-critical research, even though he obviously regards it as an event in time and space. He does so because the event of the resurrection calls into question the concept of history as it is conceived of within the limits of the modern scientific approach. The proper way to approach the resurrection is to connect it with the future eschatological hope; to believe in the reality of the resurrection, one must let oneself be thrown into active hope.

The importance of the resurrection for Moltmann arises out of his focus on the cross and does not negate the cross. For him, the theology of the cross is nothing other than the reverse side of the Christian theology of hope, if this theology has its point of departure in the resurrection of the one who was crucified. The most controlling idea here is a dialectical interpretation of the cross and resurrection: There is a tension between death and life, between the absence and the presence of God in Jesus. Even though there is a complete contradiction between the crucified Jesus and the risen Jesus, there is also a full identity between the crucified Christ and the risen Christ, and this identity also gives hope for the future. The hope of resurrection is always based on an eschatological promise, pointing to the future and finally to God's promise of a new creation.

In the spirit of Martin Luther, Moltmann maintains that the only way to know God is to know God hidden in the cross and shame. Moltmann calls the crucified Christ alone "humanity's true theology and knowledge of God."[5] This presupposes that while an indirect knowledge of God is possible through his works, the being of God can be seen and known directly only in the cross of Christ. In that sense, the cross is the criterion and standard for all theology.

5. Ibid., 212.

The Suffering Christ and Our Suffering

Traditionally, theology has had a difficult time talking about the suffering of a perfect God. Anselm of Canterbury of the thirteenth century argued that a perfect, infinite God is not able to suffer or feel pain. For traditional theology, supposing that God is passible seemed to compromise his infinity and perfect nature. Many recent theologians, especially after the World Wars, have wondered whether this reservation to speak of a suffering God owes more to Greek philosophy than to the Bible. The Old Testament clearly speaks of God in terms of being involved with the life of his people, rejoicing and sorrowing, even repenting and changing his mind.

Moltmann argues that there are several reasons why theology should talk about divine suffering. If we regard Jesus' passion as real, we have to say that God himself was involved in the suffering of Christ on the cross. How can Christian faith understand Christ's passion as the revelation of God if the deity cannot suffer? God is decisively and definitively revealed in the shame and suffering of the cross. Moltmann is critical of the traditional understanding of the two natures of Christ, which distinguished the impassible divine nature from the passible human nature and attributed the suffering of Jesus only to the latter, excluding passion from the deity. This could lead only to paradoxical talk about the suffering of Christ, the God-man. "Within the Christian message of the cross of Christ, something new and strange has entered the metaphysical world. For this faith must understand the deity of God from the event of the suffering and death of the Son of God and thus bring about a fundamental change in the orders of being of metaphysical thought and the value tables of religious feeling."[6]

The nature of love also requires us to take seriously the idea of the suffering of God. Suffering does not make God less God but rather a truly loving, passionate, involved person. Moltmann lays down his understanding of divine love in these words:

> A God who cannot suffer is poorer than any human being. For a God who is incapable of suffering is a being who cannot be involved. Suffering and injustice do not affect him. And because he is so completely insensitive, he cannot be affected or shaken by anything. He cannot weep, for he has no tears. But the one who cannot suffer cannot love either. So he is also a loveless being.[7]

For Moltmann, therefore, God-forsakenness stands at the center of theology. Every Christian theology and every Christian existence fundamentally responds to the question addressed by the dying Jesus to his God: "My God,

6. Ibid., 215.
7. Ibid., 222.

my God, why have you forsaken me?" The God who is able to feel and experience the pain of the world is part of the cross and suffering. This is God's loving solidarity with the world in Christ. And the Christian church is invited to participate in this loving solidarity.

Christ and His Church

One of the distinctive features of Moltmann's Christology is that it is integrally connected with the church, the body of Christ. The church is the church of Jesus Christ. Moltmann describes his doctrine of the church as a messianic and relational ecclesiology. "Messianic" essentially means "christological," and the christological foundation always points toward the eschaton. Therefore, his view is "a christologically founded and eschatologically directed doctrine of the church."[8] The church is the church of Jesus Christ, subject to his lordship alone. Consequently, for Moltmann, ecclesiology can be developed only from Christology. But it is important to notice that statements about Christ also point beyond the church to the kingdom, the future reign of Christ, the Messiah. Thus, Christ's church has to be a "messianic fellowship." As the church of Christ, she lives "between remembrance of his history and hope of his kingdom"; the church is not the kingdom but its anticipation.[9]

As the church of Jesus Christ, the church is bound together with the history and destiny of her Lord. The dialectic of suffering and joy characterizes the existence of the church; the cross and resurrection set the tone for her life. The church participates in the passion of Christ until God's kingdom of joy and peace arrives. God has made Godself vulnerable to the sufferings of the world, and the church is drawn to that: "God's pain in the world is the way to God's happiness with the world."[10] The dialectic of suffering and joy also becomes apparent in the dual nature of the church. The church is both the "church under the cross" and also the "church of the festival of freedom and joy."[11]

One way the church lives for the world and for others is by participating in the offices of Christ. Following traditional Reformed dogmatics, Moltmann talks about the three offices of Christ as prophet (ministry), priest (death), and king (resurrection/rule). The church participates in these in its response to God's invitation to be an instrument of salvation. In its prophetic task, the church participates in Jesus' messianic proclamation and his act of

8. Moltmann, *Church in the Power of the Spirit*, 31.
9. Ibid., 75.
10. Ibid., 93.
11. Ibid., 76–78, 97–98.

setting people free. This is the liberating ministry of the church. Participating in Jesus' passion, the church lives and ministers under the cross, in suffering solidarity with the weak. As part of Jesus' exaltation, the church lives as the fellowship of freedom and equality. To these traditional offices, Moltmann adds two more: first, Christ's transfiguration, which highlights the aesthetic dimension of worship and the "festival of freedom" (with reference to the Old Testament tradition of the Year of Jubilee, the church participates in and celebrates the freeing of social, political, and other prisoners); and second, Christ's friendship. The church opens itself and invites fellowship, as Christ did while on earth by inviting sinners and outcasts into the table fellowship.

17

Wolfhart Pannenberg

Universal Christology

Theology in Search of the Universal Truth

The two works that brought Wolfhart Pannenberg to international fame were a collection of essays titled *Revelation as History,* originally written in German in 1961, and his major christological work, published in German in 1964 and later in English under the title *Jesus, God and Man.*[1] From the beginning of his theological career, therefore, Pannenberg, whom many regard as the most influential and certainly most hotly debated systematic theologian at the beginning of the third millennium, dealt with foundational issues in Christology. The main focus of *Jesus, God and Man* was methodology, and Pannenberg argued for an approach from below. In his magnum opus, the three-volume *Systematic Theology,*[2] which was released in English in its entirety in 1997, he continued the main orientation of the earlier work, even though he did so in a self-critical manner and also moved beyond methodological issues to deal with the major topics of Christology. Since Karl Barth's

---

1. Wolfhart Pannenberg, Rolf Rendtorff, Ulrich Wilkens, eds., *Revelation as History,* trans. David Granskou (New York: Macmillan, 1968); Wolfhart Pannenberg, *Jesus, God and Man,* trans. Lewis L. Wilkins and Duane A. Priebe (Philadelphia: Westminster, 1977).

2. Wolfhart Pannenberg, *Systematic Theology,* 3 vols. (Grand Rapids: Eerdmans, 1991, 1994, 1997).

publication of his massive *Church Dogmatics,* no theologian besides Pannenberg has attempted a full-scale, comprehensive theological systematics.

For Pannenberg, theology is a public discipline rather than an exercise in piety, and he adamantly opposes the widespread privatization of faith and theology. Theology has to speak to common concerns, since there is no special "religious truth." As Pannenberg untiringly insists, if something is true, it has to be true for everyone, not just for oneself. For him, the truth question is the main question of theology. To its detriment, modern theology has by and large left the truth question behind, but Pannenberg has not been willing to surrender the quest for one truth. Consequently, Pannenberg's theology focuses on reason and argumentation; theological statements—in the form of hypotheses—have to be subjected to the rigor of critical questioning. Faith is not a blind act, a leap of faith, but is grounded in public, historical knowledge. Pannenberg's idea of truth comes closest to the coherence model in which the aim of Christian dogmatics is to show its truth both with regard to its inner logic and especially in relation to the rest of human knowledge, the sciences included. In Pannenberg's own words, as stated at the beginning of his career, "The question about the truth of the Christian message has to do with whether it can still disclose to us today the unity of the reality in which we live."[3] In his theology, God is the object and determining reality of all theology. God is the power that determines everything. If the reality of God must be able to illumine not only human life but also experience of the world, then Christology should also.

For Pannenberg, the task of Christology is to offer rational support for the belief in the divinity of Jesus; this cannot be assumed but has to be argued on the basis of historical proofs. If we rest our faith on the *kērygma* alone and not on historical facts, there is a chance that our faith will be misplaced. Even though Pannenberg believes it is necessary to engage in critical-historical study of the historical foundations of the Jesus event, he also argues that we should bring openness to historical study and not limit it by dismissing miracles and other supernatural events. Historical sources talk about the miracles associated with the life of Jesus, the greatest of which is, of course, the claim for the resurrection. Critical study into the origins and historical basis of Christology, according to Pannenberg, may not decide beforehand which events are not historically possible.

Pannenberg believes that historical study alone is not capable of leading one to a final commitment of faith in the divinity of the person of Jesus Christ. At the same time, careful study is needed before one is ready to confess, for example, that Jesus' claim of resurrection is valid or at least probable.

3. Wolfhart Pannenberg, "What Is Truth?" in *Basic Questions in Theology,* vol. 2 (Philadelphia: Fortress, 1971), 1.

This means that faith in the divinity of Christ (humanity is not the challenge to his approach) is a result of historical study and not its presupposition.

The Eschatological New Human

In his *Systematic Theology,* volume 2, Pannenberg develops his Christology in three parts, parallel to how Christology has most often been done in systematic treatments: First, he considers Jesus' relationship to humanity (chap. 9), then the support for the claim of his divinity (chap. 10), and finally Jesus' role in salvation under the rubric of reconciliation (chap. 11). Yet his treatment of these traditional christological loci is unique and betrays his distinctive approach to theology.

Even though Pannenberg's theology is God-centered and focuses on showing the ability of the Christian belief in God to illumine human experience of the world, his theology is also firmly anchored in anthropology, the doctrine of humanity. One of the basic aims of Pannenberg's approach is to demonstrate that belief in God is not foreign to the structure of the human being. Religiosity is not—as atheistic critics of religion have maintained—something foreign imposed on the human being but rather an essential part of being human. By definition, the human being is open to receive revelation from God/gods. This does not, of course, prove the existence of a distinctively Christian God, but it does show that talk about God is rational and can be advanced within the nature of human existence.

This understanding provides a crucial bridge to Christology. The idea of Christ's humanity is not foreign to theology but rather is an attempt to understand the appearance of Jesus as the revelation and fulfillment of human destiny. Significantly enough, Pannenberg titled this chapter in his systematics "Anthropology and Christology." Pannenberg develops the understanding of Jesus' humanity as the fulfillment of human destiny with the help of the Pauline concept of Jesus as the new human or new Adam. The focus on Jesus as the *eschatological* new human also connects to his all-important idea of resurrection as the validation of Jesus' claims for full humanity and divinity.

For Paul, all humans are to carry the image of the new Adam. From this Pannenberg concludes that as the new Adam, Jesus is the prototype of the new humanity and brings to fulfillment the destiny of humanity. But Jesus is the destiny not only of individual human life. According to Pannenberg, Paul also emphasizes the corporate dimension in the image of Christ as the new Adam. In other words, Jesus is the fulfillment of human destiny with regard to interhuman relationships. As a corollary, no individual person is able to fulfill human destiny; it is possible only in community.

When considering the idea of Jesus as the new Adam, Pannenberg also discusses the nature of his messiahship. First, the Messiah was expected to fulfill the hope of Israel. In Jesus' life and resurrection, that hope was expanded to the whole of humanity. Jesus as the new human is the founder of the fellowship of humans with God and one another. God's plan for creation in general and the creation of humanity in particular is communion. The Messiah brings to fulfillment this divine plan, finally uniting all people under one God to the worship of the one true God.

The Resurrection and Jesus' Divinity

The incarnate Christ claimed to be the Son sent by his Father to preach about the coming kingdom. Pannenberg begins his consideration of the divinity of Christ right here. Rather than appealing to Christology from above, which presupposes what it argues, Pannenberg begins with the historical foundation of Jesus' claims and their validation by the Father through the raising of Jesus from the dead. Jesus' proclamation of the nearness of the kingdom of God clearly implied a personal claim to authority that went beyond anything a human person can claim for himself or herself; in fact, Jesus proclaimed himself to be the mediator of God's coming lordship, which was already operative in the present. To validate his claims, Jesus looked to a future confirmation, the resurrection. For Pannenberg, the event of the resurrection was *the* starting point for the assertion of Jesus' deity, his unity with God.

The assertion of Jesus' deity on the basis of the resurrection is related to the way in which resurrection was understood in the Jewish context. Here the pervasive influence of apocalypticism is the key to understanding the meaning of resurrection. New Testament scholarship agrees that more significant than the presence of several apocalyptic passages—passages that talk about the coming end of the world in terms of cataclysmic cosmic events and divine intervention—is the fact that the whole of the New Testament grew in the soil of apocalypticism. The apocalyptic worldview provides the key to understanding the New Testament significance and meaning of Jesus and his resurrection. Three main features of apocalypticism have special significance here: First, the full revelation of God will not happen until the end of history. Second, the end of history is of universal significance: It involves both Jews and Gentiles. At the end, God will be shown to be the God of all people and all creation. And third, the end of history entails a general resurrection of the dead.

If the resurrection of Jesus can be shown to be a historical event—and Pannenberg believes it can be on the basis of the empty tomb tradition and the existence of a large number of eyewitnesses, the validity of whose testimony was not contested by their contemporaries—then that resurrection means the beginning of the resurrection of all that will take place at the end. For Pannenberg, Jesus' resurrection is the key to the insight that the human

person Jesus is one with God. In raising Jesus from the dead, the Father confirmed Jesus' pre-Easter claims with regard to the coming of the kingdom
and the Father's rule; Jesus was shown to be the eschatological Son of Man
of the prophecy of Daniel 7:13–14 and the apocalyptic expectation of the
time. After Jesus died on the cross, people could not justify belief in Jesus
and his claims without divine confirmation. Had there been no resurrection,
his opponents would have been correct: His authority claims would have
been blasphemous.

According to Pannenberg, we may now apply christological titles to him
such as Son of Man, Lord, Son of God. Even more, the end of the world has
already begun with the resurrection of Jesus. His resurrection is a "prolepsis,"
a preview of what will apply to all of us at the end. What happened in Jesus'
life as microcosm will apply to the rest of us and to creation. The definitive
revelation of God through the resurrection of Jesus took place even though its
final fulfillment awaits the end-time revelation when the God of the Bible
shows himself to be the God of all. But already now we may say that if Jesus
is ascended to God and the end of the world has begun, then God is ultimately revealed in Jesus.

But what about the cross of Christ? What is the meaning of the cross for
the personhood of Christ and our salvation? It has often been noted that Pannenberg so focuses on the resurrection that the cross does not play a crucial
enough role in his Christology. It is true that Pannenberg emphasizes resurrection and therefore places less emphasis on the cross. His approach to the
cross is through the concept of "inclusive substitution" in contrast to "exclusive substitution." For Pannenberg, in his cross and resurrection, Jesus acted
as our substitute. Jesus did not die so that we can avoid death, as the exclusive
view maintains; instead, in tasting death for us, he radically altered it. No
longer do we need to be terrified of death. Because we participate through
faith in the new life brought by Christ, we can look forward to participating
in God's life beyond death.

Christ in the Trinity

It is not surprising that for a theologian who sees the central task of theology as illuminating all human experience and the world, the doctrine of the
Triune God is the focus and foundation of his systematic presentation of
Christian faith. Pannenberg's theology is thoroughly trinitarian, and Christology is the gateway to his unfolding of this doctrine.

Pannenberg is, of course, not the first Christian theologian to place the
doctrine of the Trinity at the forefront. For example, for Karl Barth, all Christian doctrine is anchored in and dependent on the Trinity. But Pannenberg's
approach to the doctrine is unique for at least two reasons. First, the doctrine

of the Trinity precedes that of the unity of God.[4] It has been the norm in theology to talk first about God in his oneness and then to explicate the trinitarian perspectives. Pannenberg first exposits the Trinity and then the oneness of God. This reversal is significant in view of the fact that trinity is not something added to the unity of God; God in fact exists as trinity. This parallels John Zizioulas's idea that God does not first exist as being to which personhood is added but rather that God is person, communion. Second, rather than building his doctrine of the Triune God on speculation, as has often been the case, Pannenberg bases everything he says about the Trinity on revelation, namely, the way the Father, Son, and Spirit appeared in the event of revelation. Therefore, the point of departure for Pannenberg's trinitarian doctrine is Jesus' message of the fatherly care of God and the kingdom of God, his rulership over all creation.[5] In this regard, Pannenberg comes close to the approach of Jürgen Moltmann. The difference is that for Moltmann the point of departure is Christ's cross whereas for Pannenberg the focus is Jesus' filial relationship with the Father and Jesus' obedience to the Father's will.

At the heart of Pannenberg's doctrine is his concept of "self-differentiation" (in line with Hegel), namely, that the essence of person lies in the act of giving oneself to one's counterpart and thereby gaining one's identity from the other. This is a correction to the traditional notion of trinitarian self-differentiation, which refers to the bringing forth of the second and third trinitarian persons through the Father and so implies the priority of the Father. In Pannenberg, the one who differentiates oneself from another is dependent on the other for one's identity. In that sense, the Father's fatherhood is dependent on the activity of the Son and the Spirit and vice versa. In this understanding, Pannenberg follows the ancient view of Athanasius, according to which the Father would not be the Father without the Son and vice versa; once again it is manifested that the Trinity is essential to God's ontological being. Jesus differentiated himself from God and voluntarily submitted himself to serve God and his kingdom, giving place to the Father's claim to deity (Phil. 2:6–8). Conversely, the Father handed over lordship to the Son, who will hand it back in the eschaton (1 Cor. 15:24–25; Phil. 2:9–11). The Father's kingdom is dependent on the Son and his obedience.

This paradigm also explains the differentiation of the Spirit from both the Father and the Son. Pannenberg appeals to the Johannine statements concerning the glorifying of the Son by the Spirit (John 14:26; 15:26; 16:13–15). He notes that the trinitarian conception of the Spirit likewise developed from the coming of Jesus; the early church viewed the Spirit of God as the mediator of Jesus' community with the Father and of believers' participation in Christ. This act constitutes the Spirit as a distinct person alongside the Father and the

4. Pannenberg, *Systematic Theology*, 2:280–99.
5. Ibid., 259–80.

Son; as Jesus glorified the Father, not himself, and thereby is one with him, so the Spirit glorifies the Son and with him the Father.[6]

It should now be evident that Pannenberg rejects the *filioque* view (that the Spirit proceeds from both the Father and the Son). He believes it is wrong because it presupposes that Father-Son is the primary relation of origin to which the spiration of the Spirit is added. This makes the Spirit secondary and represents subordinationism of the Spirit.

In his trinitarian Christology, Pannenberg also emphasizes the mutual and interdependent relationship between Christ and the Spirit. This comes to focus first in his trinitarian doctrine of creation. The key to understanding creation is that it is the Son who is the model of an "otherness" different from the Father. The fact that there is creation, the world, distinct from the Creator, owes to the Son's self-differentiation, yet not total separation, from the Father. In other words, the Son's self-differentiation from the Father is the basis for the existence of the world independent from the Father. In that sense, the Son is the mediator of creation. The Spirit is the principle of the immanence of God in creation and the principle of the participation of creation in the divine life. There is an interesting paradox here: The goal of creation is the independence grounded in the Son, but participation in God—in the divine life—is likewise necessary; the latter is the role of the Spirit.

According to Pannenberg, "The christological constitution and the pneumatological constitution do not exclude one another but belong together because the Spirit and the Son mutually indwell one another as Trinitarian persons."[7] Everywhere the work of the Spirit is closely related to that of the Son, from creation to salvation to the consummation of creation in the eschaton. The reciprocity, rather than the asymmetry (usually in the form of Christology taking precedence), is accentuated by the fact that in the New Testament Jesus Christ himself is seen as a recipient of the Spirit and the Spirit's work in conception (Luke), baptism (Mark), and resurrection (Rom. 1:4; 8:11). According to John, the Spirit is given to Jesus Christ "without limit" (John 3:34). Since the risen Lord is wholly permeated by the divine Spirit of life, he can impart the Spirit to others insofar as they have fellowship with the Lord.

Christ and Religions

Pannenberg's historically anchored and thoroughly trinitarian Christology also has something decisive to say to the most urgent problem facing Christian theology in general and Christology in particular, namely, its relation to

6. Ibid., 314–16 especially; see also 304–5.
7. Pannenberg, *Systematic Theology*, 3:16–17; this emphasis is evident throughout his discussion of the foundations of the church in the earlier part of volume 3.

other religions. In theological terminology, this is the question of the theology of religions. The main question is this: What is the role of Christ with regard to other religions and their view of salvation?

On the basis of his understanding of mutual intra-trinitarian relations, according to which the task of the Spirit is to glorify the Son and through the Son to give honor to the Father's claim of unique lordship, Pannenberg is able to maintain that everywhere the divine mystery is at work, the Son is too. Now, it may be that distortions and misrepresentations are present in religions, but still the Son as the mediator of all creaturely existence is "behind" this quest for meaning and truth. And the same Spirit of God who is the principle of human beings' participation in God and divine life is at work in the world and religions along with the Son.

Pneumatology represents universality while Christology in a sense is the point of tension between the historical particularity and the eschatological universality, not in an exclusive way but in a way that opens up Christianity for dialogue with others. "The rule of God which Jesus proclaimed and pioneered in his own life, death, and resurrection can be seen in light of the apostolic message as the power at work in all the religions of humanity."[8]

What is Pannenberg's understanding of the fate of nonbelievers? He leaves the question open. For him, Jesus is "the universal criterion of judgment or salvation, but not the indispensable historical means of salvation."[9] This understanding coincides with Pannenberg's understanding of election, according to which election does not mean sealing the eternal fate of certain individuals but rather bringing about the divine goal through the involvement of the people of the world. "This view serves to move the focus of interreligious dialogue away from the question of who ultimately belongs to the people of God and toward the task of looking for the activity of the divine reality in the world and engaging all peoples in the mandate to foster the divine program."[10]

For Pannenberg, Christ represents the final revelation of God, although not in an exclusive way. Unpromising as this attitude might sound to most pluralists of our age, Pannenberg's theology of religions in fact carries a great deal of potential for a sustained dialogue. Even though he believes Christ represents a unique revelation of God in the history of religions, his Christology is by no means restrictive. In Jesus' resurrection, which was the Father's con-

8. Carl E. Braaten, "The Place of Christianity among the World Religions: Wolfhart Pannenberg's Theology of Religion and the History of Religions," in *The Theology of Wolfhart Pannenberg: Twelve American Critiques with an Autobiographical Response*, ed. Carl E. Braaten and Philip Clayton (Minneapolis: Augsburg, 1988), 305.

9. Wolfhart Pannenberg, "Constructive and Critical Functions of Christian Eschatology," *Harvard Theological Review* 77 (April 1984): 136.

10. Stanley J. Grenz, "Commitment and Dialogue: Pannenberg on Christianity and the Religions," *Journal of Ecumenical Studies* 26, no. 1 (1989): 206.

firmation of the claims of Jesus of Nazareth, a proleptical definitive insight into the final eschatological resurrection and new creation was given. In retrospect, one can see that the coming eschatological kingdom and the Father's claim for lordship over all creation and all people were already present in other religions in their function as witnesses to the coming fullness of the truth.

There are challenges for the future of theology of religions and interreligious dialogue on the basis of Pannenberg's program. If, as Pannenberg seems to believe, the unique place of Jesus Christ in the history of religions can be more or less objectively affirmed—based on the historically verifiable fact of his resurrection, which validates his earthly claims—without a commitment to any definite set of beliefs, then theology of religions could have the potential of becoming a truly interreligious endeavor. Even when theologians from various backgrounds hold to their personal convictions, their theological work could ideally be based just on "facts" and the assessment of their weight. Even though this kind of systematic work is not easily imagined, vision and utopias should not be discarded too hastily. Consequently, religious dialogue, rather than being just an encounter between two or more parties, could become an avenue for a true "ecumenical exchange of gifts."

18

Norman Kraus

Disciples' Christology

Christology from the Disciples to the Disciples

It has been customary for the writers of church history and Christian theology either to ignore or to downplay contributions from the "margins," as the mainline theologians have seen them. Even at the end of the nineteenth century, most church historians still divided Western Christianity into Protestant and Catholic types without remainder. An array of legitimate Christian churches and communities were left out, mainly descendants of the Radical Reformation such as Anabaptism and later Free Church movements. Whereas Catholics and Magisterial Reformers regarded the Radical Reformers, the "left-wingers," as dissenters, the latter considered themselves the true church of God on earth, guardians of the apostolic doctrine and practice.

C. Norman Kraus, in his book *Jesus Christ Our Lord,* offers a Christology from a disciple's perspective.[1] Kraus, a theologian who has taught in Asia and Africa and interacts with non-Western concerns in his writings, represents the Anabaptist tradition going back to the time of the Radical Reformation. His focus is on the meaning and significance of Jesus Christ to discipleship, the main emphasis of Anabaptism. For Anabaptism, mere belief or orthodox con-

---

1. C. Norman Kraus, *Jesus Christ Our Lord: Christology from a Disciple's Perspective* (Waterloo, Ontario: Herald Press, 1987).

victions are not enough; a practical Christian lifestyle in obedience to the Lord's commands must be visible. In addition to interacting with his Anabaptist heritage, Kraus challenges the standard Western interpretations of Christ that use the categories of guilt and penalty and looks at Christ's work in light of the Asian concept of shame. Standing as he is in the tradition of Anabaptism, Kraus also intends to write a "peace theology" from the perspective of Christology. The starting point is the biblical affirmation, "He is our peace" (Eph. 2:14).

Kraus finds the concept of self-identity and self-revelation most helpful to his Christology. Jesus, the self-revelation of God to us, is God-giving-himself-to-us. That self-revelation comes to us only in the form of a genuinely personal, historical relationship.

To write a Christology from a disciple's perspective, Kraus begins by listening to the biblical testimony of the first disciples of Christ. Out of that he creates a Christology that is firmly embedded in the existing cultures of the global world. In fact, Kraus writes not only a full-scale Anabaptist Christology but also a prolegomenon, an introduction to Christian theology as a whole. Christology is the gateway to studying God.

Christology or Jesusology?

The nineteenth-century and subsequent quest of the historical Jesus raised the question of whether we should talk about Christology or Jesusology. After all, the focus of the quest was to inquire into the historical and psychological origins of the person by the name of Jesus from the town of Nazareth. While Kraus acknowledges the value of the approach from below, in his reading of the New Testament, he sees a synthesis of the approaches from below and from above. This is encapsulated in Ephesians 4:20–21, which talks about Christ and "the truth that is in Jesus." In other words, this passage combines the earthly Jesus and the Christ of faith. From this Kraus draws an introductory conclusion, a framework that serves the rest of his Christology:

> Christology begins with the faith conviction that the man Jesus can be rightly understood only in the unique categories of biblical messianism and attempts to explain how and why this is so. But it also begins with the firm conviction that this messianic image must be understood in light of the fact that the Christ is none other than Jesus of Nazareth. Christology moves beyond the biographical categories of a historical Jesus in its attempt to assess his significance, but it must never abandon its historical referent. The historical revelation in Jesus remains the norm for defining the authentic Christ image and the Christian's experience of God.[2]

2. Ibid., 25.

The Christ of the Ephesians letter, Kraus reminds us, is not a mystical figure, a mythical symbol, or a philosophical principle but precisely the one who is identified with and known in Jesus, the historical figure of apostolic tradition.

In trying to understand the Jesus of the first disciples—in an attempt to offer a Christology for current disciples—Kraus asks, Why should we not simply read the New Testament Gospels for an account of the historical Jesus? Why must we theologize about Jesus at all? The obvious reason is that the Gospels contain more than one theological picture, more than one interpretation of Christ. Which one should we choose for the purposes of our current needs? The loving savior blessing the children? The healer and miracle worker? The rabbi-prophet who teaches with authority? The nonresistant suffering servant? Or the preexistent prototype of all creation?

For Kraus, the existence of both a history of Jesus and theological interpretations of its meaning in one and the same canon point to the methodology of Christology: It is not either/or but both/and with regard to the approaches from below and from above. What is clear is the need for multiple, distinctive theological interpretations of Christ to do justice to the varied cultural and religious needs of our times:

> This Christ may come in the semblance of an American savior whose image merges into that of the Statue of Liberty welcoming the distressed of the world to a land of freedom and opportunity. Or he may be presented as the 900-foot-high miracle worker which Oral Roberts claims to have seen in his vision.[3]

Or he may be the Christ of the standard evangelical theologies, the substitutionary sacrifice for the guilt of sin. Or he may be the liberator of South American revolutionary and liberationist theologies.

The context for such a search of meaningful contextual Christologies is the missionary work of the church among various cultures of the world. The assumed purpose of disciples' Christology is to help the church understand the implications of its message both for its life of discipleship and for its proclamation of the gospel to the nations. The context and purpose of the original witness to Christ in the Gospels and the rest of the New Testament was missionary proclamation. The task of such a Christology is to employ images and languages of existing cultures to express its message in various culturally appropriate ways. For example, the concept of incarnation was quite common in the ancient world. Polytheistic mythology contains many examples of divine heroes born to human mothers. The *avatara* (incarnations of deities) of Hindu tradition are also widely known and have often been compared favor-

3. Ibid., 27.

ably to the Christian idea of incarnation. In many cultures, the king or emperor has been considered a divine incarnation.

But a criterion is needed, Kraus argues, and that is the New Testament, the testimony to the original disciples' view of Christ. "We need a theological description that will provide a norm for using the New Testament images in shaping the message of the gospel for the many cultures of the world. It must also give a clue to our own self-understanding as followers of Christ and guide us into a relevant discipleship."[4]

Jesus, a Word about Humanity

It hardly comes as a surprise that Jesus' full humanity is a key point for a disciples' Christology. The Anabaptists of the sixteenth century, who put great emphasis on following Christ in faithful obedience, clearly understood this point. They focused their attention on the sinless and nonviolent humanity of Jesus as the prototype for a new humanity of obedience and purity. Some Anabaptist sources from the seventeenth and eighteenth centuries talk about the "holy Manhood" of Christ. The man Jesus is the gateway to the ethical renewal of humanity. Metaphysical explanations about his divinity were not the focus, even though all Anabaptists strongly affirmed the classical orthodoxy of the creeds.

Anabaptist sources looked at Christ's humiliation, death on the cross, and subsequent descent into Hades as the process of salvation. Salvation does not come by power but by the humble submission of the Servant of God unto death. "The Man Jesus Christ (who alone accomplishes in the believers the good pleasure of his Father) . . . is Lord, Ruler, Leader, and Director of His saints." This Son of Man is the "hominized" Word of God to us.[5]

According to Kraus, implicit in the Anabaptist insistence on the full humanity of Christ are two basic convictions: first, that God is a self-giving Creator who fully identifies with us in our need, and second, that our humanity finds its true fulfillment in this one who is the prototypical image of God. The Word become flesh is not just another kind of "contextual" communication but God's love coming to us as one of us. Incarnation at the same time also affirms the creation of humanity. The humanized Word of God is God's image and therefore points to the way God wanted human beings to be. This destiny to be like God is the true meaning and destiny of human existence. In this regard, Kraus makes basically the same point as Pannenberg (though without reference to him).

4. Ibid., 29–30.
5. Ibid., 63.

For Kraus, the heart of the Christian message is the conviction that Jesus is the fulfillment and thus the revelation of God's intention for human life. All Docetic attempts to attenuate Jesus' humanity detract from this central tenet of Christian theology. Writing at the end of the first century, the author of 1 John equated Docetism with the spirit of the antichrist (2:22–23; 4:1–3).

The way the sinlessness of Jesus was defended in the past created a problem in appreciating his full humanity. Especially the Augustinian understanding of sin as sensuality and inherited guilt motivated theologians to defend Christ from all taint and influence of sin. For Kraus, the focal point of the sinlessness of Jesus is his refusal to assert his self-will in opposition to God's will; this is the core of Jesus' being the perfect image of God, which "from the biblical perspective . . . is what it means to be fully human!"[6] In his humanity, Jesus totally identified himself with humanity. He lived in solidarity with human beings. The cross for Kraus represents the consummation of God's solidarity with the world.

If *incarnation* is a word about humanity, at the same time it is also a word about God. Incarnation speaks of the self-disclosure of God in the God-man, Jesus Christ. Jesus' claim of unity with God was established and validated by his resurrection from the dead. Here again, Kraus follows the path of Pannenberg; for both of these theologians, the resurrection is the divine confirmation of Jesus' claim that he is the mediator of divine life and the coming kingdom of God. Resurrection for Kraus is *the* sign pointing to the reality of the deity of Christ. Jesus' resurrection also confirms our salvation. Salvation means overcoming death, and had Jesus not been raised from the dead, our hope beyond death would be vain.

The Cross, Shame, and Guilt

In his search for appropriate images of salvation, Kraus considers some that are less familiar in standard Christologies. One image that seems to capture much of the *agapē* love of God is the parent-child analogy. The true nature of genuinely moral responses is best seen in our most intimate human relationships, which is why the parent-child metaphor has potential for illuminating God's way with his children. In the New Testament, Jesus' special name for God was the Aramaic *abba*. In light of this—and the fact that the early church used this designation, "father," for Jesus Christ—it seems strange that so little use has been made of this metaphor. This approach can illumine the passionate yet mature love of the heavenly Father for his wayward and erring children. Sin means the rejection of love; therefore, Fatherly love means restitution for sin and open arms to the repenting son and daughter.

6. Ibid., 72.

Kraus uses many other metaphors from the New Testament and Christian tradition that highlight the loving solidarity between Christ and us. One of the main images in the Bible, especially in the New Testament, is the restoration of covenantal relationship. The covenant that God made with Israel and later with us in Christ is an offer of salvation based on the faithfulness of God. It is about relationships, trust, love. Another image, widely employed especially outside Western culture, presents salvation as deliverance from alien authorities. Deliverance from the power of sin and bondage to the demonic are both part of this image.

The Eastern concept of salvation as the renewal of the image of God is one of Kraus's favorite images in his Christology and soteriology. This is understandable in light of the importance he attaches to the humanity of Christ as the fulfillment of human destiny. The early Christian tradition talked about the restoration of the image as divinization or deification: Christ became human so that we may become deified. The moral renewal of Wesleyan and Holiness movements was a later appropriation of this image.

The most distinctive approach to the work of Christ in Kraus's *Jesus Christ Our Lord* is related to Asian cultures, especially the Japanese context. There is a pronounced difference between the Western idea of guilt and the Asian idea of shame as the main category for the human predicament. Guilt focuses on the act; shame focuses on the self. The nature of fault in shame cultures is the failure to meet self-expectations. Guilt arises out of offenses against legal expectations. The internal reactions vary too. In guilt cultures, there is remorse, self-accusation, and fear of punishment. In shame cultures, embarrassment, disgrace, self-deprecation, and fear of abandonment abound. The remedy for guilt is often a demand for revenge or penalty, while for shame it is identification and communication; love banishes shame, while justification banishes guilt. Out of these two paradigms emerge different views of the cross of Christ. For the Asian, the cross represents an instrument of shame and God's ultimate identification with us in our sinful shame; it is an expression of God's love. In standard Western soteriologies, the cross has often been an instrument of penalty and God's ultimate substitute for our sinful guilt; the cross expresses God's justice.

These two approaches are, of course, not exclusive of one another. The cross of Christ is related to both shame and guilt. Reconciliation means overcoming shame and freedom from guilt. In his self-sacrifice, Jesus acted vicariously for us in two ways. He bore the consequences of our sin in order to be our servant (Mark 10:45). Jesus also took the place of all humankind inasmuch as his revelation is a universal one. As one totally identified with and representing humanity, he faced his destiny of death on the cross. Furthermore, the crucified Christ not only effects the resolution of shame anxiety but also reveals the normative ethical-social dimensions of shame: "The cross exposes false shame as an idolatrous human self-justification and, in exposing it, breaks its power to instill fear."[7] Shame is expressed in the taboos and norms of society. In theological terms, that means, according to Kraus, that the expressions of shame are negative indicators of a society's concept of the image of God reflected in humanity. They define what is considered truly human. Thus, when Christian theology says that the cross exposes false shame and reveals the true nature of human shame, it means that the crucified Christ reveals God's authentic image for humanity. In other words, Kraus concludes, the crucified Jesus demonstrated God's standard of right human relations and became the truly universal norm for humanity.

7. Ibid., 220.

19

Stanley Grenz

Evangelical Christology

Theology for the Community of God

The term *evangelical* in its current usage, especially in the English-speaking world, is ambiguous. Following the Reformation, the term originally meant Protestant theology as opposed to Catholic theology. Another meaning was added in the twentieth century when it came to mean those Protestants who adhered to the more orthodox version of Christianity as opposed to the liberal left wing. Thus, there arose an "evangelical doctrine of Scripture" that held that the Word of God is divine in its origin and trustworthy in all regards. In still more recent decades, the evangelical movement, which is transdenominational and global and represents not only all sorts of Protestants from Lutherans to Presbyterians to Baptists to Pentecostals but also Anglicans, has distanced itself from the more reactionary fundamentalism, even though most fundamentalists regard themselves as the true evangelicals.

Reference to "evangelical theology" here follows the main usage in the English-speaking world, namely, various Protestant Christian traditions that are open to dialogue with other Christians and cherish classical Christianity as explicated in the creeds and mainstream confessions, yet are also open to new developments in theology and other academic fields.

Stanley Grenz's *Theology for the Community of God*,[1] as the title suggests, approaches the nature and task of systematic theology from the perspective of

1. Stanley Grenz, *Theology for the Community of God* (Grand Rapids: Eerdmans, 1994).

171

the community of God, the church. Too often theologies in general and Christologies in particular are written for and from the perspective of individuals in need of salvation. This work attempts to overcome that reductionism and reflect on the communitarian implications of theology and Christology. Christology for Grenz is reflection on the role of Jesus of Nazareth, whom Christians acknowledge as the Christ, "in the reconciling, community-building work of the Triune God."[2]

Grenz's Christology follows the traditional path in that he first considers the divinity of Christ, his humanity, and the union of the two natures before entering into a discussion of the work of Christ in his cross and resurrection. At the same time, Grenz's treatment is up-to-date, creative, and open to most current developments in the field while being anchored in basic evangelical convictions. The influence of Wolfhart Pannenberg is visible in the background; this is understandable given that Pannenberg was Grenz's *Doktorvater,* doctoral mentor (even though Grenz rarely refers to Pannenberg).

Characteristic of Grenz's approach is his effort to find a balance between Christology from below and from above. At times he seems to support one-sidedly the approach from below, but in his final conclusions the approach from above is also visible.

The Fellowship of Jesus the Christ with God

If Grenz were a typical evangelical theologian of the past, he would simply allude to biblical statements about the claims, miracles, and other ministries of Jesus to affirm Jesus' unity with God, his deity. But that is not the approach of Grenz. In the footsteps of Pannenberg, he sets himself the tedious task of establishing the divinity of Christ on the basis of historical inquiry. Grenz argues that we cannot separate the Christ of faith from the Jesus of history, although that would be tempting because it would free us from historical research.

Grenz considers several proposals as to what aspect of Jesus' life can provide the foundation for his deity. Traditionally, Jesus' sinlessness has been a good candidate. However, this aspect lacks an objective historical foundation and was questioned even during Jesus' life. An even more serious objection to this proposal is that even if we could establish the claim for Jesus' sinlessness, it would not guarantee his divinity: Sinlessness is not the same as being divine. At its best, sinlessness could make a person an extraordinary individual. Using Jesus' teaching as the foundation for his divinity results in the same problems associated with his sinlessness. His teaching was contested during his life, and even had it not been, authoritative teaching does not make one divine.

2. Ibid., 244.

A weightier proposal concerns the death of the Messiah, which has often been seen as *the* foundation for his deity. His death reveals his identity. As the soldier at the foot of the cross observed, "Surely he was the Son of God!" (Matt. 27:54). However, in isolation, Jesus' death is ambiguous. Was Jesus' death the death of a political victim or a sacrificial martyr? Only in light of a prior faith commitment (the assurance that he was divine) can the death of Christ serve as foundational.

What about his own claim for divinity? Gospel criticism has questioned many, if not most, of the passages that contain such a claim. The scholarly consensus maintains that Jesus was aware of his divinity, but this awareness does not guarantee his divinity; he may have been wrong. Furthermore, other religious leaders have made similar claims. What makes Jesus' claim distinctive, however, is that he looked for a future vindication that would establish the truthfulness of his claim: the resurrection.

The resurrection is, in fact, another aspect that has been seen as the foundation for Jesus' divinity. Resurrection alone would not make a person a god; Lazarus was raised from the dead, but he was not considered divine. What makes resurrection a valid foundation in Jesus' case is its relationship to Jesus' claim of divinity. Grenz concludes that Jesus' claim and his resurrection taken together provide evidence for his divinity. Through his teaching and actions, Jesus made a claim for his own uniqueness; this claim called for a future confirmation. If the resurrection did take place, it constitutes the needed confirmation. And there is also the wider context of the eschatological coming of the kingdom that was inaugurated by the resurrection: "The resurrection is God's declaration that through his ministry, Jesus had indeed inaugurated the divine reign. In him God is truly at work enacting his eschatological purpose, which is the establishment of the community of God."[3] From this we can work backward to other proposals. As divine, Christ is sinless, his teaching has divine authority, and in his death he acted for our salvation.

For Grenz, in order for his argumentation to hold, he has to establish the historical nature of the resurrection. Once again, following Pannenberg, he maintains that the empty tomb tradition and the existence of independent witnesses provide historical evidence for the factuality of the Gospel claims. While using the resurrection as the means to establish Christ's deity, however, Grenz also wants to avoid an adoptionistic interpretation according to which Jesus was made God's Son by virtue of the resurrection. Jesus was already divine; the resurrection merely provides the historical evidence for that fact.

In this way, Grenz affirms the fellowship of Jesus Christ with God on the basis of historical inquiry. In addition to the historical evidence, though, the birth of faith also requires personal experience of the living Lord. But even

3. Ibid., 260.

that is based on the conviction of the historical foundation and not vice versa. In 1 Corinthians 15:17–19, the historicity of the resurrection is Paul's criterion for the reliability of the Christian message.

What, then, are the implications of Jesus' unity with God? In theological history, there has been a dualism between two approaches, functional and ontological. The functional approach argues on the basis of the task given to Christ, and the ontological proceeds with reference to his being (ontology is that branch of philosophy that inquires into the question of "being"). For Grenz, these two options are not mutually exclusive but complementary. The biblical concept of Jesus as the revealer of God (John 14:9–10) has the potential of transcending the function-versus-ontology demarcation. Christological understanding of Jesus is functional in that he reveals God and ontological in that he is the self-revelation of God. To reveal God, Jesus Christ has to be God, ontologically one with God.

In his fellowship with the Father, Jesus reveals to us both God's compassionate, loving heart and Jesus' special *abba* relationship with his Father. As the self-revelation of God, he is able to bring us into the most intimate relationship with the Father. At the same time, Christ also reveals the Father's lordship. Once again, this title is both functional and ontological: Because Jesus is one with God, he functions as God present in the world. He is the cosmic Lord (Phil. 2:9–11), the Lord of history, and our personal Lord.

The Fellowship of Jesus the Christ with Humankind

According to Grenz, Jesus is not only essential deity but also essential humanity, "man for us." Jesus shares in our true humanness. Grenz develops this line of thought by looking at Jesus' earthly life. Jesus obviously participated in the conditions of normal human life, experienced growth, and lived the life of a particular Jewish person at a particular time. The Bible also affirms that he completely identified with us in all respects (Heb. 2:14, 17).

What is the foundation for affirming Jesus' true humanity? Grenz does not find the foundation just by considering Jesus' earthly life. The resurrection in isolation shares the same ambiguity with regard to Jesus' humanity as with regard to his divinity, but combined with Jesus' claim for true humanity, it shows that God gave his approval to that claim. Therefore, Jesus' claim for true humanity in conjunction with his resurrection serves as the needed historical foundation for Jesus' fellowship with humanity. If there had been no resurrection following the cross, God's plan for eternal fellowship with humans would have been made void. But Jesus' resurrection shows what our path can be too, in the newness of life. In this context, Grenz talks about the "paradigmatic nature of Jesus' humanness in an ontological sense": Jesus reveals the transformed ontological reality that we will one day become.[4]

The fellowship of Jesus Christ with humankind points not only to the hope beyond death but also to God's intent for our future lives that goes beyond individual life. It points to community. Jesus is the paradigm for human fellowship. Jesus as the New Human expresses the true humanity intended for us. As such he shows us the nature of the "Universal Human" with regard to the marginalized, women, and the individual. Jesus' humanity encompasses and gives room to women and men, young and old, rich and poor.

The Fellowship of Deity and Humanity in Jesus

It is one thing to affirm separately the divinity and the humanity of Jesus Christ and another thing to consider the unity of these two natures. For Grenz, the foundation for affirming the unity lies in two New Testament titles: the Word and Son. The term *word, Logos,* which appears roughly 330 times in the Bible, was rooted in both Greek culture and the corresponding Hebrew term *davar,* which has the dual meaning "word" and "event." In the first chapter of the Gospel of John, two roles are assigned to the Word. On the one hand, the Word has a creative role ("through him all things were made" [1:3]); on the other hand, he has a revelatory role ("we have seen his glory" [1:14]). Another biblical passage, Colossians 1:15–16, employs the same idea. For Grenz, the declaration that Jesus is the Word:

> therefore constitutes a theological statement concerning the significance of this historical life. In him, God's revelation is disclosed and God's power is operative. As a result, the title asserts that in Jesus of Nazareth the power of God is at work revealing the meaning of all reality—even the nature of God. To refer to Jesus as the Word is to affirm that as this human being, he is the revelation of God.[5]

The related New Testament references to Jesus as the Son are, of course, based on the biblical notion of the "Son of God," which is rooted in the Old Testament and the ancient Near East. In the ancient Near East, the title "son" was given to those thought to be the offspring of the gods such as kings or those with extraordinary, "divine," powers. To the Hebrews, "son" indicated election to participate in God's work, a special agent elected to obedience in carrying out God's mission in the world. In the Gospels, the title Son of God in reference to Jesus indicated his unique obedience to God's will and mission. On the basis of Jesus' unique sonship and earthly life of obedience, he

4. Ibid., 283.
5. Ibid., 301–2.

was seen as divine, as conveyed in the epistles. The title Son, therefore, came to carry exalted aspects similar to those of Word. In fact, Hebrews 1:3–4 shows a connection between the two by describing the Son as the one through whom God made the universe and as the revelation of God's essence.

Taken together, the titles Word and Son offer the basis for explaining the unity of Jesus' two natures. This basis is their common connection with the idea of revelation. As the Word and the Son, Jesus is both essential deity and essential humanity and reveals both natures. The unity of the two natures, therefore, is a revelatory unity. As this revelation, Jesus brings the two natures together in his one person. According to Grenz, this appeal to revelation as the focus of the unity of the two natures is not merely functional, as some critics suggest. Inherent in revelation is participation. Jesus not only reveals but also participates in divine and human life. His revelatory unity, therefore, leads to his ontological unity with God and humanity.

Incarnation

From the time of the early creeds, the church has unanimously confessed that the person of Jesus Christ contains a union of human and divine natures; he is a true human and a true God. But Christian theologians have had a difficult time putting that confession in a satisfactory theological form. When considering the formulation of an evangelical Christology, Grenz is critical of the way the Chalcedonian creed incorporated the central features of what he calls incarnational Christology. Incarnational Christology focuses on the condescension and self-humiliation of the divine *Logos,* the Son, in taking to himself human nature. It also includes the exaltation of human nature to inseparable (in technical theological language, hypostatic) communion with the divine *Logos* because of that act. Therefore, in the incarnation:

> the Son did not unite with a human person, but with human nature, which gained existence in its connection with the Logos *(enhypostasis).* As a consequence of the incarnation, the one person Jesus Christ enjoys the properties of the two natures *(communicatio idiomatum).*[6]

This traditional approach to incarnation shares several common features. Jesus combines in one person a divine and a human nature, and the incarnation was the means of effecting the union of these two natures. This act was the work of the Second Person of the Trinity, the *Logos,* and resulted in a "hypostatic union" of deity and humanity in Jesus. In other words, in this union, the personal center of the earthly life was the eternal Son, with the human na-

6. Ibid., 306.

ture existing only through its union with the *Logos.* The historical act of incarnation took place in the conception of Jesus in the womb of Mary. While this post-Chalcedonian Christology has good intentions in trying to defend the full humanity and the full divinity of Christ and their coexistence, it is beset with serious problems, Grenz argues, and therefore has to be modified.

Some of the most typical criticisms targeted at incarnational Christology are the following: similarity with other mythological stories of contemporary religions; dangers of Docetism (which compromises the full humanity of Christ) or Apollinarianism (which regards the human nature of Christ as nonpersonal); and the most serious of all, the separation between *Logos* and Jesus. What was the *Logos* doing before the incarnation?

On the way to a more satisfactory formulation of the doctrine of the incarnation, Grenz goes back to the central biblical passages from which theologians have built the concept of incarnation: John 1:1–4 and Philippians 2:5–11. In Grenz's reading of these passages, there was no historical descent of a preexisting divine *Logos.* In fact, Paul does not even mention the *Logos;* rather, he writes about Jesus Christ. The historical person Jesus refused to clutch his divine prerogatives but was God's humble, obedient servant to the point of death, and as a consequence, he achieved the highest name. Therefore, Paul drew the incarnation view from the history of Jesus. Similarly, Grenz contends that even John, though he mentions the *Logos,* builds on the historical life of Jesus. John does not mention Jesus' birth as the vehicle that facilitated the incarnate state of the eternal *Logos.* John appeals to eyewitnesses who observed Jesus' earthly life and testified that they "have seen his glory," the glory of the one who became flesh. The Johannine prologue does not focus on how Jesus came into existence. More importantly, it is a theological declaration of the significance of Jesus' earthly life. When he confesses Jesus as the incarnate Word, John is claiming that as this human being, Jesus is divine; he is God's revelation.

As a remedy, Grenz suggests once again Christology from below. He searches for the answer to the identity of Jesus by looking at his historical life. The confession of the incarnation, rather than being the presupposition of Christology, is the conclusion drawn from an examination of the earthly life of Jesus Christ, which is the presupposition and beginning of Christology.

Preexistence

If one claims to work with Christology from below and yet is not willing to set aside the classical affirmation of the preexistence of Christ, how does one hold the two together? To call Jesus Christ the *Logos,* the Word of God, necessarily implies his preexistence and has been so understood from the first centuries. By now it should be clear that for Grenz preexistence should be linked to Jesus rather than directly to the *Logos*. Grenz disagrees with the traditional way of understanding preexistence as the preexistence of the *Logos* prior to his assuming human form in the incarnation. The question, then, is twofold: In what sense was and is the eternal Son active apart from the historical person Jesus of Nazareth? And in what sense is the *Logos* active beyond the action of Jesus? A corollary question is whether there are other religious figures, saviors, apart from Jesus Christ.

The foundational guiding principle for Grenz is that in the New Testament, preexistence is an attribute describing Jesus of Nazareth, not a purported eternal being—whether the *Logos* or the Son—apart from Jesus. There is no separating the Son from Jesus of Nazareth. Doing so would destroy the importance of the title *Logos,* by which the New Testament writers confess the meaning of the historical person of Jesus. Grenz also reminds us of the original intent of the doctrine of the incarnation in the early church. It was a polemic against adoptionism, which asked, When did Jesus become the Son? Did he become the Son at his ascension, resurrection, baptism, or conception? Or will he become the Son at the second coming? Seeing all these options as potentially adoptionistic, early theology came to the conclusion that Jesus was the Son from eternity. Hence, they attributed preexistence to him. But now, of course, we have another problem: How do we predicate preexistence to a historical person? According to Grenz, there are three senses in which we should understand this assertion.

First, Jesus belongs to God's eternity. Jesus' preexistence speaks about his relationship with God. By confessing his preexistence, we declare that this human being is eternal deity. Though his earthly life was short, it was the revelation of the eternal God. According to Colossians 1:19, "God was pleased to have all his fullness dwell in him."

> By confessing Jesus' preexistence—that Jesus belongs to God's eternity—we affirm the uniqueness and finality of his earthly life. Thereby, our affirmation of preexistence carries far-reaching implications for human beliefs and religion. We declare through our confession that Jesus is the embodiment of truth. His life is the truly religious life. And his teachings are true teachings, revealing the eternal truth of God himself. As a result, Jesus is the standard for measuring all religious truths. All other truth claims must be weighed in accordance with his one historical person.[7]

Second, the historical life of Jesus carries significance beyond the boundaries of his brief life. He gives meaning to all history. Jesus is the divine principle of creation (John 1:3; Col. 1:16). And third, Jesus' life is the story of history itself: His life narrative includes more than the thirty-three years of his earthly life. All history—whether the preparation for his coming or for his second coming—is his story, Grenz concludes.

7. Ibid., 313.

20

John Hick

Universalist Christology

The Copernican Revolution of Religions

John Hick, the most noted and hotly debated defender of religious plural-ism, has gleaned many insights from Asia through his extensive travels and short-term teaching stints in India (1974, 1975–1976), Sri Lanka (1974), and elsewhere. Hick began his theological career as a conservative, almost fun-damentalist, believer following his dramatic conversion experience, but dur-ing his years of teaching and doing research in the field of theology, he has become the leading spokesperson for a universalist, mythical Christology and an extremely pluralistic theology of religions.

In 1970, Hick and his colleagues published a critical manifesto titled "The Reconstruction of Christian Belief for Today and Tomorrow"[1] in which they questioned the literal meaning of most traditional Christian beliefs. This manifesto also meant a new approach to Christology, for most of the tenets had to do with Christ:

1. divine revelation
2. creation ex nihilo

1. John Hick, "The Reconstruction of Christian Belief for Today and Tomorrow," *Theology* 73 (1970): 339.

3. substitutionary death of Christ
4. virgin birth
5. miracles of Christ
6. resurrection
7. need for new birth to be saved
8. no other chance after death
9. hell and heaven

Hick also questioned the old paradigm according to which there is no salvation outside the church, and therefore, missionary work is needed. His own emerging pluralistic view, according to which there is more than one way of salvation, was inspired by considering factors that challenge exclusivism: the diversity of religions (Christians are the minority in many areas of the world), the tie between ethnicity and religion, the lack of missionary success, the quality of religious life in non-Christian religions, and the phenomenological similarity of religions. He came to the conclusion that religion is a human interpretation of reality, not absolute fact statements, and consequently, all religions are in contact with and describe the same reality.

Hick has published a number of books that argue for a pluralistic Christology and theology, the most well known of which is *God and the Universe of Faiths*.[2] Hick compares his pluralistic theology of religions to Copernicus's astronomical model. Rather than Jesus Christ of the traditional view, it is God, the Ultimate Truth, who is the center of all religions around whom they revolve in the way of planets:

> And the needed Copernican revolution in theology involves an equally radical transformation in our conception of the universe of faiths and the place of our own religion within it. It involves a shift from the dogma that Christianity is at the center to the realization that it is God who is at the center, and that all the religions of mankind, including our own, serve and revolve around him.[3]

In Hick's view, the essence of pluralism means that there is "both the one unlimited transcendent divine Reality and also a plurality of varying human concepts, images, and experiences of and responses to that Reality."[4]

The challenge to Christian theology, as well as to, for example, Hindu or Buddhist theology, is to move from the "Ptolemaic" view in which Christianity or any other religion stands at the center and in which other religions are

2. John Hick, *God and the Universe of Faiths: Essays in the Philosophy of Religion* (London: Macmillan, 1973).
3. John Hick, *The Second Christianity*, 3d ed. of *Christianity at the Centre* (London: SCM, 1983), 82.
4. Ibid., 83.

judged by the criteria of that center. To accomplish this task, Hick contends that the views of the adherents of religions cannot be taken at face value; rather, each religion has to deemphasize its own absolute and exclusive claims.

To illustrate his point, Hick uses an allegory from Buddhist sources according to which ten blind men touch an elephant and each describes what an elephant is on the basis of his limited experience. Various conceptions of God/god(s)/divine such as Yahweh, Allah, Krishna, Param Atma, or the Holy Trinity are but aspects of the Divine. They are like maps or colors of the rainbow. All religions in this estimation have the same basic orientation and share the hope of salvation. The main biblical-theological reason for pluralism is God's love, which is best expressed in the person of Jesus Christ. The task of the Holy Spirit is to open followers of various religions to the idea of openness. On the basis of these considerations, Hick calls for a recognition that "the basic common ground of the world is a result of empirical, phenomenological observations." The pluralist, according to Hick, does not claim to possess the final word about religions.[5]

Later in his career, to do justice to his understanding of the nature of religious language, Hick shifted from speaking about "God" to "the (Ultimate) Reality," a term that is more flexible than the personal term *God*. For Hick, the great religions of the world are different—and one may say complementary—ways of approaching this Reality, which exists beyond the human capacity of knowing. The Sanskrit term *sat* and the Islamic term *al-Haqq* are expressions of this Reality, as are *Yahweh* and *God*.

Myth and the Nature of Religious Language

To better understand Hick's theology and Christology, one has to know how he understands the nature and function of talk about religion and the divine. While many other contemporary pluralists deny the cognitive function of religious language, Hick does not do so completely. Instead, he uses two approaches to deal with the existence of competing truth claims.

In his first approach, Hick divides the seemingly contradictory claims of various religions into three levels. The first level relates to historical conceptions, such as the Christian belief in the death of Jesus on the cross vis-à-vis the view of the Qur'an, according to which it only seemed actual. The only way to solve a conflict on this level is by an appeal to historical evidence, which, of course, is lacking. The second level is that of suprahistorical claims, or as Hick also calls

5. John Hick, *Problems of Religious Pluralism* (London: Macmillan, 1988), 37; Matti T. Amnell, *Uskontojen Universumi: John Hickin uskonnollisen pluralismin haaste ja siitä käyty keskustelu,* Suomalaisen Teologisen Kirjallisuusseuran Julkaisuja 217 (Helsinki: STK, 1999), 49.

them, "quasihistorical" claims, such as the doctrine of reincarnation. Obviously, there is no way to reconcile the differences between religions that support the idea (Buddhism, Hinduism) and those that do not (Islam, Judaism, and Christianity). Consequently, the only sensible way to deal with this level of conflicts is to adopt an attitude of mutual respect and acceptance. The third level concerns conceptions about the Ultimate Reality. Ideas about personal god(s) such as Yahweh, Siva, Vishnu, and Allah and ideas about impersonal concepts such as Brahma, Tao, nirvana, Sunyata, and Dharmakaya cannot be easily reconciled. Thus, according to Hick, we should treat these seemingly contradictory descriptions of the divine as complementary to one another.

Hick's second approach to easing the conflict between contradictory truth claims is to appeal to the mythical nature of religious language. The "myth" is based on "metaphor," which means that we speak "suggestive of another." In other words, metaphors that are not meant to be taken at face value still convey meaning, though in terms of eliciting emotions and associations familiar to a group that shares a common context of meanings. In an important sense, myth is an expanded metaphor. Even though it is not literally true, it "tends to evoke an appropriate dispositional attitude."[6] Its purpose is to change attitudes and thus influence thinking in a real way. The story about Buddha's flight to Sri Lanka, the creation story of the Old Testament, or the legend of the dance of Siva function in this manner.[7] As long as myths are understood literally, conflicts arise, but if they are treated mythologically, they function in "separate mythic spaces" and do not conflict with one another. Rather than inquiring into the truth of a myth, one should ask whether it functions in the life situation and context for which it was created.

On the basis of his understanding of language, Hick divides the basic elements of religions into two categories, those that are essential and those that are not. Even though religions seem to differ dramatically on the surface level, deep down they have a common foundation. For Hick, the differences on the surface level, even when they are to some extent cognitive in nature, do not create insurmountable conflicts, and here the two strategies described above are of help.

Mythical Christology

Hick's Christology is the result of his understanding of myth and religious language. It illustrates his understanding of the relationship between seemingly

6. John Hick, *The Metaphor of God Incarnate: Christology in a Pluralistic Age* (London: SCM, 1993), 105; see also John Hick, *An Interpretation of Religion: Human Responses to the Transcendent* (London: Macmillan, 1989), 99–104, 348; and Amnell, *Uskontojen Universumi,* 79–81.

7. Hick, *Interpretation of Religion,* 103, 347–72.

conflicting truth claims and highlights the importance of his idea of language. Traditional talk about incarnation has to be demythologized and set in harmony with other major religions, Hick contends. The incarnation is about making the presence of the Divine real to all men and women. It is not about a god becoming a human being; that idea is repulsive to contemporary people.

In traditional Christianity, incarnation language has been taken for granted, and it entails exclusivism: God is present in Christ in a specific, unique way. Mythical interpretation, on the other hand, sees continuity rather than contradistinction between religions. According to Hick, a demythologized Christianity has the advantage of being compatible with genuine religious pluralism. Doctrines are time- and context-bound; myths and metaphors are dynamic, subject to change. Talk about incarnation is therefore not indicative but expressive. Hick refers to the way two lovers express themselves to each other. Even though expressions such as "I love you more than anybody else" seem to be absolutistic, they are not exclusive. Other lovers may freely use them as well; yet they are true in their own context and for the purpose they were meant.

Against the traditional view, Hick argues that it is extremely unlikely that Jesus thought of himself, or that his first disciples thought of him, as God incarnate. Jesus would have regarded such a claim as blasphemy. Sayings such as "I and the Father are one" (John 10:30) are not sayings of Jesus but of the early church. Jesus regarded himself as an end-time prophet sent to proclaim the imminent coming of the kingdom or, so to speak, a Buddha who had attained true knowledge of and access to pure reality; he was aware that God was present in his life. This presence of God in his life was channeled to others through, for example, occasions of "healings," which were psychosomatic healing influences.

Furthermore, the traditional view of the sinlessness of Jesus has to be reevaluated. Although Jesus was above other humans because of his special God-consciousness, he was not perfect morally. For example, he displayed racist attitudes toward the Canaanite woman (Matt. 15:21–28), violence in the temple by driving out the merchants, and so on.

Jesus' divinity has to be understood metaphorically. A mythological interpretation of Christology has the potential of serving a pluralistic theology of religions, Hick argues. In that view, Christ is depicted as the embodiment of divine love, complementary to the intense experience of the release from suffering in Buddhism or the source of life and purpose in Hinduism. *Logos* for Hick transcends any particular religion and is present in all of them.

Degree Christology

According to Hick, the development of the doctrine of the incarnation had little to do with Jesus or his early disciples. Echoing the opinions of classical liberalism and the quest of the historical Jesus, Hick maintains that neither Jesus nor his disciples saw Jesus as God incarnate. The early church later elevated Jesus to the status of God because of the power of the Christ event. In the process, the church made use of the Old Testament concepts of divine sonship and the Suffering Servant. Early Christians had encountered God in a specific way, and as the message spread into the Greco-Roman world, the language and philosophy of that culture were employed to give meaning to the experience. In that sense, the development of Christology was a historical accident. Had it spread to the East, it might have taken another path of development. Hick's vision for an Eastern Christ is this:

> Instead of Jesus being identified as the divine *Logos* or the divine Son he would have been identified as a Bodhissattva who, like Gotama some four centuries earlier, had attained to Buddhahood or perfect relationship to reality, but had in compassion for suffering mankind voluntarily lived out his human life in order to show others the way to salvation.[8]

Hick's preference for a pluralistic understanding of Christ is "degree Christology" in contrast to "substance Christology," which holds that Jesus is unique. According to degree Christology, Christ differs from other humans only in degree. Hick claims that substance Christology must be rejected because theology no longer treats the incarnation factually. The metaphorical or mythical understanding is in line with degree Christology:

> Incarnation, in the sense of the embodiment of ideas, values, insights in human living, is a basic metaphor. One might say, for example, that in 1940 the spirit of defiance of the British people against Nazi Germany was incarnated in Winston Churchill. Now we want to say of Jesus that he was so vividly conscious of God as the loving heavenly Father, and so startlingly open to God and so fully his servant and instrument, that the divine love was expressed, and in that sense incarnated, in his life. This was not a matter (as it is in official Christian doctrine) of Jesus having two complete natures, one human and the other divine. He was wholly human; but whenever self-giving love in response to the love of God is lived out in a human life, to that extent the divine love has become incarnate on earth.[9]

Instead of *homoousios,* the term of the ancient creeds that establishes the divinity of Christ and his equality with the Father, Hick prefers the term *homo-agapē.* And this work of the Holy Spirit, to be a channel of God's love, can be found everywhere, not only in Jesus incarnate. It is incarnated in other world religions as well. From this perspective, incarnation is the activity of God's Spirit or God's grace in human lives so that the divine will is done on earth.

8. Hick, *God and the Universe of Faiths,* 117.
9. John Hick, *God Has Many Names* (Philadelphia: Westminster, 1982), 58–59.

For degree Christology, there is no need for a trinitarian doctrine. The Trinity is merely an expression of a threefold experience of God in the human mind as Creator, Redeemer, and Sanctifier. Neither is there a need for a two-nature Christology in the traditional sense. Christ's "divinity" means that he had a specific God-consciousness, but that does not mean that other religious leaders could not share the same consciousness.

Consequently, one is not surprised to hear that for Hick, different religions lead to salvation; regardless of differences in beliefs, ultimately their purpose is the same: the salvation of all. He posits a unified soteriological structure in all religions. This he calls a move from self-centeredness to reality-centeredness.

Of course, various religions have their own distinctive ideas about the fall, out of which one has to be saved. Mahayana Buddhism requires an awakening to the realization that the way to salvation comes by the release from one's own self and transformation into the manifestation of Dharmakaya. In the monistic tradition of Hinduism, salvation is depicted as the freeing of *atman* (the eternal self) from the empirical self through the enlightening insight that it is identical with Brahman. In Christianity, the fall is missing one's calling to be a more loving and accepting person and failing to reflect Jesus' heightened God-consciousness.

Hick's interpretation of the fall and of Christ, like his entire mythological approach to religions, elicits critique not only from traditional Christian theologians but also from other major religions who likewise claim true access to the divine. An investigation of these criticisms is outside the realm of an introductory Christology text. For now, we can note that to a greater or lesser extent, each of the theologians in this section critiques the others for different reasons.

Part 4

Christ in the Contemporary World: Contextual Christologies

Perhaps no other field of study in theology is as integrally connected to culture and worldview as Christology. The foreword to a recent study in intercultural Christologies encapsulates well the significance of cultural context for Christologies in various contexts and global settings:

> If any single area of theology is especially poised to raise questions about the nature and practice of inculturation [the influence of culture on theology and vice versa], it is surely Christology. The fact of the Incarnation itself places us already on a series of boundaries: between the divine and the human, between the particular and the universal, between eternity and time. The questions raised for culture span the entire range of Christological discourse, from what significance Jesus' having been born in a specific time and place might have, to the cultural and linguistic differences that plagued the Christological controversies of the fourth and fifth centuries.[1]

Therefore, it is understandable that when African, Asian, and Latin American churches and theologians dared to strip off the Western clothing of the

---

1. Robert J. Schreiter, foreword to Volker Küster, *The Many Faces of Jesus Christ: An Intercultural Christology* (Maryknoll, N.Y.: Orbis, 2001), xi.

gospel they had inherited from Western missionaries and theological academies, they began to develop culturally appropriate and relevant Christologies.

The term *contextual* implies that the Christologies to be studied in this section are firmly anchored in a specific context, be it cultural, intellectual, or related to a specific worldview. To call these Christologies contextual does not mean that the Christologies already studied are free from contextual influences. Even classical Christologies in the West, including the classical christological creeds, are not immune to surrounding philosophical, religious, social, and political influences. Ironically, the more Western theologians have studied theologies outside the West, the more knowledgeable they have become about their indebtedness to factors in the context in which the early creeds and christological interpretations arose. However, it has become commonplace to use the term *contextual* for theologies not based more or less on classical Western ones. These theological interpretations, emerging out of new contexts and questions, most of which were unknown when the basic christological formulations were developed, are important topics of current theology.

Contextual Christologies are not found only outside the West, namely, in Africa, Asia, and Latin America. Contextual interpretations of Christ are also found in North America and Europe. These include feminist, process, black, and postmodern Christologies. In what follows, these North American and European contextual Christologies will be discussed first, followed by Latin American, African, and Asian interpretations. For each of these three main geographical areas, a chapter provides a general description of its central christological ideas and orientations. Then, to make the study more specific, a second chapter examines one particular Christologist to highlight the distinctive features of that context. It goes without saying that choosing *one* theologian from each region is an extremely selective exercise. To remedy this necessary limitation, the introductory chapter for each region refers to several of its main christological theologians and theological movements.

21

Process Christology

The World in Process

The often-quoted dictum of the ancient philosopher Heraclitus (540–475 B.C.) expresses much about the twentieth-century worldview called process thought: "You cannot step twice into the same river; for fresh waters are ever flowing in upon you." Several philosophers and scientists of the modern era have elaborated on this thought. They include Albert Einstein, who developed the principle of relativity, which finally discredited static Newtonian physics; the philosopher Henri Bergson with his organic view of reality; and philosopher William James, who views human consciousness as a stream whose later moments are able to grasp their predecessors. The mathematician Alfred Whitehead wrote *Process and Reality*,[1] which outlined in 1957 the main approach of process thought.

One of the leading ideas of process thought is the contingency of all things. We live in an interdependent world in which each event is part of an endless flow of preceding causes and succeeding consequences. Nothing exists in isolation. Everything is related to some degree. Process thought applies the idea of Einstein's principle of relativity to reality as a whole. Nothing in the universe is static—either at the inorganic or the organic level. We find ourselves in a world of becoming in which things, events, societies, and especially persons come to be and pass away. In opposition to the older static view, process

1. Alfred Whitehead, *Process and Reality* (New York: Free Press, 1957).

philosophy sees reality as something that exhibits novelty and self-creation. Consequently, process thought challenges the traditional understanding of cause and effect.

The goal of process theology, based on the analysis of process philosophy, is to determine the relevance of the Christian faith for a culture increasingly imbued with the sense of becoming. In doing so, it also borrows concepts and approaches from Eastern philosophies and religions.

Process theology, based on the philosophy of Whitehead and others, has developed its own language. The most important concept is "actual entity" or "occasion of experience." Everything in the universe, from God to the smallest puff of existence, is an entity. Each entity has two sides: mental and physical. According to process theology, even God is dipolar and consists of a "primordial" and a "consequent" dimension. The primordial dimension (nontemporal or mental) refers to God's grasp of all possibilities. This dimension of God is the principle of the process of the world with an infinite range of possibilities. The consequent (physical or concrete) pole in God is "God's feeling of the world," "a fullness of physical feeling": God is the fellow sufferer who understands. God is the repository of each occasion once it perishes. Each entity not only becomes the predecessor for the next occasion but also adds to God's experience. Thus, God exists in genuine, dynamic interaction with the world. God is part of the world experience, perhaps a "bigger" entity than others, but still an entity. God provides the initial aim to every occasion. God does not work by coercion but as a "lure" from the future to persuade other entities to join the process of becoming toward their intended goal.

Process theology, of course, has roots in classical theism (in which God is part of the world yet totally sovereign and transcendent) but also serves as its critic. According to proponents of the process approach, the main problem with the classical view is its denial of reciprocity between God and the world. Traditional Christian theology qualifies the reciprocity to an extent that makes it almost meaningless. Classical theological assertions such as the aseity, immutability, and impassibility of God have truncated the concept of mutual reciprocity.

Whitehead sought at any cost to avoid dualism (or as he calls it, bifurcationalism): "The universe, assumed to be ever-changing, is the only reality."[2] Theologically, this idea eliminates the traditional dualism between God and the world. Even though there is a distinction between God and the world, there is also an intimate, two-way relationship. It is Whitehead's contention that unless placed within a unified metaphysical schematization, the concept of God acquires a meaning so indefinite and indeterminate as to be unintelligible. God and the world require each other for the intelligibility of each.

2. Quoted in Blair Reynolds, *Toward a Process Pneumatology* (Selingrove, Pa.: Susquehanna University Press, 1990), 13.

God in the Experience of the World

In process theology, God is present in human experience. God is accessible, close at hand: "God dwells within the universe, among us, not in some remote atemporal realm above and beyond the world."[3] If this principle holds, then to experience the world, we also at some level experience God—God encountered within our experiences.

Some process theologians have detected common elements in Christian mysticism. In both traditions, God's touch is exercised gently. Feelings of sweetness, gentleness, and tenderness characterize the life of the mystics. Process theology also focuses on the sensitive, tender elements of God. The mystics tended to allegorize God as an artist, as does process theology. Both the mystics and many process thinkers also allegorize God in the feminine form. Another noteworthy feature is that in the mystical tradition, ecstasy is a process, not a static repose. Blair Reynolds argues with regard to mysticism that the "fundamental mystical intuition of God as diffuse in the cosmos provides the basis for a spirituality in which purity is not found in a separation from the temporal-material world but is formed in a deeper penetration of the universe."[4]

Process theologians have also looked to the Eastern Christian tradition in hopes of finding convergence with mainline Christian theology. For example, certain aspects of the thought of the second-century church father Irenaeus reveal a concept of divine immanence, what has been named "process soteriology." Irenaeus's refutation of Gnosticism suggests that Irenaeus attempted to transcend any sort of spirit-matter dualism. In this effort, he strove to synthesize or unify nature and spirit, body and soul, creation and redemption. Irenaeus's recapitulation theory (according to which Christ in his incarnation "recapitulates" all the stages of human life and so heals it) suggests a dynamic rather than a static view of the world and creation. Furthermore, his view of salvation as maturation and fulfillment (rather than the standard Western view of guilt and satisfaction) may lend itself to a "process notion of an empathic bond between God and the world and also of the Holy Spirit as creative transforming love."[5]

Process Christ

In process theology, the doctrine of the Trinity suggests that "there are elements of relativity, complexity, or multiformity and change within an oth-

3. Ibid., 35.
4. Ibid., 103.
5. Ibid., 111.

erwise simple, immutable, self-contained deity."[6] The incarnation of one person of the Trinity shows that God can take material form and can overcome the dualism so prevalent in theism. In process theology, the doctrines of incarnation and atonement focus on Jesus suffering as a temporal being.

Several types of process Christologies have been developed during the past three decades or so. Process theology seeks to maintain faithfulness to tradition not in the sense of repeating old dogmas but by continuing their doctrinal aims, which can lead to new ideas. In doing so, the current scientific context serves as an important dialogue partner.

Process theology stresses the humanity of Jesus. Thus, questions about the historical Jesus are important in helping to place him in a specific place and context. David Griffin's main work, *A Process Christology*,[7] is a good example of a process Christology that takes its point of departure from the tradition, including the history of Jesus, and yet goes beyond it. His aim is to bring together several traditions: the new quest of the historical Jesus, neo-orthodoxy (Karl Barth), the existentialism of Paul Tillich and Rudolf Bultmann, and the process philosophy of Whitehead and others, such as Charles Hartshorne.

With regard to the role of Christ, two groups of process theologians can be detected. On the one hand, there are those to whom Christ is just an extraordinary person, not a special revelation in the classical sense of the term. Therefore, Christ is different only in degree, not in kind, from God's other revelations. Process writers such as Norman Pittenger, Schubert Ogden, and Peter Hamilton belong to this orientation. Pittenger's comment in his book *Christology Reconsidered* makes this clear:

> Jesus, in the dynamic existence which was his, fulfilled the potentialities which were also his in a manner that impressed those who companied with him as being extraordinary without being a violation of the ordinary conditions of manhood. . . . His degree of realization was not the same as that of other men whom his companions knew; it was immeasurably different yet not utterly removed from the experience of manhood elsewhere seen.[8]

Pittenger employs the distinction, from the British New Testament scholar C. F. D. Moule, between the uniqueness of exclusion, in which Jesus has no equivalent, and the uniqueness of inclusion, which may be shared by others in addition to Jesus. Pittenger rejects any conception of Jesus that denies salvation or authentic existence to any who do not accept him. Pittenger opposes "false Christocentrism" (that God limits his love to those who know Christ) because it seems to contradict the idea of God being love. What is unique about Christ is the extraordinarily intense and most generous revelation of God that he shared.

6. Ibid., 132.
7. David Griffin, *A Process Christology* (Philadelphia: Westminster, 1973).
8. Norman Pittenger, *Christology Reconsidered* (London: SCM, 1970), 119–20.

On the other hand, writers such as John Cobb Jr. and David Griffin acknowledge that Jesus is special in his personhood and can be referred to as unique, though he is not an "absolute savior" in the sense of traditional orthodoxy. They, too, represent pluralistic Christologies, as Cobb's main book on the topic indicates: *Christ in a Pluralistic Age*.[9]

A Process Jesusology

Cobb, who used the worldview of the end of the twentieth century as the starting point for his pluralistic, process Christology, prefers to call his approach "Jesusology." Cobb acknowledges contemporary orientations, such as the commitment of the modern mind to the profane and to pluralism, openness to other religious traditions, ecological concerns, and the need to live together on earth. Two of his interests have been the relationship between process theology and ecology and between process theology and politics. In other words, Cobb wants to locate Christ in contemporary experience. Rather than following the guidelines of traditional orthodoxy, which have their starting point in the Bible, he begins with the present experience of Christ and works backward to history and the Bible.

Cobb takes into consideration the classical christological concept of *Logos* but gives a specific meaning to it. The primordial nature of God from which all initial aims emerge is *Logos*. Employing the concept of "creative transformation," he suggests that the *Logos* supplies each event or actual entity with its initial aim, its potentiality, and lures it to do more than simply repeat habitual existence. The *Logos* entices each event to realize its full potential. The ultimate agent of this transformation is the incarnate *Logos*, the Christ. The *Logos* in Christ is the cosmic principle of order, the source of purpose and growth. In its transcendence it is boundless and eternal, but as immanent in creation it provides the proper creative lure for every changing situation in the process.

Cobb's idea of the *Logos* coming to fulfillment in Christ does not deny Jesus' full humanity. In process theology, humanness is not a fixed mode of being. Thus, when God was present in Jesus of Nazareth, he did not displace part of that person. A person is a dynamic, changing set of relationships. According to Cobb, "The one God was thus uniquely present in him. At the same time, Jesus was fully human and no aspect of his humanity was displaced by God. It was a thoroughly human 'I' that was constituted by God's presence in him."[10] Christ's humanity implies that Christ is present within all human

---

9. John Cobb, *Christ in a Pluralistic Age* (Philadelphia: Westminster, 1975).
10. John Cobb, "A Whiteheadian Christology," in *Process Philosophy and Christian Thought*, ed. Delwin Brown et al. (Indianapolis: Bobbs-Merrill, 1971), 394.

beings and even within all of reality; thus, if Jesus cannot be fully human, neither can we. Christ's humanity, as ours, is dynamic.

Cobb's view of incarnation is typical of other pluralistic Christologies. It is too limited to say that the *Logos* is incarnate only in Jesus; the *Logos* is also incarnate in all things. What makes Christ's incarnation unique is that the lure or the aim does not come from without, as in the case of other human beings, but from within. Jesus is the Christ in that Jesus brought into history a distinctive structure of existence:

> The distinctiveness of Jesus can be spoken of in terms of Christ. Christ is the incarnate Logos. As such Christ is present in all things. The degree and kind of Christ's presence varies. The fullest form of that presence is that in which he coconstitutes with the personal past the very selfhood of a person. That would be the paradigm of incarnation. In that case Christ would not simply be present in a person but would be that person. The distinctive structure of Jesus' existence was characterized by personal identity with the immanent Logos. . . . In all things Christ is present. Jesus was Christ.[11]

One of the driving forces of Cobb's theologizing is to find a balance that allows religious pluralism while avoiding total relativism. Christ should not be identified with any one system of belief that came into being under historically conditioned circumstances but rather with the creative transformation of the whole theological enterprise, which is moving beyond every established denominational form. The special significance of Jesus as the "bearer" of the *Logos,* who lures each person toward constant growth to reach full potentiality, is his exemplary love. Jesus' life was permeated by love and reflected a concern for others, particularly the outcast and downtrodden. Another leading process theologian, Charles Hartshorne, also emphasizes the significance of Jesus as a unique symbol of the Christian view of love. Jesus invites his followers to participate in this unconditional love, but it means total trust and obedience. Christ's preaching focused on the coming of the kingdom, which calls for a decision now for repentance and a change of heart.

The most important image for salvation and our relationship with Christ is the Pauline concept of being "in Christ." Through his life, ministry, death, and resurrection, Jesus created "a force field" into which believers may enter. For Cobb, to be in Christ means that one realizes Christ as the center of one's existence and participates in grace, peace, and joy with God.

Future Prospects

A central tenet of process theology is openness to the future, which consists of unlimited potentialities. Because the whole of existence is in process, our

11. Ibid., 142.

future is also in the process of becoming. God has not predetermined the course of the future; it unfolds during the course of the world process. Christ and his transformation opened prospects for the emerging of ever new possibilities. This entails both hope and threat. On the one hand, all experiences have some intrinsic value. Those experiences with greater harmony, variety, and intensity are intrinsically better than those with less. God's subjective aim is that the entities of the world constantly experience greater value. In that sense, total openness to the future provides the basis for hope that progress will occur.

But on the other hand, this openness to the future is also risky. Human beings may choose self-annihilation in terms of ecological catastrophe caused by human actions or nuclear war, for example. Even God cannot guarantee the future of the creation, according to process theology, though the hope of the kingdom of God is a vision for the future.

What is the eschatological hope of the kingdom of God that Jesus preached? Process theology and Christology are vague about that. Perhaps, by definition, the process never comes to an end and therefore "becoming" never becomes "being." What about an afterlife? Whitehead's concept of "objective immortality" is the standard answer. It means that occasions of experience, even though they constantly come and go, do not perish in the final analysis but remain in the "memory" of God and form the basis for the emergence of ever new occasions. Human beings do not enjoy immortality or experience resurrection in the traditional orthodox sense but rather add to the enjoyment of God and are "remembered" by God.

Process theology is more specific about the this-worldly hope. In considering Christ as the image and source of hope, Cobb refers to Friedrich E. D. Schleiermacher, the father of liberal theology from the nineteenth century. Schleiermacher was one of the first theologians to portray Christian faith as the full realization of our potentialities in this present life rather than an anticipation of an existence beyond death. Fidelity to Christ now calls Christians to deepen their involvement in the transformation of the secular world, for it is right there that the power of Christ's transformative influence is to be found.

22

Feminist Christology

Can a Male Savior Be the Savior of All?

> I have always found it difficult to walk away from the church, but I have also found it difficult to walk with it. . . . The alienation is shared with many other women and men whose pain and anger at the contradictions of church life lead them to challenge the very idea of talking about a feminist interpretation of the church. It is also increased by knowledge of the disdain and anger of those theologians and church officials who consider women like me to be the problem rather than the church itself.[1]

This quotation from one of the leading American feminist thinkers, Letty M. Russell, reveals the anguish many women—and men—feel concerning the way the Christian church and theology have treated women. Feminist and other liberationists also share a concern about the locus of the Christian message, the message about liberation and love in the person of Jesus Christ: "It is impossible for me and for many other alienated women and men to walk away from the church, however, for it has been the bearer of the story of Jesus Christ and the good news of God's love."[2]

Living as we do in an age of "hermeneutics of suspicion," we find many conventional ways of talking about religion threatening. Many feminist

1. Letty M. Russell, *Church in the Round: Feminist Interpretation of the Church* (Louisville: Westminster John Knox, 1993), 11.
2. Ibid., 11.

thinkers insist that the personification of God as Father is a form of patriarchy and makes mechanisms for the oppression of women appear justified; from this grows male dominance. There is no denying that most images of God in religions are modeled after the ruling class of society.[3] Even though, generally speaking, it may be an overstatement that the symbol of divine fatherhood has been the source of the misuse of power for violence, rape, and war, it is true that language not only reflects reality but also constructs it.

Even though Christian theology has been slow to change its traditional masculine language, the problem is not really new. Gregory of Nazianzus ridiculed his opponents who thought God was male because God is called Father, or that deity is feminine because of the gender of the word, or that of the Spirit is neuter because it does not have personal names. Gregory insisted that God's fatherhood has nothing to do with marriage, pregnancy, midwifery, or sexuality. God is not male, even though we call God *him*. It is just a conventional way of using language. Christian theology believes that none of the divine Persons has a gender, but in their actions in humanity and the world, each Person is manifested under names borrowed from the genders.

Sallie McFague has tried to escape the problem of sexist talk about God with the help of metaphorical talk. Attempting to avoid literalism, so rampant in our time, she suggests piling up metaphors to relativize the Father symbol and provide room for complementary symbols, such as God as mother, lover, or friend. Elizabeth Johnson's approach shares many similarities with that of McFague. Johnson argues in her book *She Who Is: The Mystery of God in Feminist Theology* that we need to envision and speak of the mystery of God with female images and metaphors in order to free women from a subordination imposed by the patriarchal imaging of God. Her own preference is "She Who Is."[4]

Questions posed by feminist theologians with regard to Christology are pointed: How can a Son of God be a Savior and representative of God's sons *and* daughters? How does Jesus' "maleness" relate to the other half of humankind? Is God the Son masculine or feminine or beyond? The image of Christ is ambiguous for many contemporary women because it has served both as the source of life and as the legitimator of oppression. Women have found comfort and strength through their faith in Christ, while at the same time they have also experienced christological interpretations and practices that are male dominant and suppressive of feminism. Some extreme voices ask whether Christian theology can ever overcome this built-in tension. According to Naomi Goldenberg:

> Jesus Christ cannot symbolize the liberation of women. A culture that maintains a masculine image for its highest divinity cannot allow its women to ex-

3. Rosemary Radford Ruether, *Sexism and God-Talk* (Boston: Beacon, 1983).
4. Elizabeth Johnson, *She Who Is: The Mystery of God in Feminist Theology* (New York: Crossroad, 1992).

perience themselves as the equals of its men. In order to develop a theology of women's liberation, feminists have to leave Christ and the Bible behind.[5]

This "critical principle" of feminist analysis, which has liberation and equality as its goal, borrows from liberation theologies of various sorts; it is what the liberationist Gustavo Gutiérrez has called "theology from the underside of history."[6] Feminist thinkers join this liberation tradition in moving from the questions of those at the center of society to the questions of those considered less than human because they are powerless and unimportant.

The Experience of Women

Even though women's experiences vary from culture to culture and context to context, there are some uniting features, three of which seem to be the most important in terms of implications for Christology. First, women from different situations have experienced their embodiment as something negative in many Christian traditions. Western theology in particular has been based on a dualistic worldview that placed soul over body and male over female. Female caricatures in early Christian writings abound. For example, women were called "the gateway to hell" and "less than male." Even though Christianity is an incarnational religion, it has too often been uncomfortable with the body, especially with the task of women to give birth to the next generation. With regard to the doctrine of the incarnation, Jesus' maleness has often been used as an argument against the full humanity of women. "The doctrine that only a perfect male form can incarnate God fully and be salvific makes our individual lives in female bodies a prison against God and denies our actual, sensual, changing selves as the locus of divine activity."[7]

Second, women from different contexts have experienced oppression. Patterns of domination and submission vary, but they are present worldwide. The headship of Christ over his body the church, reflected in the headship of the husband over his wife, has often legitimized the subordination of women.

Third, interrelatedness has been part of the experience of women. Women have traditionally found identity in relation to others as mothers, wives, sisters, daughters. In the past, a single male individual could represent all humanity. In current times, however, the interrelatedness of all life, including creation, has come to the fore; one of the impetuses has been the emergence of process thought.

5. Naomi Goldenberg, *The Changing of the Gods: Feminism and the End of Traditional Religions* (Boston: Beacon, 1979), 22.

6. Gustavo Gutiérrez, *The Power of the Poor in History: Selected Writings* (Maryknoll, N.Y.: Orbis, 1983), 183.

7. Rita Nashima Brock, "The Feminist Redemption of God," in *Christian Feminism: Visions of a New Humanity,* ed. Judith L. Weidman (San Francisco: Harper & Row, 1984), 68.

In line with the idea of interrelatedness, Jürgen Moltmann places the question of sexism in relation to God in a wider perspective, namely, that of community. Theologically, it is not enough to criticize traditional theologies for neglecting feminine terminology and attempt to replace the masculine terms with other limited, exclusive terms. Moltmann insists that according to biblical ideas, what makes us *imago Dei* is not the soul apart from the body. The image of God consists of men and women in their wholeness, in their full, sexually specific community with one another. God is not known in the inner chamber of the heart or at a solitary place but in the true community of women and men. As a result, the experience of God is "the social experience of the self and the personal experience of sociality."[8] One could also express the core of feminist ecclesiology by describing the church as "connective"; in it there is a living, dynamic connection between men and women and between God and human beings. "If the table is spread by God and hosted by Christ, it must be a table with many connections."[9]

Searching for Inclusive Images of Christ

Feminist Christology has been in the forefront in looking to replace the older male-dominant, hierarchical, exclusive images with new, complementary, and inclusive ways of speaking about Christ, the Savior of all. To re-image Jesus may involve letting go of old images or transforming them to fit the current context and experience of women. Ellen Leonard suggests five ways of referring to Christ as inclusive of both men and women:

1. envisioning Christ's humanity in female terms, as "Woman Christ"
2. envisioning Christ as the incarnation of female divinity
3. beginning from the Jesus of history as prototype
4. beginning from the Jesus of history as iconoclastic prophet
5. relocating Christology in the community[10]

The image of Christ as a woman is shocking to some twenty-first-century Christians. Christian theology, however, contains a historical precedent for depicting Christ as female. There are references to Christ as mother in the writings of early fathers such as Clement, Origen, Irenaeus, John Chrysostom, Ambrose, and Augustine, as well as medieval theologians such as Bernard of Clairvaux and

8. Jürgen Moltmann, *The Spirit of Life: A Universal Affirmation* (Minneapolis: Fortress, 1992), 94.
9. Russell, *Church in the Round*, 18.
10. Ellen Leonard, "Women and Christ: Toward Inclusive Christologies," in *Constructive Christian Theology in the Worldwide Church*, ed. William R. Barr (Grand Rapids: Eerdmans, 1997), 326–33.

Anselm of Canterbury. Especially in medieval times, female images of Christ were popular. Divinity was associated with maleness, humanity with femaleness. Julian of Norwich in the fourteenth century spoke of Christ as "our true Mother Jesus" who "alone bears our joy and endless life."[11]

Another way of highlighting female aspects in Jesus is the use of the female image Sophia (Wisdom) as an image of Jesus. Jewish tradition personified the wisdom of God as female. The so-called wisdom Christology, which takes its point of departure from the Gospels, especially Matthew and John, is an alternative to the view of Jesus as male.

Some feminist thinkers have claimed Jesus and the praxis of the earliest church as a *prototype* rather than an archetype. This means that the biblical tradition of a male Jesus addressing his male Father is not an exclusive source but a re-source (only one way) for thinking about Jesus. Feminist theologians also remind us of the great extent to which Jesus carried out his vision for inclusive attitudes even in the ancient Jewish culture in which women were subordinate to men. Jesus' vision of the kingdom was all-inclusive; he opened up table fellowship—the primary sign of inclusion in that culture as it still is in many third world cultures—to sinners, the poor, women, even prostitutes.

Yet another way of addressing Jesus in feministic thought is to depict the Christ of the Gospels as an iconoclastic prophet speaking on behalf of the marginalized and despised groups of society and challenging the social and religious hierarchical structures of his day. Women in the Gospels often represent the lowly, the last who will be first in the reign of God. Some feminist thinkers look at Jesus' maleness from this perspective and speak of the *kenōsis* (self-emptying) of patriarchy.

The last image suggested by Leonard is that of Christa/community. Some feminist theologians highlight the role of Jesus in cocreating liberation and enhancing community. They prefer to refer to Christ with the female term *Christa* rather than with the masculine *Christ*. These female theologians point to the role of the unnamed woman in the Gospel tradition who anointed Jesus: "This woman, as a woman, represents the revelatory and healing power of heart. She becomes prophet and healer by her act as representative of the Christa/community that would survive Jesus' death and witness his resurrection."[12]

Black Women's Liberating Christology

Women do not all live in identical situations and contexts. Their circumstances and needs vary as much as those of men. Therefore, feminist theology in general and Christology in particular are shaped by particular contexts. For

11. Ibid., 327.
12. Rita Nashima Brock, *Journeys by Heart: A Christology of Erotic Power* (New York: Crossroad, 1988), 97.

example, in the Americas, one may find feminist interpretations rooted in various traditions such as African American, Asian American, Hispanic American, and Native American. How do black women, women of African descent and the current African American culture, speak of Jesus Christ as their Savior? While many, especially among the younger generation, do not see a need for a black feminist theology separate from feminist theology in general, other black women—and men—believe the phenomenon of feminism originated from and serves white middle-class women's agenda. They see no other option than to call for a responsible black feminist theology and Christology.

Naturally, emerging black feminist Christologies share the overall concern of black theology: to liberate from white oppression and to cry for freedom and self-fulfillment. They also share the general aim of feministic thought: to set women free from patriarchy and male dominance. An important corollary to black feminism is the longing for a holistic theology and Christology that integrate into a single theological vision all aspects of human life. African American cultures, as most two-thirds world cultures, lean toward holism more than do most dualistic Western worldviews.

Black women do theology out of their tridimensional experience of racism/sexism/classism. To ignore any aspect of this experience is to deny the holistic and integrated reality of black womanhood. In reading the Bible narrative about Christ, who was inclusive in his love toward women and other marginalized people in society, black women found a Jesus they could claim and whose claim for them affirmed their dignity and self-respect. Jesus means several things to black women; chief among these, however, is belief in Jesus as the divine co-sufferer who empowers them in situations of oppression.

> Black women identified with Jesus because they believed that Jesus identified with them. As Jesus was persecuted and made to suffer undeservedly, so were they. His suffering culminated in the crucifixion. Their crucifixion included rapes, and husbands being castrated (literally and metaphorically), babies being sold, and other cruel and often murderous treatments. But Jesus's suffering was not the suffering of a mere human, for Jesus was understood to be God incarnate.[13]

Jesus is seen not only as the divine co-sufferer but also as the one who empowers the weak. His love is not sentimental, passive love but a tough, active love. Thus, not only Jesus' divinity but also his life has immense meaning in black feminist thought and spirituality. Jesus was a political Messiah whose task was to set all people free.

13. Jacquelyn Grant, "Black Women's Experience as a Source for Doing Theology," in *Constructive Christian Theology*, 346.

Jesus Christ, the Savior

Feminist approaches to the work of Christ, the salvation Christ brought about, are shaped by their inclusive, holistic approach to life and are often critical of white male theologians' perspectives. Many feminist thinkers entertain serious doubts about what they call the "traditional/mythological" view of Jesus as the unique and exclusive incarnation of God because this idea has been used to reinforce male supremacy. Jesus was male, and therefore, the traditional argument has gone, God could not have become incarnate in the so-called inferior sex. The idea of original sin (that Eve sinned first and prompted Adam to eat) has also been tied up with this view. The idea of Jesus as the supreme scapegoat, a role projected on women, has contributed to their victimization. Qualities such as sacrificial love, humility, and meekness, characteristically associated with women, have not been given due attention in the picture of Jesus' role as the Savior.

Feminist readers of the Bible remind us that the biblical notion of salvation entails liberation, wholeness, peace, and blessing of all life. Aligning with liberation theologians, feminist theologians recognize salvation as holistic *shalom,* social and physical wholeness and harmony. Salvation is understood relationally, between human beings and in relation to God. Only that kind of holistic approach can equip the church to fulfill its task in promoting justice, peace, and wholeness.

In the early centuries of the church, Christian theology showed a tendency to reduce and narrow the understanding of shalom in light of the Hellenistic separation of body and soul. In liberation and feminist theologies, there are two overlapping motifs of shalom—liberation and blessing—as God's intention for the full humanity of women together with men for the healing of all creation. The larger meaning of salvation as shalom includes not only blessing and liberation but also justice and righteousness.

Feminist theology is weary of the prevailing hierarchical dualism in Christian theology that leads to abuse of nature, the other sex, and one's own body. It has also plagued the Christian understanding of God and Christ; often the Trinity has been depicted in hierarchical terms, which leads to hierarchical conceptions of the community.

An even wider perspective on the feminist theology of salvation in Christ is provided by the emerging "ecofeministic" thought in which the concerns of creation and ecology are merged with theology. In the past, male-dominated theology separated the feminine, nature, the body, sexuality, and women. Elizabeth Johnson has argued that:

> the exploitation of the earth, which has reached crisis proportion in our day, is intimately linked to the marginalization of women, and that both of these pre-

dicaments are intrinsically related to forgetting the Creator Spirit who pervades the world in the dance of life.[14]

Ecofeminist theology sees its task as seeking a new wholeness, a new community of equals. Ecofeminist theology emphasizes unity between nature and people, between women and men, between us and our bodies, and so looks favorably toward "kinship models" of thought that emphasize interrelatedness and community.

14. Elizabeth Johnson, *Women, Earth, and Creator Spirit* (Mahwah, N.Y.: Paulist Press, 1993), 2.

23

Black Christology

Black Experience

Black Christology refers to a varied group of theological approaches found mainly in the African American context but also in Africa—for example, in South Africa. These approaches address Christology in light of the challenges faced by people of African descent. Though it is often unclear whether black Christology includes only African American Christologies or also African Christologies, this chapter focuses on the African American context. The final section, however, considers black Christology in the South African context as an example of the shared values of black theology in various parts of the world.

The starting point for black theology in general and black Christology in particular is black experience. The proponents of this contextual theological movement argue for the uniqueness of black history and current experience, which have to be taken into consideration in doing theology. Too often, they say, theology has been done by white males of the West, and Christianity has justified black suffering.

The most characteristic feature of black theology is its relation to the idea of liberation. In fact, black theologians see their way of doing theology as liberation. James Cone, the most noted black liberationist, defines liberation as working so "that the community of the oppressed will recognize that its inner thrust for liberation is not only consistent with the gospel but is the gospel of

Jesus Christ."[1] Thus, to speak of liberation as God's work and intention in the world means that one must understand liberation as a permanent, final, and ultimate feature of one's existence. Many black theologians insist that all Christian hope stands or falls with this conviction and that liberation is God's irresistible will. The task of theology, therefore, is to identify with the humiliated and the abused. Biblical starting points are found in liberationist passages such as Exodus 3 and Luke 4:18–19.

Black theology is a creative, engaging, responsible dialogue with several sources and influences. According to Cone, there are six sources:

1. black experience: the totality of black existence in a white world of oppression and exploitation; blacks making decisions about themselves, affirming the value of blackness
2. black history: not only how whites have treated blacks but also how blacks have resisted that oppression
3. black culture: the self-expression of the black community in music, art, literature, and other kinds of creative forms
4. revelation: not only a past event (and Cone emphasizes the nature of revelation as an *event*) but also God's present redemptive activity on behalf of blacks
5. Scripture: In line with the neo-orthodox, Barthian view, Cone thinks that the Bible is not to be identified with revelation; the Bible has the capacity to become revelation in the event when God and human beings meet in an event initiated by God. The Bible is a testimony and guide to God, who acts as the liberator.
6. tradition: a critical appropriation of how the church has understood the gospel in varying contexts[2]

Black theology differs from traditional theology in much the same way that African American Christianity differs from the Christianity of Europe and white North America. It is based on African heritage and cultural roots. Perhaps the most distinctive features of that heritage are the legacy of slavery and the struggle to survive under harsh and unjust oppression. "African slaves who embraced Christianity also modified and shaped it to meet their existential needs and saw, even in the contorted presentations of the gospel by some white people, a continuity between what they knew of God in Africa and the God of the Bible."[3] The sociopolitical context for black theology in African

1. James H. Cone, *A Black Theology of Liberation,* 2d ed. (Maryknoll, N.Y.: Orbis, 1986), 1.
2. Ibid., 33–34.
3. James H. Evans Jr., *We Have Been Believers: An African-American Systematic Theology* (Minneapolis: Fortress, 1992), 3.

American Christianity in the twentieth century is the civil rights or the "black power" movement.

Like many typical non-Western-originated theologies, black theology is based on stories and the story of God in the Bible. African Americans and other blacks bring their own stories to bear on the Bible and tradition. Their folk stories are means of expressing their fears, anxieties, and struggles in their longing for freedom and liberation. According to James Evans, "The two stubborn facts of African American Christian existence are that God has revealed Godself to the black community and that this revelation is inseparable from the historic struggle of black people for liberation."[4]

Based on the starting point and the sources of black theology, the foundation for doing black theology may be summarized as follows: First, the people's social location conditions their biblical interpretation. The status of African Americans as outsiders within American society has shaped their perspective on the Bible, and their marginality has made them sensitive to the misuses of Scripture. Second, what the Bible means for today takes priority over what the Bible meant in the past. This does not mean ignoring rigorous historical-critical study of the Bible but merely that studying the original, past meaning of the text is not enough. Third, the story takes priority over the text. The religious experience of African Americans serves the text. Fourth, an African American theologian must articulate the liberating hermeneutic that grants authority to Scripture in the experience of black Christians.[5]

The "Figura" of Christ in African American Experience

Evans employs the term *figura*, borrowed by early and medieval Christian writers from Greek and Roman thought, to express an idea of something that both reflects something that already exists as well as projects something yet to be. This concept can be applied to Christ. The key to understanding who Jesus Christ is for African Americans is the relationship between the biblical notion of the Messiah and the various heroic figures that populate their cultural landscape:

> The Messiah embodies the nationalist hopes and dreams of an oppressed people. . . . It is noteworthy that continued oppression and travail did not destroy the messianic dream but intensified it. Indeed, the more evil abounded the more powerful the idea of the Messiah became. As the actual historical liberation of Israel seemed to recede into the remote provinces of probability, the Messiah became one capable not only of transforming the historical situation of the people, but of transforming history itself.[6]

4. Ibid., 11.
5. Ibid., 51–52.
6. Ibid., 79.

The Messiah was vested with the authority to usher in a new age in which the power structures of this world would be overturned and freedom would prevail. This messianic age would include the in-gathering of the people of God. Given these hopes of the messianism of the Bible, it is not surprising that African American Christians laid hold of messianic themes in Scripture in formulating their christological beliefs. The idea of the in-gathering of the people of God seemed to support the hopes of pan-Africanism and the radical transformation of the world order and gave hope for the coming of justice and peace.

What makes the idea of "figura" even more appealing in African American religious and political contexts is the existence of a pantheon of heroes and heroic figures. For example, the African American community has many exceptional performers in the fields of sports, politics, and the arts. In her *I Know Why the Caged Bird Sings,* Maya Angelou describes the powerful effect on the black community of the victory of black boxer Joe Louis over a white opponent. Heroic actions in the African American tradition are seen as events that help blacks deal with obstacles and overcome the boundaries and limitations of their present context. Heroic actions also function to bind and preserve the culture and to enhance solidarity.

Many African American scholars point to spirituals as the form for expressing their religion's core values. These hymns reflect the heroic resources for black Christology. Old Testament stories and christological stories of the New Testament expressed in these songs pull the history of God's dealings in the past into the present struggle for freedom. Biblical heroes, not only the Messiah but also Moses, Joshua, and a host of other leaders, are elevated as the models to follow.

Evans states that "at the center of the African heroic epic is the epic hero."[7] This heroic figure bears astonishing resemblances to the messianic hero of the biblical saga. Like the superhuman Messiah of the Bible, the epic hero is empowered by gods to restore the state of his people. This African mode of figural interpretation allows African American Christians to see in Jesus not only an epic hero who embodies the values that promote the liberation of the oppressed but also a mediator who is concerned about their daily survival.[8]

Black Messiah

Already in 1829, Alexander Young's "Ethiopian Manifesto" referred to the appearance of a black Messiah. The first book to consider in detail the meaning of a black Messiah for African American theology was Howard Thur-

7. Ibid., 82.
8. Ibid.

man's *Jesus and the Disinherited*, published in 1949.[9] Thurman combines biblical and historical ideas about Jesus as the Messiah with cosmic and mystical notions of Christ. Thurman's main questions are, What is the significance of Jesus for people "against the wall"? and Why is it that the "white" religion of Christianity has been so impotent in dealing with this problem? Thurman underlines the fact that Jesus is able to identify with oppressed black people because he himself belonged to a people under oppression; Jews of that time were threatened by Romans and subjugated under their tyranny. However, unlike many later black Messiah manifestos, Thurman does not refer to an active political stand but rather to the idea of the kingdom of God in Jesus "in us." Its emphasis lies in the role of Jesus the Messiah in bringing about liberation by virtue of being a mediator among the forces of evil, the effects of sin, and the powers of redemption. Salvation was still essentially spiritual, but blacks did not relegate it to the future as much as white Christianity of that time was accused by blacks of doing.

Albert Cleage's *Black Messiah*[10] from 1968 promotes a more politically and socially active approach. Many consider this collection of sermons and essays the most extreme left wing of black Christology. According to Cleage, the idea of a "white" Christ is a product of the white dominant class in society and has little to do with the Bible. The most controversial claim of Cleage is that Jesus of Nazareth, as a member of his people, was literally black. He insists that the Bible was written by black Jews and argues that Jesus identified himself with the ultranationalistic Zealot movement, which was committed to bringing about a black nation of Israel. Few scholars are convinced of the historical basis of this claim, but it was later appropriated by several black Christologists in a less literal way.

Tom Skinner's *How Black Is the Gospel?*[11] published in 1970, is more conservative and looks for a "black Messiah" who is beyond racial divisions. Christ is a liberator but does not identify with a particular color of people. Jesus' only allegiance was to his Father and the kingdom of God he preached. Jesus came to preach spiritual dimensions of salvation.

Many other black Christologists fall between the extremes of Cleage and Skinner. J. Deotis Roberts and James Cone are the most well-known, the former being less radical than the latter. Roberts's *Black Theology in Dialogue*,[12] as the name suggests, strikes a more conciliar tone: Instead of promoting parochialism, his black theology is ready to dialogue. Roberts makes reference to Paul Tillich's idea of theology as a correlation between revelation and current questions. He also acknowledges that blacks are *African* Ameri-

---

9. Howard Thurman, *Jesus and the Disinherited* (Nashville: Abingdon, 1949).
10. Albert Cleage, *Black Messiah* (New York: Sheed & Ward, 1968).
11. Tom Skinner, *How Black Is the Gospel?* (New York: J. B. Lippincott, 1970).
12. J. Deotis Roberts, *Black Theology in Dialogue* (Philadelphia: Westminster, 1987).

can, and therefore, African roots are important. As a result, African experience has to be brought to Bible reading. When black slaves were introduced to the Bible, they readily embraced it because of their understanding of life as sacred, as whole, as community. There is no presuppositionless exegesis; therefore, reading the Bible from a distinctively black perspective is just as justified as reading it from any other perspective.

Roberts regards the idea of a black Messiah as symbolic rather than literal; he believes in an actual historical Jesus. Roberts's task is "psychocultural": to restate the teaching about the universal Christ in such a way as to particularize God's redemptive act for a specific group. Christ is the redeemer of all, but he is also the redeemer of each and every specific group. "The black Christ participates in the black experience. In some sense Christ makes contact with what the black Christian is aware of in his unique history and personal experience."[13]

The central idea of Roberts's thought is the relationship between the black Messiah and the Christ of faith. The black Messiah is a mythical construct that helps blacks overcome the negative views associated with being black. But ultimately, the black Messiah has to give way to a "colorless Christ." The black Messiah is particular, while the Messiah of the Bible is universal. There is a dialectical relationship between the particular and the universal Christ: The universal Christ is particularized for the sake of the particular people of the black race, while the particular black Christ points to the universalization of Christ for all people. The ultimate goal of the black Messiah is reconciliation. He is the reconciler of both black and white.

What to Do with the "White Jesus"?

For James Cone, Christology begins and ends with Jesus Christ, who is the starting point for talking about God and humankind. Christ is the center of Christianity, and talk about Christ can never take place abstractly. It has to be concrete and rooted in the actual life situations of people. Because the Christ of the dominant forms of Christianity is presented as a white Christ tailored to the values of modern white society, there is a need for a black Christ:

> If Jesus Christ is to have any meaning for us, he must leave the security of the suburbs by joining blacks in their condition. What need have we for a white Jesus when we are not white but black? If Jesus Christ is white and not black, he is an oppressor; and we must kill him. The appearance of black theology

---

13. J. Deotis Roberts, *Liberation and Reconciliation: A Black Theology* (Philadelphia: Westminster, 1971), 139–40.

means that the black community is now ready to do something about the white Jesus, so that he cannot get in the way of our revolution.[14]

Later on, Cone softened his attack on the "white Christ" and acknowledged that his early theology was too much a reaction to the theology of the dominant class rather than a distinctively black talk. But still, the norm of all God-talk that "seeks to be black-talk is the manifestation of Jesus as the black Christ, who provides the necessary soul for black liberation."[15] This is appropriate in view of the fact that from the very beginning of his history with the people of Israel to the present day, God has taken the side of the poor and oppressed. Cone argues that God freed his people by means of the exodus event and continued to do so in the life, death, and resurrection of Jesus Christ. Cone speaks of the "new black man" whose newfound identity is manifested in Christ.

Cone emphasizes the importance of knowing the historical Jesus. Without knowing who Christ was, we cannot know who he is now. The New Testament pictures Jesus as a man identified with and speaking for the oppressed. Jesus' ministry focused on the oppressed. His message that the kingdom of God was at hand meant that slavery was about to end; the divine reign would displace all human authorities. The cross and resurrection confirmed his ministry: God is not defeated by oppression but transforms it into the possibility of freedom.

For Cone, the idea of a black Messiah is not literal, nor is it to be understood merely as a cultural symbol. It is a theological statement of the truth about Christ among the oppressed. Cone is not indifferent to the function of the myth of the black Messiah, but he insists that it has to be grounded in the history of Jesus of Nazareth. He also states that the blackness of Christ is not only about the fact that he was a victim; it also testifies to Christ's victory over destroying powers. The black Christ links the past and the present meanings of Jesus the Christ and also points to the future coming of Christ and the victory of the kingdom over all racial, social, and political boundaries.

The Reconciling Christ

Many of the leading ideas of Cone and his colleagues found their way into the church in South Africa under the oppression of apartheid. Yet many South Africans, especially Allan Boesak, have also taken a critical stand against some of the ideas presented by Cone. Boesak is a South African pastor who also became the President of the World Alliance of Reformed Churches. For

14. Cone, *Black Theology of Liberation*, 111.
15. Ibid., 38.

him, black theology is the theological reflection of black Christians on the situation in which they live in South Africa. Blacks ask what it means to believe in Jesus Christ when one is black and lives in a world controlled by white racists. Boesak is not prepared to separate the reality of the historical Jesus from the reality of his presence in the world today. In line with Cone, Boesak also affirms that the idea of liberation is not just *part* of the Christian gospel; it *is* the gospel of Christ. For Boesak, Christ is the center not only of Christology but also of all theology. He even uses the expression "christological theology."

Boesak offers his understanding of the terms "black consciousness" and "black power." He says that confining black consciousness to the process of discovering one's black identity limits the concept. It should also lead to the act of overcoming the institutionalized oppression of apartheid in South African society. To clarify his view, he criticizes Cone's understanding of black theology. According to Boesak, Cone makes the black experience "revelatory" in the sense that he bases his theology on that experience rather than on the revelation of God in Christ and therefore virtually identifies black power with the gospel. Not all agree with this reading of Cone's position;[16] Boesak's criticism reflects his own struggle to find a balance that he sees lacking in Cone. But the way in which Boesak finally conceives of black power remains unclear. For example, he does not clearly present his standpoint concerning the use of violence. He is not an advocate of violence, but to what extent he would allow its use is not clear in his writings. What is clear is that he is critical of the tendency of white theologians to make the issue of violence *the* theme of black theology.

The central feature of Boesak's thought is the idea of Christ as the reconciler of both black and white. "Liberation and reconciliation presuppose one another."[17] For reconciliation to happen, white racism must be abolished. In agreement with Cone, he maintains that blacks must drop their internalized slave mentality and accept themselves in their blackness. They can then claim the promise of God for their own dignity before God in Christ.

16. For a critique of Boesak's understanding of Cone, see Volker Küster, *The Many Faces of Jesus Christ: Intercultural Christology* (Maryknoll, N.Y.: Orbis, 2001), 148–49.

17. Allan A. Boesak, *Farewell to Innocence: A Socio-Ethical Study on Black Theology and Black Power* (Maryknoll, N.Y.: Orbis, 1977), 92.

24

Postmodern Christology

Christ for the Post-Christian Era

Perhaps no term is used as widely as *postmodernism*. Most movements today appeal to postmodernism, whether with affirmation or with criticism. On the one hand, all kinds of problems are attributed to postmodernism, from the fragmentation of society to desperate isolationism to a loss of the meaning of life. On the other hand, Christian theologians and philosophers of almost every persuasion envision an (unholy?) alliance between their faith and this concept, which defies a strict definition. The life of a postmodern person living in a "city," whether literally (as most do!) or figuratively with regard to the lifestyle of the third millennium, looks something like this:

> The irony is deep, pervasive, and seemingly all-encompassing. In virtually every corner of the globe human beings spin round and round, living out their lives as individuals paradoxically compelled in their "private" lives to make choices from a range of options that are enumerated and managed by institutions they cannot see and people they never meet face-to-face. . . . The groove of the City is decisive, making its inhabitants believe they can do what they want and get away with it. A peculiar mix of permissiveness and supervision thus character-izes the comings and goings of the global Cosmopolis, as people do exactly what it wants them to do, yet all the while saying to themselves that they are free.[1]

Theological analysts of postmodernism acknowledge that the spell of post-modernism lurks above the Christian church and makes a majority of Chris-

---

1. Barry A. Harvey, *Another City: An Ecclesiological Primer for a Post-Christian World* (Harrisburg, Pa.: Trinity Press, 1999), 2.

tians "retain a vague notion of religious identity" while "their lives are distinctively secular, with the experience of God in worship and prayer not figuring very prominently in all that they do."[2] However, it has to be acknowledged that those who envisioned the birth of postmodernism did not set out to deliver a monster. Rather, these descendants of classical liberalism wanted to realize the dream of an earthly paradise made by the hands of men and women and not gods.

Contrary to the prophecies of atheists and secular theologians of the 1960s, spirituality has not vanished from the modern and postmodern world. Of course, the goals and ethos of spirituality in this culture are very different from those of the early church or even the modern church. The postmodern notion of religion is characterized by consumerism: "The individual in the role of consumer is encouraged to pick and choose from a vast inventory of religious symbols and doctrines, to select those beliefs that best express his or her private sentiments."[3] Such spirituality is individualistic; it does not require a form of communal direction or oversight but may be enjoyed in the privacy of one's own life. This kind of spirituality is effectively delivered within the marketplace of desire. The church of the third millennium finds itself in the midst of a culture that has become "nothing but a meeting place for individual wills, each with its own set of attitudes and preferences and who understand that world solely as an arena for the achievement of their own satisfaction, who interpret reality as a series of opportunities for their enjoyment and for whom the last enemy is boredom."[4]

Philosophers and theologians also talk about a post-Christian era. The place and role of the Christian faith have permanently changed as a result of the emergence of postmodernism, and it is not easy for the Christian church to come to terms with such a radical transformation. The church no longer occupies the privileged position it held in the past. Indeed, its current social status more closely matches that of the early church than its status at any other time and place in history. The nostalgia for what was in the past often takes one of two forms. Some Christians desire to go back to the institutional and cultural synthesis between Christianity and society. Others try to adjust to the present culture by resorting to a secularized notion of the Christian message. So where do we put Christ in this chaos? What does it mean to talk about the humanity and divinity of the Son of God for a postmodern, post-Christian, post-anything world? An attempt to respond to these questions requires an analysis of the phenomenon of postmodernism from a theological perspec-

2. Vigen Guroian, *Ethics after Christendom: Toward an Ecclesial Christian Ethic* (Grand Rapids: Eerdmans, 1994), 89.
3. Harvey, *Another City,* 128–29.
4. Alasdair MacIntyre, *After Virtue: A Study in Moral Theory,* 2d ed. (Notre Dame: University of Notre Dame Press, 1984), 25.

tive. But first we must acknowledge that a definitive answer to the question of the role of Christ in the postmodern era may not be possible, for even an initial postmodern treatment of Christology (let alone alternatives for comparison) does not yet exist. Other topics in theology have been studied quite extensively from the postmodern perspective, for example, the nature of the church and its mission, but no major christological proposal has been written from a postmodern perspective.

Postmodernism as a Critique of Modernism

Postmodernism is usually regarded as cultural sensibility without absolutes, fixed certainties, or foundations. Postmodernism cherishes pluralism and divergence and encourages consideration of the radical "contextuality" or "situatedness" of all thought forms and philosophies. Whatever postmodernism encompasses, it is overall a criticism of modernism, its predecessor, the intellectual orientation that goes back to the Enlightenment. Even though much of public life and scholarship continues the agenda of modernism, many believe that modernism came to an end with the collapse of the Enlightenment confidence in the power of reason to provide universal knowledge of the world, including theological knowledge. The modernist, "foundationalist" epistemology (that is, theory of knowledge) assumes that it is philosophy's job to find an indubitable foundation on which all knowing rests. In the attempt to justify a given belief, one looks for a justification that requires no further justification. Various foundations have been posited, such as the sensory experience of logical positivism at the beginning of the twentieth century, to support the scientific paradigm. But the possibility of the foundation failing undermines human knowledge and leads to skepticism. Skepticism grows out of the suspicion of the absence of an epistemological foundation.

Various movements are related to and helped to give birth to postmodernism. They include continental (especially French) literary theory and criticism, some orientations of physics (such as that of Fritjof Capra), American neopragmatism, and many others.

In contrast to modernism, postmodernism is committed to relativism or pluralism in relation to questions of truth. To use more technical terminology, the "signifier" has replaced the "signified" as the focus of orientation and values. This point of view not only recognizes the arbitrariness of linguistic signs but also sees a lack of interdependence among signs, which denies the possibility of fixed, absolute meaning. Many postmodern writers, in opposition to modern authors, argue that language is whimsical and capricious and does not reflect overarching, absolute linguistic laws. Consequently, one of the major tasks of postmodernist study is to deconstruct language; there is virtually no relationship between what the author meant and how the reader understands and appropriates the text. The emphasis is on the "con-text" in the mind and orientations of the reader. All interpretations, then, are equally valid—invalid for that matter—with regard to what the text once meant. Some postmodernists even go so far as to say that the very idea of "meaning" is a forced concept, implying that somebody had the authority to define the meaning.

The [Im]Possibility of Christology in the Postmodern Era

What about the possibility of theology in general and Christology in particular in such an intellectual environment? Several implications follow. First, the postmodern way the Christ story is read and interpreted is vastly different from the modern way, let alone the premodern way. Instead of taking the Gospels' stories at face value (premodern) or attempting to uncover the "real history" of Jesus of Nazareth with the help of critical-historical methods (modern), the postmodern deconstructionist and/or structuralist hermeneutic challenges all notions of the correct (meaning the only right) meaning of the biblical text. The notion that there is a meaning to a biblical text—whether ascertained by church authority as in the premodern period or by critical scholarship as in the modern period—is blasphemy to the postmodern mind-set. There are no institutionally legitimized or scholarly approved interpretations of the Christ story. It is a story told anew each time it is encountered in a new context. Postmodern Bible readers fear that the demand for an authoritative interpretation is "authoritative" and so betrays a misuse of power.

Second, understandably, the postmodern outlook eschews all kinds of "systematic" theology, including Christology. Postmodernism by definition is hostile to claims concerning a determined meaning. Mark Taylor's study *Erring*,[5] to be examined in what follows, is an excellent illustration of the avoidance of any kind of systematization. "Erring"—Taylor's construction—leads to a/theology (Taylor's designation for a sort of anti-theology) rather than to any kind of system. For him, theological language does not refer to anything, and truth does not correspond to anything.

Third, postmodernism involves a striving for wholeness. Modernism separated self and object, visible and invisible, physical and spiritual:

> The problem with modernity is that it is divisive. It isolates human subjectivity from the physical or objective world. Persons are separated from things. The human self is thought to be autonomous; it dictates its own standards of value

5. Mark Taylor, *Erring: A Postmodern A/Theology* (Chicago: University of Chicago Press, 1984).

and beauty on the basis of its own arbitrary taste. This is done amidst an objective world which is in itself thought to be meaningless if not godless. The modern mind so fragments knowledge into separate disciplines that no one any longer has a vision of the whole. Everyone specializes. No one integrates.[6]

According to postmodernism, rather than analyzing and systematizing about Christ, the influence of Christ is to be lived again in any new context. Theology is participation in life rather than the act of analyzing concepts. The postmodern theologian Harvey Cox was fascinated with liberation theology and its idea of "changing" the world (in the spirit of Marxism) rather than "explaining" it. This view pointedly illustrates this ideal.

Fourth, any claim for a definitive Christology is to be discarded at the outset. There are no correct or false interpretations. There are just various deconstructions, or interpretations, of Christ.

Fifth, postmodern Christology is based on what Paul Ricoeur, the grand old man of postmodern philosophical hermeneutics, called "second naivete" or "postcritical naivete." According to Ricoeur, premodernism operated at the level of first naivete, where one's mind, it was assumed, participated directly in the thinking processes of the world and where one interpreted texts and concepts in terms of literal reference. Paul Tillich called this "natural literalism." Modernism operated at the level of critical consciousness by making critical thinking the main guide into the mysteries of reality. Using this method, one distanced oneself from the text in a critical sense, assuming distance between the original meaning and its meaning for the present. The concept of historical-critical Bible study worked according to this paradigm. Postmodern theology approaches the text from the postcritical standpoint. "Scientific" or distanced knowledge gives only a glimpse into some parts of reality; it is incomplete. Modernist knowledge has to be complemented with a form of participatory knowledge, affective or aesthetic knowledge, perhaps even mystical knowledge. In this scheme, the story of Christ is not read from a distance by an objective researcher but from inside the community of participation in the narrative of Christ.

Three theologians, namely, Harvey Cox, Mark Taylor, and Ted Peters, are discussed below to illustrate various postmodern approaches to Christology. While their approaches are vastly different, they all attempt to make sense of Christology for the postmodern world. Yet one should keep in mind that a definitive postmodern Christology does not exist and that by definition, postmodernism opposes a definitive, dominant approach to theology. What follows, then, are merely sketches.

6. Ted Peters, "Toward Postmodern Theology, part 1," *Dialogue* 24, no. 2 (1985): 6.

The Postmodernism of the Liberationists

Harvey Cox of Harvard University wrote a controversial book in the 1960s in which he prophesied the end of religion in the "secular city." His prognosis, however, was premature, and so in his subsequent book, *Religion in the Secular City: Toward a Postmodern Theology,*[7] he envisioned a spirituality commensurate with the end of the second and the beginning of the third millennium.

According to Cox's revised prediction, postmodern theology will arise out of the movements that still appear on the fringes of society and that in themselves serve as critiques of modernity. He considers two candidates: mass-media fundamentalism in the camp of right-wing Protestantism (Jerry Falwell and others) and liberation theology and the Base Christian Communities of Latin America (a Catholic renewal movement that tries to make church communities open, egalitarian, and welcoming). The first one is a less likely candidate because of its focus on the past, while the latter holds much promise because of its accent on the community and future.

What is there in the Base Communities that points to postmodernism? They emphasize active participation in small groups and the organization of community life in organic rather than hierarchical and mechanistic terms. Cox sees in the interpersonal life of the Base Communities the rebirth of "corporate community." This contrasts with modernism, in which churches became "collections of discrete persons . . . who created a church through a kind of social contract." Base Communities, on the other hand, have the ethos of being "members one of another."[8] These communities create a new style of selfhood and community life badly needed in the postmodern world. Liberation theology and Base Communities affirm social justice, the rights of the poor, a communal understanding of salvation, and democracy not only in society but also in the church. "Rather than thinking of the church as modern Protestants do, i.e., as a conglomerate of individuals, these base communities follow the Roman Catholic tradition and think of themselves as belonging to a corporate community understood as a 'mystical body.'"[9] In contrast to classical theology, which is oriented to the world of ideas, liberation theology is concerned with participation, community, social sources, and political life.

Radical Christology

One of the leading postmodern theologians, Mark Taylor, has tried to be more consistently postmodern in his style of writing theology than Cox and

7. Harvey Cox, *Religion in the Secular City: Toward a Postmodern Theology* (New York: Simon & Schuster, 1984).
8. Ibid., 214.
9. Peters, "Toward Postmodern Theology," 6.

many others. His sketch of postmodern theology, *Erring*, eschews any notion of a standard theology textbook and enters into play with words, etymological derivations, and impressions. It is an a/theology that on first reading seems to have been written by an atheist. Taylor takes his point of departure from the death of God theologies of the late 1960s as they were developed by Thomas J. J. Altizer, William Hamilton, and others, and says that his thought is based on a "radical Christology" rather than on humanistic atheism.

What does the term "radical Christology" mean here? It goes back to the thinking of Altizer, who spoke of the absolute immanence of God in humanity in contrast to the classical idea of transcendence. Altizer viewed the death of God, the "self-annihilation of God," as an event in history. Beginning in the incarnation and culminating at the cross, God emptied himself in the person of Jesus Christ. God became fully identical with humanity by negating his own objective existence through finite life and death. This "passage" of God in history to total immanence, in Altizer's analysis, was an act of grace for the sake of the creature and creation. This is what Taylor also affirms, and his task is to deconstruct classical Christology and its language; an earlier work of Taylor was significantly titled *Deconstructing Theology*.

Taylor approaches his task from the perspective of "elimination." He argues for the elimination of the concepts of self, truth, meaning, good, and evil. The only meaning of the term *self* is as a subject constituted entirely by its relations. Without God—since God is "dead"—there is no central perspective, no objective truth of things, no "real thing" beyond language. In the biblical texts about Christ, one discovers no meaning such as the intention of the author; meaning can be found only in the reader and his or her idea of what the text means.

Taylor utilizes the narrative in Luke 24:13–25 according to which the disciples of Jesus did not recognize their Master when he was present with them but only after he had left. Thus, "they recognized presence in absence and absence in presence." It was the "vanishing act that really opened their eyes."[10] This is the a/theology after the death of God, the "truth" that has been so slowly understood and appropriated by most modern theologians. The idea of the death of God leads to the heart of Taylor's radical Christology. Radical Christology is "*thoroughly* incarnational—the divine 'is' the incarnate word. Furthermore, this embodiment of the divine is the death of God."[11] According to Taylor, the divine is forever embodied. Incarnation, therefore, is not a once-and-for-all event, restricted to a specific time and place and limited to a particular individual. Rather, it is continual, though not necessarily a continuous process.

10. Taylor, *Erring*, 103.
11. Ibid., italics in text.

It is crucial for Taylor to try to overcome the antithesis between the transcendence and the immanence of God that he sees as so prevalent in classical theology. In his postmodern Christology, he overcomes this antithesis by affirming the death of God and arguing for an incarnation that is not a once-and-for-all event but rather an example, an illustration of God's continual relating to the world. Incarnation is an eternal occurrence.

What makes Taylor's radical Christology and idea of the death of God different from the ideas of his predecessors (especially the so-called death of God theology of Altizer) is that there is no grief over the loss of God. There is an acknowledgment of the loss but no regret. Neither is the longing for the God of classical theology replaced by the joyful acknowledgment of the incarnation of Jesus Christ in all human beings, as it is in some death of God theologies (for example, Hamilton). For Taylor, incarnation is "a diffused presence of God rather than a concentrated, once-for-all event."[12] This dispersion of divinity, one might be inclined to say, is Taylor's Christ. Taylor, understandably, is not happy with the term *C/christ* or, perhaps surprisingly, the term *Jesus*. The reason is obvious: Because of the death of God and the loss of transcendence, the traditional tasks of Jesus Christ as they were explicated in (pre-)modern theology, such as revelation and reconciliation, are totally meaningless to him.

An Evangelical Version of Postmodern Christology

By its very nature, postmodernism enhances and cherishes pluralism. Therefore, it is not surprising that theologians from widely differing perspectives have attempted to construct proposals for the postmodern era. Ted Peters, a Lutheran ecumenical theologian who places himself in the evangelical camp, has attempted a systematic theology for a postmodern era (the subtitle of his book *God—The World's Future*).[13] The title of the book illustrates the radical difference between this and Taylor's death of God theology.

According to Peters, the postmodern consciousness embraces a vision of wholeness as a remedy to the mind-set of modernism, the critical world that tore apart the relationship between the human mind and objective reality. "Emerging schools of postmodern thought . . . are searching for ways to reunite what has been separated, to fix what has been broken apart." So the task that Peters sets for himself in light of this postmodern consciousness is to "ask how God's promise of future wholeness for all creation affects our life now amid a world of brokenness."[14]

12. Millard J. Erickson, *The Word Became Flesh* (Grand Rapids: Baker, 1991), 325–26.
13. Ted Peters, *God—The World's Future: Systematic Theology for a Postmodern Era* (Minneapolis: Fortress, 1992).
14. Ibid., xii–xiii.

In total deviation from the approach of Taylor and other deconstruction-ists, Peters bases his explication of Christian doctrine on the Bible and classi-cal creeds. Peters also criticizes the modern mind and its "critical conscious-ness," which distances us from the "objects" of our study. But his conclusions are vastly different from more liberal postmodernists. In fact, Peters is doubt-ful of many tenets of mainline postmodernism, certainly disbelief in the living God. Peters, in fact, confesses that his primary motive for addressing postmo-dernity arises from the contextualization principle, according to which the church's theology and ministry need to be made intelligible and effective in each context to which Christians are called to bear witness to the gospel of Jesus Christ.

But what then is the justification of postmodernity for theology? Peters's response is practical: Postmodernity belongs to our current context, and that alone justifies addressing it theologically. But Peters also believes that postmo-dernity has constitutive value as well. "The medium of postmodern thinking itself draws theological explication in directions of greater comprehensiveness and coherence than were possible during the modern period."[15] Postmodern-ism's call for wholeness especially appeals to him.

Evangelical postmodern theology focuses on Christ. According to the bib-lical narrative, the gospel of Jesus Christ is essentially a promise for the future. But Peters reminds us, it is more than just a promise:

> It actually embodies ahead of time the future God has promised for the whole of creation, namely, new creation. If the gospel be the key to understanding re-ality, which I believe is the central Christian commitment, then it seems to fol-low that what is real is future-oriented. Destiny determines and defines what things are. Further, only at the fulfillment of the divine promise will reality it-self become a whole, and only with this whole of wholes will the true nature of all the participating parts—including ourselves—be revealed. . . . Of course, that God-determined whole is not yet actual. It does not yet exist. But it has been revealed—it has been incarnated—ahead of time in the life, death, and resurrection of the Nazarene. Hence, it is to Jesus Christ that one must look to find human destiny, to gain a vision of the whole, and according to which peo-ple can integrate the disparate elements of their lives.[16]

According to Peters, a life integrated with Christ is a "proleptic life." It is the future life actualized ahead of time. In fact, it is new life in the midst of old life; Peters calls it "beatitudinal."

Peters's evangelical version of postmodern Christology, based on these un-derlying principles, then takes a surprisingly classical form. For him, Jesus Christ brings the forgiveness of sin and a proleptic foretaste of new creation.

15. Ibid., 18.
16. Ibid., 19.

On the basis of the Easter victory, Jesus is the Christ, the bringer of the new era. Creatively appropriating the classical Reformed typology, Peters discusses the threefold office of Christ as the final prophet, the final priest, and the final king. He argues for the factuality of the cross and resurrection. The resurrection was the needed confirmation of the Father for the work accomplished at the cross. Peters's Christology recognizes the two natures of Christ in line with ancient Christian symbols, and he finishes his sketch of Christology by relating the doctrine of incarnation to the doctrine of the Trinity.

This brief survey of three postmodern Christologies shows clearly that a new paradigm is emerging, but no one yet knows what it will be and whether it will be long-lasting. Postmodernism embraces all sorts of approaches to theology; the only uniting core, if there is one, is disappointment with the program of modernism. But how this disappointment is addressed with regard to theology in general and Christology in particular differs so vastly from one author to another that one wonders if an umbrella term such as *postmodernism* is justified.

25

Christology in Latin America

Search for Freedom

The Christ of the Poor

Since the time of Vatican II (1962–65), liberation theologians of the Roman Catholic Church—followed by many in the Protestant churches as well—have come to see Christ as one who identified with the poor and oppressed and have focused on the self-understanding of the church as the church of and for the poor and underprivileged. The 1971 Catholic Bishops Synod took up the topic of "Justice in the World" and produced a notable declaration on the integral relationship between action for justice and evangelization: "Action on behalf of justice and participation in the transformation of the world fully appear to us as a *constitutive dimension of the preaching of the Gospel,* or, in other words, of the church's mission for the redemption of the human race and its liberation from every oppressive situation."[1] This was the first official Catholic document to describe social justice as a "constitutive" dimension of the preaching of the gospel. Christian love of the neighbor and justice cannot be separated, for love implies a demand for justice.

Given Latin America's many social and economic problems as well as its political upheavals and uncertainties, it is no wonder that the Latin American

1. "Declaration from the Roman Bishops Synod of 1971," in *Mission Trends,* vol. 2, ed. Gerald H. Anderson and Thomas F. Stransky (New York: Paulist Press, 1975), 255, emphasis added.

church has pioneered an emphasis on social justice. CELAM, the Second Conference of Latin American Bishops at Medellín, Colombia (1968), meeting in the presence of Pope Paul VI, placed three interrelated themes on its agenda: efforts for justice and peace, the need for adaptation in evangelization and faith, and the reform of the church and its structures. This regional conference, with its clear articulation of the people's cry for justice and liberation, its espousal of the cause of the poor, and its recognition of Base Christian Communities as primary centers for Christian community and evangelization, was actually a turning point in the identity and mission of the Catholic Church in Latin America. To bring about justice, however, it is not enough to change political structures; people need to be converted to the kingdom of justice, love, and peace.

Out of the liberation theologies' struggle for freedom, justice, and economic sharing arose a new type of ecclesiological experimentation that has contributed to the renewal of the church in Latin America, namely, the Base Christian Communities. The term *base* means the poor, the oppressed, and the marginalized. These communities, in which lay leadership and lay ministries have taken on a new significance, represent a grassroots cry for the liberation of the poor and other outcasts in society. In other words, Base Communities champion freedom and liberation. The significance of these communities goes beyond sociological or political definitions, however, even though they share a firm commitment to social concerns. According to Leonardo Boff, one of the leading liberationists, theologically, these communities "deserve to be contemplated, welcomed, and respected as salvific events."[2] The Base Communities argue not just for the ecclesiality of the church (what makes the church the church) but for a specific type of ecclesiality, namely, the birthing of the church community from below, from the people of God.

According to the Base Communities, Jesus' preaching can be seen as an effort to awaken the strength of the community for the people. In the horizontal dimension, Jesus called human beings to mutual respect and generosity, to a communion of believers and simplicity in relationships. Vertically, Jesus sought to open up human beings to a sincere filial relationship with God, characterized by openness, love, and trust. These same features of relationships are to characterize the church of Jesus Christ. By recovering these characteristics, the church reclaims its apostolicity.

The Base Communities not only identify with the poor and the weakest in society but *are* a church of the poor. As such, the Base Communities resist the widespread Christian ethos of reducing Christianity to the intimate sphere of private life. "Jesus preached and died in public, out in the world, and he is Lord not only of the little corners of our hearts, but of society and the cosmos

---

2. Leonardo Boff, *Ecclesiogenesis: The Base Communities Reinvent the Church* (Maryknoll, N.Y.: Orbis, 1986), 1.

as well."[3] The preaching of the gospel, good news to the poor, kindles in the poor the fire of hope and transforms their lives.

Theology in the Liberation Style

The term *theology* has a different connotation for Latin American and other liberation theologians than for classical theology. Medieval scholastic theology attempted to construct a finished theological system in which the language was more or less stable and in which all the major doctrines were examined. Theology in the liberation style bears marks of a pragmatic nature, in the spirit of Karl Marx's statement that his aim was not to explain the world but to change it. It is, indeed, from socialist and Marxist philosophies that liberation theology has borrowed some insights and tools for an analysis of society. The liberationists argue for the epistemic nature of praxis, which means that praxis is not only functional but also cognitive: Committing ourselves to the betterment of society is itself a means of gaining reliable knowledge of reality. This is the insight of a new epistemological style, often called the "sociology of knowledge," according to which knowledge is never neutral or value free but betrays the influences of context and circumstances. Naturally, a commitment to the poor, often called the "preferential option for the poor," is the leading principle of liberation theology.

At the beginning of the 1970s, following CELAM (1968), a Catholic Peruvian priest and theologian Gustavo Gutiérrez published a landmark book titled *A Theology of Liberation*.[4] This marked the beginning of a new style of theology called liberation theology. In his book, Gutiérrez argued that what is most distinctive about liberation theologians is the perspective from which they engage in theological reflection. Liberation theologians take as their point of departure the experience of the poor and the struggle of the marginalized for liberation. Their foundational conviction is that Christ, through his Spirit, is present everywhere that people engage in struggle for the poor and the weak. According to Gutiérrez, this kind of theological and pastoral work goes back to the Spanish priests at the time of the Spanish conquest of Latin America. In that era centuries ago, the pastors defended native peoples against the conquistadors, the foreign oppressors. Bartolomé de Las Casas and others reminded the rulers that the indigenous people, who were denied their full humanity, were also created in God's image and therefore deserved to be treated with honor and justice. A more recent advocate of liberation theology

3. Ibid., 38.
4. Gustavo Gutiérrez, *A Theology of Liberation: History, Politics, and Salvation* (Maryknoll, N.Y.: Orbis, 1973).

is the famous Tübingen theologian Jürgen Moltmann, who has called theologians to engage in political and social activism as part of their vocation.

In the past, the church fulfilled "religious" needs but not earthly ones; therefore, it failed its calling amid the poverty of Latin America. The church of Christ became captive to the ruling class and, with the rest of the powerful elite, neglected native peoples and tolerated corruption and injustice, at least by its silence. To be relevant, the church has to respond to the questions asked by the poor. Consequently, liberation theology calls the church to direct political action.

Gutiérrez and other liberationists such as Juan Luis Segundo have proposed a hermeneutic to guide theological work that is liberationist in its nature and goals. The starting point is the context rather than the text. Based on this insight, the "hermeneutical circle" takes place in four interrelated stages:

1. ideological suspicion: an emerging notion that perhaps something is wrong in society, especially among the underprivileged
2. analytical reflection on the social-value system: asking penetrating questions such as whether a situation is justified by Scripture and whether God's purposes are fulfilled in it
3. exegetical suspicion: an acknowledgment of the fact that theology is not relevant because of a one-sided and biased style of reading the Bible that neglects the perspective of the poor and oppressed
4. pastoral action: articulating an appropriate response to what is determined to be one's personal biblical responsibility

Rubem Alves goes back to the Hebrew concept of truth, which—in contrast to the Greek idea of truth, which relates to the realm of pure ideas—takes shape as action and relationships. Liberationists champion this preferred notion of truth, which arises from a critical reading of the Bible and leads in Alves's terminology to "messianic humanism," the goal of which is the humanization of life.[5] The paradigm is the exodus event in the Old Testament in which God manifested himself as the power of liberation. This goal emerges because, according to Gutiérrez, in a continent such as Latin America:

the main challenge does not come from the nonbeliever but from the nonhuman—that is, the human being who is not recognized as such by the prevailing social order. These are the poor and exploited people, the ones who are systematically and legally despoiled of their being human, those who scarcely know what a human being might be. These nonhumans do not call into question our

5. See Donald K. McKim, *The Bible in Theology and Preaching: How Preachers Use Scripture* (Nashville: Abingdon, 1994), 140–42.

226 Christ in the Contemporary World: Contextual Christologies

religious world so much as they call into question our *economic, social, political, and cultural world*. Their challenge impels us toward a revolutionary transformation of the very bases of what is now a dehumanizing society.[6]

Many analysts concur that the major problem with regard to the dehumanizing aspects of the Latin American context is dependency. On the one hand, most Latin American countries are dependent on foreign countries and investments; on the other hand, within the countries, the poor and other marginalized people depend on the ruling, affluent, politically powerful elite. Naturally, these two forms of dependency are mutually intertwined and feed each other. The majority of the population, estimated at 85 to 90 percent of most Latin American countries, is directly affected by this marginalizing dependency and its implications, such as poverty, lack of human rights, lack of access to education, and so on. For Christian theology to address this situation, people need to listen to the voices of the liberationists.

The Jesus of Real History

One of the preferred terms of liberation theology is *praxis* (instead of inquiring into the ontology of Christ [traditional theology], liberation theologians look at what Jesus did and taught and want to put that into practice). Out of this concept arises the main focus of its Christology: the meaning of the historical Jesus, who lived a real life under real human conditions. Interest in the historical Jesus leads to the study and appropriation of the Gospels. Latin American liberationists usually prefer Mark and Luke to Matthew. The reason is obvious: The Jesus of the Gospel of Mark is a suffering, humble Christ, and the Christ of Luke is a compassionate, loving figure. Matthew's Christology, to many liberationists, echoes the reign of the kingdom with its dark side of ruling and power. A relevant illustration for the liberationist is the saying of Jesus, "Blessed are you who are poor," in Luke 6:20, in comparison to Matthew's version, "Blessed are the poor in spirit" (5:3).

But it has to be noted at the outset that the interest of Latin American liberation theologians in the Jesus of history differs from the quest of the historical Jesus. For the liberationists, the historical facts of the life of Jesus as such are not the focus, as in the quest, but rather of the relevance of the history of Jesus to the struggles in Latin America. "*Understanding* Jesus, as opposed to recovering Jesus, requires holding together in creative fusion two distinct horizons: the historical Jesus of the Gospels and the historical context of contemporary Latin America."[7]

6. Ibid., 140–41, italics in text.
7. Priscilla Pope-Levison and John R. Levison, *Jesus in Global Contexts* (Louisville: Westminster John Knox, 1992), 31.

Boff has extended the inquiry into the identity of the historical Jesus by exploring the question of the authority Jesus assumed for himself while on earth. Unlike other rabbis, Jesus taught with authority (Mark 1:22). His miracles prompted a reaction of both astonishment and excitement. According to Boff, Jesus came to the realization of the decisive breakthrough of the kingdom of God in his life and ministry. Even though he never adopted the title Son of God directly during his ministry, he claimed a unique relationship with his Father. Boff believes that at least three times in the New Testament Jesus was called God (John 1:1; 20:28; Heb. 1:8); thus, this was but a logical conclusion of the authority and unique identity Jesus assumed during his earthly life. But how, then, can we put together the ideas of Jesus as "the human God and the divine human"? Boff believes the ancient formulae are insufficient. For example, the formulation of the Council of Chalcedon does not account for the gradual growth and development in Jesus's consciousness that he is unique. The ancient formulations also do not pay enough attention to the "nature" of Jesus (for example, as Liberator) but simply delve into philosophical questions about his personhood.

What about the risen Lord? What is the meaning of the ascension for liberation Christology that focuses on the Jesus of history? In Boff's vision, the risen and ascended Christ has penetrated the world in a profound manner: He is now ever present according to his own promise (Matt. 28:20). Boff also refers to the Pauline idea of Christ as the "pneumatic body," spirited body (1 Cor. 15:44). The resurrection revealed the cosmic dimension of Christ, for in him all creation has come into existence, and he is the goal of all. From this perspective, the significance of the incarnation can be seen in a new light. For Boff, the main focus of the incarnation is the completion of creation rather than the remedy for sin, which is the focus of classical theology. "The eternal person of the Son was always acting in the world from creation, but his presence was concentrated in Christ and was spread throughout the cosmos after the resurrection. Jesus is portrayed as the focal being in whom the total manifestation of God takes place within creation."[8]

Jesus Christ the Liberator

As the name liberation theology suggests, the main role in which Jesus Christ is depicted is that of Liberator. Jesus' ministry encompasses several forms of liberation, beginning with the fight against unjust economic structures, as liberationists see evident in the parable of the workers who labored for different lengths of time but earned the same wage (Matt. 20:1–16). Jesus

8. William J. LaDue, *Jesus among Theologians: Contemporary Interpretations of Christ* (Harrisburg, Pa.: Trinity Press, 2001), 175.

also fought social structures by inviting those who were outside the religious law, such as prostitutes and tax collectors, into table fellowship. In that culture, as in many non-Western cultures even today, table fellowship is the most honorary and inclusive means of welcoming another person. Jesus also:

> fought dehumanization by placing human need above even the most sacred traditions such as Sabbath purity (Mark 2:23–3:6). Therefore the oppressed were conscientized in his presence. Blind Bartimaeus, whom the crowds silenced, was given voice and healed by Jesus (Mark 10:46–52). An unnamed woman with a flow of blood and no financial resources touched Jesus and subsequently "told him the whole truth" (Mark 5:25–34). Jesus fought sin by denouncing everything—whether religious, political, economic, or social—that alienated people from God and from their neighbor.[9]

The term "integral liberation," coined by the Latin American bishops in the Puebla Document subsequent to the Medellín conference, has been used for this all-encompassing ministry of Jesus. It denotes Jesus' liberating ministry, which takes into consideration different dimensions of life, whether social, political, economic, or cultural, and the entire web of factors affecting human life. The idea of integral liberation is the key to understanding the agenda of liberation theologians. They insist that "spiritual" and "earthly" belong together and can never be divorced from each other, as has often happened in classical theology. Fighting economic and political injustice is a spiritual act.

Liberation theologians talk about liberation in relation to the central concept in Jesus' teaching, namely, the kingdom of God. Jesus himself made explicit the link between his own ministry and the coming of the kingdom: "But if I drive out demons by the finger of God, then the kingdom of God has come to you" (Luke 11:20). Those Jesus delivered—the sick, the demon possessed, those outside the covenant community—were signs of the coming kingdom and its power of liberation and reconciliation. The kingdom is a "world in which the creative plan of God is finally fulfilled; where hunger, poverty, injustice, oppression, pain, even disease and death have been definitively overcome; it is a world from which evil has been rooted out forever."[10]

This is the thrust of the book *Jesus Christ Liberator*[11] by Boff, the Brazilian liberationist who has experienced great pressure not to speak for the poor and other marginalized. Christ's message concerning the kingdom of God actually amounted to the promise of the full realization of the whole of reality. Boff complains that the revolutionary message of Christ has been reduced in many cases to a decision of faith made by individuals without much relation to the

---

9. Pope-Levison and Levison, *Jesus in Global Contexts,* 35.
10. José Miguez Bonino, *Room to Be People* (Philadelphia: Fortress, 1979), 41.
11. Leonardo Boff, *Jesus Christ Liberator* (Maryknoll, N.Y.: Orbis, 1978).

social and political aspects of life. Boff argues that the liberation proposed by Jesus relates to the public realm as well as to the personal sphere. He even contends that over the years "the church has fallen into the temptation of adopting the customs of pagan society, with authority patterns reflecting domination, and with the use of lofty and horrific titles by those in positions of power over others."[12] By doing so, the church has been hiding its true identity as the community of Christ.

How did Jesus attempt to accomplish his task of liberation? According to Boff, two interrelated calls served the liberating aim of his ministry: the call to personal conversion and the call to restructure human relationships in society. Jesus attacked those who were self-righteous and ignorant of their own sins and misgivings. He also warned those, such as the Pharisees, who were in the business of placing burdens on other people in the name of religion or culture. For Jesus Christ, participation in the worship life of the covenant community of Israel was no guarantee of one's right relationship with God or fellow people. If love is missing, Boff reminds us, everything else is worthless.

It was obvious that Jesus Christ in his role as Liberator would eventually come into conflict with the ruling religious and political establishment of his time. For liberation theologians, this conflict is one area for study and reflection. Jesus clearly presented himself as a danger and a threat to the ruling class. It was also predictable that, after Jesus' death at the hands of the establishment, Jesus' followers would not at first see any salvific significance in his death; rather, the disciples were struck by the disappointment concerning the death of their Master and his project of liberation. Only after the resurrection did the disciples see the significance of the cross. The fact that Jesus, who challenged the establishment, was vindicated by God provides encouragement for the followers of Jesus.

The Socioanalytical Presentation of Christology

According to Justo L. González, an American-Hispanic liberation theologian, early in Christian history, the interpretation of Christ became tuned in with the wishes and hopes of the ruling class, and the role of Christ as the one who identifies with the outcasts, the poor, and the oppressed lost its dynamic:

> Great pains were taken to mitigate the scandal of God's being revealed in a poor carpenter. His life and sayings were reinterpreted so as to make them more palatable to the rich and powerful. Innumerable legends were built around him, usually seeking to raise him to the level that many understood to be that of the divine—that is, to the level of a superemperor. Art depicted him as either the

---

12. LaDue, *Jesus among Theologians,* 170.

Almighty Ruler of the universe, sitting on his throne, or as the stolid hero who overcomes the suffering of the cross with superhuman resources and aristocratic poise.[13]

But even so, González reminds us, there still remained the very real and very human figure of the carpenter, crucified by the ruling powers, crying when abandoned by God and his fellow people, yet being "very God." Liberation Christology has had to remind traditional theology of the inadequacy of its categories and orientations with regard to uncovering the biblical message about Christ.

Boff says there are two current approaches to Christology. The first he calls the "sacramental approach." Its aim is to offer a reinterpretation of Christology in terms of classical dogmas and concepts with some liberationist leanings. Boff thinks that even though this type of Christology is helpful in its acknowledgment of the need for liberation, it falls short in its analysis of the Latin American context and is not able to help remedy its massive social and political challenges. The second type of liberation Christology is called the "socioanalytical presentation of Christology." This is genuinely liberationist in that it not only offers an incisive analysis but also attempts sociopolitical structural change. This type of liberation theology uses the tools of social and political sciences and is not afraid to borrow from socialist or Marxist analyses of society.

In this latter approach, social, economic, and political liberation is seen as constitutive of the preaching of the kingdom of God. In light of the socioanalytical approach, for example, the exploitative nature of capitalism and its corollary problem of economic dependency are exposed, and measures are taken to counteract them.

Socioanalytical Christology aims for a liberating *orthopraxis* (literally, "right action") rather than *orthodoxy* (literally, "right worship," though the current meaning is "right belief").

> Like other liberation theologians, Boff affirms that access to God is not attained primarily through cultic worship or religious observance, but through service to the poor and the oppressed, for God lies hidden in those segments of society. The poor are declared blessed because poverty is the end product of unjust and enslaving relationships among human beings.[14]

Socioanalytical Christology may or may not lead to taking political, even violent, action to further the cause of the poor and oppressed. Liberation theologians acknowledge that Jesus did not intend to occupy a position of po-

---

13. Justo L. González, *Mañana: Christian Theology from a Hispanic Perspective* (Nashville: Abingdon, 1990), 140.
14. LaDue, *Jesus among Theologians*, 177.

litical power; yet they also believe that a takeover of political power should not necessarily be ruled out of the picture. One reason Jesus and his followers were slow to take political action was the intensive expectation of the imminent coming of the kingdom. Because in our own times that kind of expectation has waned, striving for social and political justice is a mandate for the followers of Christ.

Salvation as Liberation

As mentioned earlier, Christology has traditionally been divided into two sections: Christology proper, which deals with the person of Christ, and soteriology, which deals with the work of Christ, the salvation Christ accomplished. Naturally, these two areas are integrally related; what one believes about the person of Christ carries over to what one affirms about the nature of salvation in Christ. In liberation theology, this connection between Christology and soteriology comes to focus in that, as a result of looking at the person of Christ from the perspective of liberation, salvation is understood as liberation. The term *liberation* here does not necessarily mean only this-worldly social and political liberation, as liberation theologians are sometimes unjustly charged of believing, especially by their more conservative colleagues. Rather, it emphasizes that salvation is not *only* about saving the soul. Salvation in the biblical sense of the term—based on the Old Testament concept of *shalom,* "peace," "well-being," "harmony"—encompasses the fulfillment of God's promise in a holistic sense. Liberation theology is a form of *Christian* theology and as such, even when it takes on social and political forms, even acknowledging the use of violence in extreme cases (as, for example, Gutiérrez does, though reluctantly), it seeks a Christian answer to the problems in society. The controversial figure of early Latin American liberation theology, Camilio Torres, once a priest and then a guerrilla fighter who was killed, once said, "I am revolutionary because I am a priest." For him, "Revolutionary action is a Christian, a priestly struggle."[15]

It has been the task of liberation theology in general and Christology in particular to remind Christian theologians of the often-too-narrow outlook they have regarding salvation and to insist that sociopolitical aspects not be overlooked. In Gutiérrez's terminology, traditional theology errs in viewing salvation as exclusively "quantitative," that is, as guaranteeing heaven for the greatest number. According to him, in the Latin American context, there is an urgent need to reinterpret salvation in qualitative terms, as a way of social, political, and economic transformation. The careful analysis of Gutiérrez

15. Cited in José Miguez Bonino, *Doing Theology in a Revolutionary Situation,* ed. William H. Lazareth (Philadelphia: Fortress, 1975), 43–44.

leads him to the conclusion that the Christian sense of salvation has three interrelated facets:

1. personal transformation and freedom from sin
2. liberation from social and political oppression
3. liberation from marginalization (which may take several forms, such as unjust treatment of women and minorities)

The task of the Christian church is to cooperate with God in shaping society in light of the values of the coming kingdom of God, the kingdom of equality, justice, and peace. To accomplish this noble task, the church has to give preference to the poor and marginalized. Even though final, all-encompassing justice and peace may not come until the full arrival of the kingdom, the followers of Christ are called to do whatever is in their power to reach for the noble goal. It is here that the "church finds its full identity as a sign of the reign of God to which all human beings are called but in which the lowly and the 'unimportant' have a privileged place."[16]

Jesus' role as the Liberator was accentuated by the way he treated the poor. He not only expressed the "preferential option for the poor" and not only identified himself with the poor; he also was poor. As liberation theologians remind Christians who often depict Jesus in idealistic terms, he belonged to the ordinary working class of the society.

One of the key sayings of Jesus—understandably precious to all those for whom the cause of the poor is dear—is the opening statement in the Sermon on the Mount: "Blessed are you who are poor, for yours is the kingdom of God" (Luke 6:20). Even earlier, in the inaugural sermon in his native town, Nazareth, Jesus counted the poor, the blind, and the oppressed as his special objects of care and ministry (Luke 4:18–19). Throughout his ministry, Jesus welcomed the poor, held them up as examples of piety, denounced the dangers of wealth, and called for self-renunciation and sharing with the underprivileged. Most of his followers were marginalized people and economically deprived.

A Hispanic Rereading of the History of Christology

González, the writer of a recent Hispanic interpretation of systematic theology, including a fresh discussion of Christology from a Latino perspective, years ago wrote a comprehensive three-volume *History of Christian Thought*. Being well versed in the history of Christology, González offered an engaging,

16. Gustavo Gutiérrez, *A Theology of Liberation*, rev. ed. (Maryknoll, N.Y.: Orbis, 1988), xlii.

critical account of the development of the christological tradition in light of the ancient creeds and heresies. This he did from the perspective of both the oppressed and the oppressors.

There are always those among the oppressed who deem it necessary to find a justification for their condition of oppression—particularly for their subservient attitude. Challenging the structures of oppression and injustice, trusting that the living God shares in the struggle, requires taking a risk. Those who do not dare to do so have a tendency to understand their faith in a way that minimizes their oppression. In González's view, this is the mechanism that explains the appeal of Gnosticism for early Christology:

> The Gnostics were well aware of the evil and injustice that abound in this world. Their solution, however, was not to oppose that evil but rather to surrender this world to the powers of evil. And to turn to a wholly different realm for their hope for meaning and vindication. According to them, original reality—and therefore also ultimate reality—was purely spiritual. The physical world is not part of a divine plan of creation but is rather the result of a mistake. In this world, and in the material bodies that are part of it, our souls are entrapped, although in truth they belong to the spiritual world. Salvation thus consists in being able to flee this material world.[17]

The appeal of Gnosticism was often coupled with its cousin, Docetism (from the Greek *dokeō,* "to appear" or "to seem"), according to which Jesus was not a real human being; he only appeared to be human. The true God, in this view, can never appear in the form of evil matter, flesh. Likewise, according to the Docetists, suffering and death, as well as injustice and evil in the world, are not significant; what matters is the world of the heavenlies. According to González, this view held for the dispossessed of the second and third centuries the same appeal that Egypt held for the Israelites.

> There is comfort in believing that whatever happens in this world has no ultimate significance, and that for that reason one is not to be too concerned about the evil one sees in the world. If the emperors and the aristocracy now live in comfort while the masses toil, or if someone owns our bodies as slaves, this is nothing to be concerned about, for in the end we shall flee from this vale of tears.[18]

In sum, both Gnosticism and Docetism have always been a temptation for the oppressed, and this has been the case in the Latino context, González reminds us.

17. González, *Mañana,* 140–41.
18. Ibid., 141.

Yet another early heresy has had some, though less, appeal for the oppressed, according to González's Hispanic rereading of Christology's history. That heresy is adoptionism, which maintains that Jesus was not God "in nature" but was adopted as God's son at a definite point in his life, whether at conception, baptism, or resurrection. González explains the rationale behind this view, which he calls a "christological expression of a myth":

> Adoptionism is the Christological expression of a myth that minorities and other oppressed groups have always known to be oppressive. This is the myth that "anyone can make it." Those who belong to the higher classes have a vested interest in this myth, for it implies that their privilege is based on their effort and achievement. But those who belong to the lower classes and who have not been propagandized into alienation from their reality know that this is a myth, and that the few that do make it are in fact allowed to move on in order to preserve the myth.[19]

In other words, adoptionism is seen as an alienating doctrine by those who realize that their society is in fact closed.

González also considers the implications of other early heresies such as Apollinarianism, which did not recognize the full humanity of Jesus but only a truncated form, a sort of "semi-humanity." The danger of Apollinarianism from the Hispanic vantage point is that such a doctrine would undo the saving power of Jesus. If the human mind is not in need of salvation—as Apollinarianism implies—then problems in life are relegated to the bodily nature as opposed to the spiritual.

As the church and Christian theology struggled in the early centuries with these and related views, they established christological affirmations in the form of creeds. González acknowledges the value of the Chalcedonian formulation but finds it wanting because it expresses christological beliefs in static terms. The Chalcedonian formula speaks of the humanity of Christ in a language foreign to the dynamic language of the Bible, which describes Jesus as a child growing up (Luke 2:52) or a young man having to make difficult decisions (Mark 1:12 and par.).

The One for Others

In his exposition of a Hispanic Christology, in light of historical and current trends in international, ecumenical theology, González posits that the heart of Christology for Latinos is that Jesus Christ is entirely for others. At his birth, the announcement was made by the angels that *"to you"* the Savior is born (Luke 2:11). One of the most beloved Gospel texts affirms that in the

19. Ibid., 144.

coming of Jesus, God so loved "the world" (John 3:16). The Gospels, especially John, often talk about Christ laying down his life for others.

Jesus' "for-otherness," however, is not a self-deprecation or the cowardice often found among the oppressed but rather a strong, assertive living for others. "He was for others, not only when he healed the sick, forgave those who condemned him, and died on the cross but also when he cleansed the Temple, spoke the harsh truth to the Pharisees, and called Herod a fox."[20]

In the kingdom of God, the one who serves and lives for others is the greatest. But because Jesus Christ found himself living in a world that was less than just, his stern for-otherness was not evenhanded. He dared to challenge the social conventions and prejudices by reaching out to the marginalized, even religiously ostracized, such as the Samaritan woman (John 4). He also harshly criticized the political and religious establishment for the cause of the common people. His message was a mixture of blessing and curse, as is evident in the Lukan redaction of the Sermon on the Mount (Luke 6:20–26).

Being a servant did not make Jesus less divine. Servanthood and humility are not foreign qualities to the being of God but rather constitutive elements of the divine. Christian theology has had a difficult time seeing this clearly and has missed an opportunity to relate Jesus' real humanity to the needs of the real world.

The Bible also talks about God's essential nature for-others by saying that "God is love" (1 John 4:8). To love is to be and to live for others. Creation, preservation, judgment, redemption, and consummation are God's acts of love, his way of being for others. As already noticed, this being-for-others is not cheap self-abasement; it goes beyond forgiveness and pardon and includes the holy will of God in judgment and purification from all that opposes this will. "This for-otherness that is the glory of God is also the glory of Jesus Christ. John 1:14 declares that 'the Word became flesh' and that 'we have beheld his glory, glory as of the only Son from the Father.'"[21] This glory of Jesus Christ is not a halo but the glory of God that guided the Israelites in their journey from slavery to the Promised Land.

The nature of Christ for-others needs to be recovered afresh in order for Christology to make sense and gain relevance for the Latin American context. Jao Dias de Araujo speaks of various inadequate, irrelevant images of Christ prevalent in Latin American spirituality: a "dead Christ" to be venerated in crucifixes, which leads to fatalism and acceptance of one's lot; a "distant Christ," divorced from the needs of real life and relegated to spiritual devotion only; and a "powerless Christ" who has some power over so-called divine forces but cannot help with regard to poverty, class struggle, or finding one's identity. In popular Catholic piety, Araujo reminds us, the saints or Mary

20. Ibid., 151.
21. Ibid., 153.

often take the place of the Son, and the faithful find it easier to direct their prayers to them rather than to Jesus. Other Christologists from Latin America add other inadequate images of Christ prevalent in the popular piety of Protestantism, such as a "Santa Claus Christ" who preaches about a cheap and uncomplicated "gift" of Christ to every imaginable problem, whether sickness, unhappiness, or material plight; a "beggar Christ" who invites people to accept him as "Savior" so he will not be alone behind closed doors; an "asocial Christ" who encourages his followers to withdraw from the world and not to be tainted by its influence. These and many other Latin American images of Christ call for reflection on his true person in contexts of revolution and suffering. To do so more fully, we turn next to one of the ablest Christologists of that area, Jon Sobrino.

26

Jon Sobrino

Christ as Liberator

In Search of a Starting Point

Born into a Spanish Basque family, Jon Sobrino studied both in the
United States and Germany and taught for a long time in El Salvador. The
book that brought him international fame and put him at the forefront of liberation theology was *Christology at the Crossroads*.[1] Among his many later writings, the collection of essays titled *Jesus in Latin America*[2] brought to maturity
his main ideas concerning Christ and gave him an opportunity to assess the
views of his earlier work.

The first task Sobrino sets for himself is to look for an adequate starting
point for doing Christology in the Latin American context. For that purpose,
he offers a wide survey of earlier approaches and finds them wanting in light
of the need to ground Christology in the history of Jesus: "Let me say right
here that my starting point is the historical Jesus. It is the person, teaching,
attitudes, and deeds of Jesus of Nazareth insofar as they are accessible, in a
more or less general way, to historical and exegetical investigation."[3] Sobrino's
starting point is not merely the history of Jesus but the "concrete history of

1. Jon Sobrino, *Christology at the Crossroads* (Maryknoll, N.Y.: Orbis, 1978).
2. Jon Sobrino, *Jesus in Latin America* (Maryknoll, N.Y.: Orbis, 1987).
3. Sobrino, *Christology at the Crossroads*, 3.

Jesus." Therefore, his is a Christology from below. In light of this founda-tional choice, he criticizes several earlier approaches:

1. The dogmatic formulation of the Council of Chalcedon, the typical point of departure for Catholic theology, which affirms the full hu-manity and divinity of Christ, represents a Christology of "descent." It starts off with God and then goes on to affirm how the eternal Son became human. This is unacceptable to Sobrino for the simple rea-son that the approach of the Bible is the opposite—from below.

2. A biblical focus on Christ, which has often taken the form of study-ing various titles given to Christ by the New Testament writers (Son of Man, Son of God, Messiah, and so on), is not much better, be-cause the New Testament does not have one but several different Christologies, and it seems impossible to unify them into one.

3. Christology that starts from people's experience of Christ in cultic wor-ship gives valuable insight into the meaning of the Christ event but cannot offer valid information about the "concrete Jesus," especially because Christ is ascended. Cultic contact with the risen Christ, as his-tory shows, is open to all kinds of interpretations.

4. Christology from the perspective of Christ's resurrection, while prev-alent in the New Testament, is not sufficient for Christology's foun-dation, because its meaning can be ascertained only from the per-spective of the historical Jesus.

5. The Christ of *kērygma* as the starting point shares all the weaknesses of Christology divorced from historical contours, as evident in the demythologization of Rudolf Bultmann.

6. Christology that focuses on the teachings of Jesus, as classical liberal-ism did, apart from the thoroughgoing eschatological, apocalyptic nature of Jesus' own understanding, shares the ambiguities of the lib-eral quest of the historical Jesus, which took this project to its end.

7. Christology as soteriology easily leads to a Christology that arises from our own needs and makes anthropology (the doctrine of hu-manity) determinative for its agenda. However, Jesus' person and ministry not only affirmed the agenda set by his followers but also, and perhaps more so, challenged it.

For Sobrino and other liberationists, their focus on the historical Jesus is different from that of the quest of the historical Jesus. In European theology, the problem of the historical Jesus arose in the context of historical criticism and was framed in terms of what we can or cannot know about the history of Jesus. In Latin America, liberation theology focuses on the historical Jesus for guidance and orientation. "Since it arose out of the concrete experience and praxis of faith within a lived commitment to liberation, it soon realized that the universality of Christ amid those circumstances could only be grasped from the standpoint of the concrete Christ of history."[4]

One motivation for focusing on the historical Jesus as the starting point for liberation Christology is a noticeable resemblance between the situation in Latin America and that in which Jesus lived (e.g., poverty, injustice, foreign occupation, etc.). Sobrino notes that the Christologies of the first communities were not fabricated theologies but rather were made up of the testimonies of the people who had encountered the Messiah. There were two poles to these emerging Christologies: the person of Jesus Christ and the life situation. That situation shares many similarities with the Latin American context, even though the church—especially the Catholic Church—has already provided dogmatic contours that guide thinking about Christ.

The Methodology of Liberation Christology

What is the value of traditional christological doctrines for the liberation theology of Sobrino? Sobrino posits a distinctive understanding of the nature of dogma. Its purpose is not to provide additional knowledge beyond what is already known otherwise but to give a better understanding and explanation of what the Bible tells us about Christ. The intention of dogma is not to exhaust the content of faith but to defend an aspect of it, an aspect regarded as so basic that it cannot be altered without compromising faith. Scripture, then, is foundational for an understanding of Christology; dogma is secondary. It is here that we see the limitations of dogma insofar as it is meant to serve the faith of Christians. "For even when a dogma says something very fundamental, it always *says* less than Scripture does."[5] Therefore, interpretation of dogma is a necessity, not a luxury. Such interpretation is not a move backward into the past, a regressive step, but a move forward, a progressive step. In other words, liberation theology's task of reading the narrative of Christ in light of the need for liberation and justice does not do away with or adulterate the original gospel; it makes it more relevant.

Sobrino acknowledges the fact that most Latin American theologians at this time are not especially interested in delving into traditional christological questions such as the "hypostatic union" of Christ's two natures or the role of Jesus Christ in the Trinity. Many Latino theologians see traditional theology as largely uninvolved with the real issues that touch the everyday lives and experiences of common people. Yet Sobrino's own approach to liberation the-

4. Ibid., 10.
5. Ibid., 318, italics in text.

ology is characterized by an honest, informed, and critical dialogue between classical Christology and the Latin American context.

Sobrino thinks that in the development of theological methodology we are now in the second phase of the Enlightenment. While the first phase effected the liberation of reason from dogmatic faith, the second is oriented toward the liberation of the whole person from a religious view that does not take a firm stand against social, political, and economic oppression. Jesus' attitude toward helping people was expressed in concrete action: His miracles, healings, casting out of demons, and other deeds of liberation touched the lives of needy people in a tangible way.

For Sobrino, therefore, a genuine Christology of liberation encompasses three foundational aspects. First, it is important to "recall the strictly evangelical tenor of the Christology of liberation in its inception."[6] This reflection draws from the convictions that the gospel of Jesus is good news for the poor and that the poor are the key to our approach to the gospel today. Second, Christ is not only the one who moves humanity toward liberation but also the norm of liberative practice and the prototype of the new human being for whom liberation strives. In classical terminology, Jesus is *norma normans* (normative norm) of liberation. Third, a kind of ethical indignation lies at the base of an incipient liberation Christology. This ethical indignation does not originate from an attempt to quell doubts about Christ but from indignation over the use to which Christ has so often been put in the history of Latin America to justify the oppression of the poor.

Sobrino's outline of the foundations of liberation Christology accords well with that of Leonardo Boff. Boff characterizes the basic approach of liberation Christology in this way:

1. the primacy of the anthropological element over the ecclesiastical
2. the primacy of the utopian element over the factual
3. the primacy of the critical element over the dogmatic
4. the primacy of the social element over the personal
5. the primacy of orthopraxis over orthodoxy[7]

Basic Themes of Liberation Christology

In a recent study of intercultural Christologies appropriately titled *The Many Faces of Jesus Christ*, Volker Küster summarizes Sobrino's approach to

6. Sobrino, *Jesus in Latin America*, 11.
7. Leonardo Boff, *Jesus Christ Liberator: A Critical Christology of Our Times* (Maryknoll, N.Y.: Orbis, 1978), 43–47.

Christology (and the approach of Boff) under four major themes that succinctly summarize its main agenda.[8]

First, liberating Christology is hermeneutical Christology. The belief that
the hermeneutical circle is the basic structure of theological reflection is the
common property of Latin American liberation theologies. Like all theological discourse, Christology is contextually conditioned.

Second, liberating Christology is relational Christology. This perspective
acknowledges several facets. There is a relationality between the historical
Jesus and the kerygmatic Christ. Even when Sobrino wants to prioritize the
historical Jesus, he does not wish to disentangle the Jesus of history from the
Jesus of faith. Furthermore, the relationship between Jesus the Son and the
Father, as is evident, for example, in the prayer life of Jesus, is a demonstration
of implicit Christology. Jesus never preaches himself but the Father and especially the coming kingdom of the Father. Finally, there is the relationality of
God the Father, Son, and human beings. "If on the one hand God has revealed himself in Jesus Christ, so at the same time on the other hand he is the
image of the perfect human being. . . . At the same time the poor and the oppressed in whom Jesus Christ is present become the image of the 'otherness'
of God."[9] Consequently, christological statements are always at the same time
statements about God and human beings.

Third, liberating Christology is incarnational Christology. The triad of the
life, death, and resurrection of Jesus Christ forms the span of the incarnation.
Jesus' death on the cross is in line with his incarnation among ordinary people. The overcoming of death in the resurrection gives the presence of suffering an eschatological dimension. The resurrection is an impulse for the hope
of liberation.

Fourth, liberating Christology is about discipleship. Just as Jesus not only
articulates his faith by preaching the kingdom of God but also makes it visible
in his activity, so too his followers must convert and follow in his footsteps.

The Presence of Christ in the Poor

One of the basic questions of any theology, and particularly of Christology,
concerns the presence of Christ. Is Christ present in an individual believer's
life or amid the congregation by virtue of the preached Word, the mediation
of the sacrament(s), or the decision of faith? While not downplaying any of
those traditional answers, liberation Christology argues that Christ's presence
is found among the poor. Therefore, the poor are a christological criterion,

8. Volker Küster, *The Many Faces of Jesus Christ: Intercultural Christology* (Maryknoll, N.Y.:
Orbis, 2001), 51–54.
9. Ibid., 52.

not in an exclusive sense (Christ is present *only* in the poor) but in an inclusive way (Christ is present *at least* among the poor and the outcasts). The One who himself was poor and who became poor for all people is, even after his resurrection and ascension, found amid the poor. The *kenōsis*, self-emptying, of Jesus Christ offers the poor a restitution of their dignity before God and consequently before other men and women. Küster rightly interprets this foundational idea of liberation Christology:

> The adoption of the generative theme of the presence of Jesus Christ in the suffering of the poor and oppressed in liberation theology is to some extent a modern version of Luther's basic hermeneutical principle "that God is to be found only in suffering and the cross." The liberation theologians "call things by their right names" [a saying of Luther with regard to the right perspective on reality given by the theology of the cross].[10]

Küster is also correct in noticing that, unlike Luther, liberation theologians have a corporate *theologia crucis,* a theology of the cross that has ecclesiological implications. This reference to community is constitutive for liberation Christologies and comes to a full development in Sobrino's work *The True Church and the Poor,*[11] which argues for the essence of the church as the church *of* the poor, not only *for* the poor. For Sobrino, it is crucial to acknowledge that this is not a sociological or a philanthropic principle but a christological statement. The Gospel narratives clearly show that Jesus surrounded himself with and favored sinners, publicans, the sick, lepers, Samaritans, pagans, and women throughout his life.

The presence of Christ in and among the poor is also significant because today, as in Jesus' time, the poor and outcast make up the majority of the world's population; this is certainly the case in the Latin American context. Out of this fact Sobrino draws an important principle:

> If Christianity is characterized by its universal claims, whether made on the basis of creation or of the final consummation, what affects majorities should be a principle governing the degree of authenticity and historical verification of this universalism. . . . Otherwise, the universality it claims will be a euphemism, an irony, or a mythified ideologization.[12]

Those who follow Christ, Sobrino reminds us, are called to discern and affirm the presence of Christ in the poor:

10. Ibid., 55.
11. Jon Sobrino, *The True Church and the Poor* (Maryknoll, N.Y.: Orbis, 1984).
12. Sobrino, *Jesus in Latin America,* 141.

The requirements Jesus laid on others show that same movement in the direction of basic impoverishment: the call to follow him in order to carry out a mission in poverty, to leave home and family, to take up the cross; these are not arbitrary requirements that he could just as well not have imposed, or in whose place he could just as well have imposed others. They are requirements in the direct line of impoverishment. The beatitudes show the same approach, from a different angle: the poor in material things are called to appreciate their poverty and live it as poverty in spirit, thereby participating actively in the movement of impoverishment.[13]

The Kingdom of God

In his proclamation of the kingdom of God, Jesus made it clear that the kingdom is good news for the poor (Luke 4:18) and that it is made up of the poor (Luke 6:20). This establishes a basic correlation between the good news and its principal recipients and indirectly shows of what this good news consists. For Sobrino, therefore, voluntary solidarity with the poor and the outcast is the manner in which the kingdom of God is actualized and comes to us. Jesus' relationship with the poor and the outcast shows not only what the kingdom should be in action but also how it is to be brought about. This principle follows the Servant Songs of Isaiah (chaps. 42–49) and the historical structure of Jesus' life on earth. Jesus, in the specific historical reality of his life, conceived of his mission in such a way that it had to follow a historical course leading inevitably to his loss of security, dignity, and life itself—the historical course of "the voluntary impoverishment."

Sobrino follows the rule of classical liberalism according to which Jesus did not come to preach about himself, not even about God as such, but about the kingdom of God. The kingdom was the focus and the main emphasis of Jesus of Nazareth. Chapter 3 in *Christology at the Crossroads* is appropriately titled "Jesus in the Service of God's Kingdom." "The most certain historical datum about Jesus' life is that the concept which dominated his preaching, the reality which gave meaning to all his activity, was 'the kingdom of God.'"[14] The message about the coming kingdom and its victory over the powers of evil is for Sobrino the gateway to appreciating the activity of Jesus as Liberator. Both his miracles and his forgiveness of sins are primarily signs of the arrival of the kingdom of God. "They are signs of liberation, and only in that context can they help to shed light on the person of Jesus."[15]

Sobrino argues that for Jesus of Nazareth, the kingdom of God was not only about speaking but also about action; in other words, *orthopraxis* must

13. Ibid., 146.
14. Sobrino, *Christology at the Crossroads,* 41.
15. Ibid., 48.

take over orthodoxy. This principle is succinctly expressed by Sobrino's colleague Boff: "The kingdom of God means a total, global, structural revolution of the older order, brought about by God and only by God."[16] By preaching the message of liberation and the inauguration of the kingdom, Jesus reached to those without hope.

> Jesus proclaims that the arrival of the kingdom is salvation and that the kingdom . . . has the decisive connotation of liberation. But this salvation and liberation is not expressed solely in words (sermons and parables); it is also expressed in *deeds*. The need to preach the good news in deeds flows of necessity from the reality of God.[17]

From the centrality of the idea of the kingdom follows Sobrino's profound theological conclusion: "God is insofar as he acts, insofar as he alters reality; and we must view the *actions* of Jesus in that light. His actions are not simply accompaniments to his words, nor are they primarily designed to illustrate his own person. Their primary value is theological. They are meant to demonstrate the kingdom of God."[18]

Jesus' message about the kingdom was not only about liberation in the past; it also had an eschatological character. The future influences the present. This is the "historicotemporal character of the kingdom."

The prophetic and apocalyptic formulations of the kingdom in the New Testament indicate that this reign of God entails a total renovation of reality. The final, ultimate goal of the coming kingdom is to establish a just, egalitarian fellowship, a "brotherhood." This goal of ultimate peace and *shalom* is also illustrated in the way the New Testament depicts Jesus' role as the bearer of the kingdom. The Gospels place the person and message of Jesus in the midst of situations embodying divisiveness and oppression, where the good news and salvation can be understood as being in total discontinuity with them.

Even though God's kingdom as Jesus preached it proclaims the reign and inbreaking of God's power, it is about grace. Thus, Sobrino also reminds us that the kingdom is the result of God's initiative and is based on grace.

16. Boff, *Jesus Christ Liberator*, 63–64.
17. Sobrino, *Christology at the Crossroads*, 46, italics in text.
18. Ibid., 47.

27

Christology in Africa

Search for Power

Christ for Africans

In what way can Jesus Christ be an African among the Africans according to their own religious experience? Who is Christ for Africans—who do not need to change their culture in order to be called children of God—and what is the impact of this Christ? These and other related questions, such as the relationship between African culture and Christian faith in Christ as Lord and Savior, occupy the interest of current christological thinking on the African continent.

Charles Nyamiti, one of the pioneers of African Christology, explains that the twin themes of inculturation (making the gospel relevant to a particular culture) and liberation shape many of the concerns of African Christian theology today, especially its thought concerning the person of Christ. "For too long, embracing Christ and his message meant rejection of African cultural values. Africans were taught that their ancient ways were deficient or even evil and had to be set aside if they hoped to become Christians."[1] The irony, of course, is that African values and customs are often closer to the world of the Bible and its cultures than is the Western form of Christianity that has often been forced on the African mind-set.

---

1. Robert J. Schreiter, "Jesus Christ in Africa Today," in *Faces of Jesus in Africa,* ed. R. J. Schreiter (Maryknoll, N.Y.: Orbis, 1991), viii.

In addition to the themes of inculturation and liberation, the topic of healing is crucial to African culture because many Africans continue to suffer. All of these themes are related to the search for power, not so much social or political power as in Latin America (even though social and political freedom is not a matter of indifference to Africans) but power over the oppression and dominance of *spiritual* powers. The African mind-set is highly animistic and spiritualistic, and it often looks to the unseen world as the key to solving life's problems. The shape Christology takes in this context differs greatly from classical theology, much of which was birthed in the intellectual worldview of Europe and the United States.

For Africans, who are sometimes considered incurably religious, the questions of who Jesus Christ is and how he relates to humans are crucial. Christology stands at the center of African theology. In the words of John Onaiyekan:

> If it is true that Christology is at the very heart of all Christian theology, it is particularly true for African Christian theology. It is by now generally agreed by most students of African traditional religions that our peoples have always had a clear idea of and firm belief in the Supreme Being. They have a faith in God which is indigenous and cannot be attributed to foreign influences, whether Christian or Islamic. In this regard, Africa is similar to the Jewish world to which Jesus presented Himself. Although the popular slogan "Jesus is the Answer" may be true in many ways, it is also true to say that "Jesus is *the* question."[2]

Onaiyekan concludes that "most of what we call 'African Theology' really boils down to Christology from an African perspective."[3]

The rich cultural background of Africa contributes to its variety of christological approaches and trends. Furthermore, Africa has been influenced by different Christian traditions, which adds to the proliferation of conceptions and images of Jesus Christ. Generally speaking, Roman Catholic theology has found it easier than Protestant traditions to make Christian sense out of African rituals and symbols. (Catholic churches freely use local customs, clothing, rituals, and building styles in their church life. This same principle also holds in other areas such as Asia; during the years I lived and taught in Thailand, I often noticed that the Catholic Church by far made the most use of local elements.)

Traditional African cultures represent oral traditions. Therefore, the strength and variety of Christologies are not found only in learned academic

---

2. John Onaiyekan, "Christological Trends in Contemporary African Theology," in *Constructive Christian Theology in the Worldwide Church,* ed. William R. Barr (Grand Rapids: Eerdmans, 1997), 356.
3. Ibid.

discussions or books; they are also found in songs, poems, and discussions in the markets and homes. Some of the most profound christological truths may come from the mouth of an illiterate elder of the community or a grand-mother in the family.

Christ in the Bible—and in Africa

In principle, there are two starting points for a *local* Christology, in other words, for a Christology that makes sense in a given context: Either one begins with the text of the Bible and then strives to find parallels in the context, or one takes the cultural context as the leading hermeneutical principle and works backward to the Bible. Both approaches have been utilized by African Christologies.

John Mbiti's work represents the first type of approach.[4] He has attempted to find parallels between the New Testament teaching concerning Jesus Christ and the African traditional worldview and beliefs. The ancient idea of *Christus Victor,* the powerful Christ who rose from the dead and defeated the opposing powers, is obviously relevant to the African search for power. The victorious Christ is able to overcome the spell and threat of spirits, magic, disease, and death and to transform the culture of fear into a culture of hope and joy.

Mbiti also finds several other christological parallels between the Bible and African cultural ideas and beliefs. The idea of Jesus Christ as the Son of God corresponds with several tribal beliefs; the title Servant of God is similarly found in some African societies; and several other christological titles such as Redeemer, Conqueror, Lord, and others have parallels in African cultures. Mbiti is, of course, not the only theologian who has seen these parallels between the Bible and African culture. Many others have done so as well, such as Onaiyekan. He claims that several traditional titles applied to Christ in the New Testament make sense in the African context. Son of God is one such title. The idea of God having a son whom he sent to the world makes sense in a culture used to divinities and the Supreme Being. The title Lord denotes authority and power in the same way that the title "Oluwa l'oke," the "Lord on the hills" of the people of Kabba (one of the Yoruba tribes), does. Even though the idea of a Savior is not prevalent in most African cultures, it is not completely foreign to them either. For example, the Yorubas have an expectation that the divinities *(Orisha)* will save them. Redeemer is welcomed as he who rescues people from the enslavement of the evil forces that surround them.

4. In what follows, I am heavily indebted to Charles Nyamiti, "African Christologies Today," in *Faces of Jesus in Africa,* 3–23.

Africans do not approach the Bible as a collection of doctrines and philosophical speculations about Christ but as a storybook. Long before "narrative theology" emerged in academic studies (an approach that attempts to honor Scripture in its original story form), Africans listened to and told others—indeed, hearing and speaking are crucial to their culture—the story of Christ. That story is received with great fascination. In fact, the average African Christian takes the story at face value. The kind of critical-historical questioning so common in the West is foreign to African Christians. African culture is at home with the stories of unusual events, miracles, visions, prophecies, and healings. Questions such as "Did it really happen?" are replaced by amazement: "How great a God we have." A Bultmannian attempt to demythologize the story of Jesus Christ is both unnecessary and damaging to African understanding.

The context of the historical Jesus as wandering teacher, miracle worker, and prophet is much closer to African culture than to any Western culture. He had a traceable line of descent, a family with which he lived, and a village and community with which he identified. Ironically, Africans "are so attached to the historical Jesus that they often reject attempts to depict him as an African in painting or sculpture. They know that Jesus was not a Yoruba or Kikuyu. They know he was a Jew, and have accepted him in spite of that."[5] Africans are fascinated by pilgrimages to the Holy Land because such journeys bring them close to the earthly realities of Jesus.

The other approach one could take for a local Christology involves beginning with an existing cultural reality, in this case the African milieu, and working backward to the Bible. This approach was taken by Efoe Julien Penoukou in his attempt to understand the meaning of Christ in light of the Ewe-Mina tribe of Togo.[6] This tribal culture is based on a worldview in which God, human beings, and the world form a symbiotic unity. Life is seen beyond death, and death is understood as a necessary passage to life.

Christ, the one who exited before all and emptied himself by becoming one of us, is the mediator between God the Father and creation. Because everything was created through Christ, the incarnation, the coming to flesh of an eternal God, is the supreme example of the union between God and the world. Christ's resurrection, which signifies the defeat of the power of death and evil, is the sign of hope for this culture, which naturally looks beyond death even while fearing it. To the Ewe-Mina, Christ represents *Jete*-Ancestor, the source of life. "An ancestor is, according to the Ewe-Mina, co-fecundator of birth and is capable of providing to many newly born children the necessary vital energy for his apparition in them. Christ as *Jete*-Ancestor

5. Onaiyekan, "Christological Trends," 360.
6. See Efoe Julien Penoukou, "Christology in the Village," in *Faces of Jesus in Africa*, 24–51.

means that he is the Ancestor who is the source of life and the fulfillment of the cosmotheandric relationship in the world."[7]

In fact, Christology from the perspective of ancestor has been one of the main directions explored by African theologians, especially from East and Central Africa. The next chapter offers a detailed look into Benezet Bujo's theology of Christ as the Proto-Ancestor. Another noted African Christologist who has pursued this line of questioning, Nyamiti, titled his book in a way that identifies African Christology with the idea of ancestor: *Christ as Our Ancestor: Christology from an African Perspective.*[8] Ancestors are believed to acquire supernatural status and are therefore able to act as mediators between human beings and God. Because of their kinship with their descendants, they are concerned about their descendents' welfare. For the Bantus (an African tribe), Christ is "Brother Ancestor" and fulfills their expectations of an ancestor to an eminent degree.

Linked with the concept of ancestor is that of kinsman. Jesus, the biblical Christ, is "the firstborn over all creation" (Col. 1:15). Born of God (John 1:13), in participation with our Kinsman, we have the hope of becoming children of God and thus acquiring the status of kinship with Jesus. African kinship involves a relationship of strong solidarity not only horizontally among living members but also vertically with deceased members of the community.

African cultures have many symbols that highlight various aspects of Christ's personality, his relationship with humans, and his work. Bantu Christians call Christ Chief.[9] There are several facets to this role. Christ has conquered and triumphed over Satan and thus is a hero. The figure of the Bantu chief is closely associated with the role of hero. Christ is also called Chief because he is the Son of the Chief, God. The belief that God is the Chief of the entire universe is part of Bantu religion, and Bantus learned that Christ is the Son of God from Christian revelation. Bantus also call a special person chief if he is able to protect and strengthen the life of a group and its individuals. At the same time, the supreme chief is supposed to be "bicephalous," his this-worldly face concealing a region of the beyond. As a result, the Bantu chief is placed at the intersection of the earthly and the beyond, a sphere called the region of the strong. The Bantu chief is not necessarily strong in a physical, muscular way but has the strength of a "participation in being."

Christ is Chief also by reason of generosity. Bantus demand that their chiefs be examples of generosity and wisdom and have a spirit of conciliation. As a generous chief, a leader is able to be an agent of reconciliation. He is a

7. Nyamiti, "African Christologies Today," 5.

8. Charles Nyamiti, *Christ as Our Ancestor: Christology from an African Perspective* (Gwero, Zimbabwe: Mambo Press, 1984).

9. François Kabasele, "Christ as Chief," in *Faces of Jesus in Africa,* 103–15.

"*cinkunku*-who-gathers-the-hunters." He is like a giant tree in whose shade are found all who have taken part in a hunt, there to share the spoils and swap accounts of the adventures they have had.

These and other similar characteristics that can be found in Jesus Christ make him an ideal Chief in the Bantu tradition. The authority of such a Chief is expressed by various cultural means such as the leopard skin (leopards are highly respected). Great chiefs can be called "chiefs-by-the-leopard" or simply "leopard-mother." The solemn vesture of the chief includes two leopard skins, one before and one behind. Other appropriate cultural means of expressing the authority of the chief include the ax, the spear, and elephant stakes, which are symbols of brave leaders.

Incarnation as the Fulfillment of Being Authentically Black

In Christian theology, the theme of Christ's incarnation has taken several forms. In many Christologies, the idea of the eternal God becoming a mortal human being and overcoming corruption is one of the leading ideas. For Africans, the conception of personality and what makes one a human being is a crucial topic. For a culture that looks at personality in vitalistic, dynamic terms, the idea of incarnation opens up new horizons: "Incarnation is the highest fulfillment of personality as understood by the African. For the African, to achieve personality is to become truly human and, in a sense, authentically black; hence, the incarnate Logos is the black Person par excellence. There is, therefore, no genuine blackness or negritude outside him."[10]

Therefore, it is understandable that for Africans the Gospels' narrative about the life of Christ is already a local theology. Several episodes in the life cycle of Christ, such as his birth, baptism, and death, have meaning to Africans who celebrate and honor crucial turning points of life with the help of various rites. Jesus was initiated according to Jewish tradition when he was circumcised. His dedication at the temple and his passage into puberty and later into adulthood were marked by rites of passage from one life stage to another, not unlike the life cycle rituals in most African communities. Even Jesus' act of washing the feet of his disciples at the Last Supper is seen as a gesture of initiation; Jesus, the Master, initiates his followers into his own lifestyle. As such, Christ acts as the head and master of initiation: Having been made perfect, he is the head of those who obey him (Heb. 5:9). In general, African Christology discovers in Christ's life a gradual movement toward a goal, toward perfection, as mentioned in Hebrews 2:10.

---

10. Nyamiti, "African Christologies Today," 5.

Christ as the Head of the Family

The concept of communion is fundamental to understanding the African mind-set. This sense of community reflects the deeply rooted African conviction that it is only in the community that people in general and Christians in particular can find the meaning to their lives. Communal living is the way to promote and maintain the well-being of the individual and of society in general. According to Kofi Asare Opoku:

> If I gain my humanity by entering into a relationship with other members of the family, both living and dead, then it follows that my humanity comes to me as a gift. This does not mean to say that it is not mine, that my being is part of the group, so that I have no individual value and destiny. It means rather that it is not something that I can acquire, or develop, by my own isolated power. I can only exercise or fulfill my humanity as long as I remain in touch with others, *for it is they who empower me.*[11]

Perhaps no one has put this idea as succinctly as Mbiti in his delightful maxim, "I am because we are, and since we are, therefore I am."[12] Even the concept of freedom, so precious to the Western mind-set, has a special communitarian slant to it in Africa: Individuals cannot be free unless they first contribute to the freedom of the whole community and vice versa.

Some theologians, therefore, have proposed that the clan, rather than a Western structure, might be the appropriate model for looking at the nature of the human being in the African context. Often in the African context, conceptions of Christ have less to do with who Christ is than with how he relates to us. This perspective deals not as much with the titles of Christ as with a type of relation. Penoukou puts it clearly:

> Once we have been willing to posit the Christological question in a perspective of relation, it will no longer be reducible simply to the identity or entity of Jesus Christ. Now it will have to be defined as relationship with others, as a mode of being-in-relation in the overall dynamics of salvation history. Thus, Jesus Christ is important not only by reason of his function, or what he has done "for us men and for our salvation," but also for his position in the mystery of the trinitarian, communitarian God. . . . As we know, an African will readily speak of an essentially relational God, a God in solidarity, rather than of a solitary one. Christology above all, then, will be primarily trinitarian and ecclesial.[13]

11. Quoted in Cephas N. Omenyo, "Essential Aspects of African Ecclesiology: The Case of the African Independent Churches," *Pneuma* 22, no. 2 (2000): 236, italics in text.
12. John S. Mbiti, *African Religions and Philosophy,* 2d ed. (London: Heinemann, 1989), 106.
13. Penoukou, "Christology in the Village," 25.

Related to the idea of the community are family-related images of Christ drawn from African cultures and employed by African Christologies. Christ as the Elder Brother, an idea that can also be found in the biblical account of Christ as the "firstborn" (Col. 1:15–20), relates to the African conception of the family and the village as the primary network of life. Personality for Africans does not denote individuality but belonging to community. This idea comes to focus, for example, in the Akan conception of the human being who is able to fulfill himself or herself only in society. J. S. Pobee has suggested that what is most distinctive about Akan Christology is its emphasis on Christ's kinship, circumcision, and baptism as rites of incorporation into the community.[14] By emphasizing the idea of community, some African theologians have developed the idea of Christ as the founder of the great family, the church.

The Healer

African culture is oriented to healing in both the physical and the mental realms. Health means not only a lack of sickness but also well-being in a holistic sense. Sickness is not primarily a result of physical symptoms; it is a deeply spiritual event. One of the differences between Western churches and African churches grows out of the distinctive worldview prevalent in various African cultures. On the basis of their worldview, Africans see spiritual and physical beings as real entities that interact with one another in time and space. These African Christians reject both the secularist worldview and Western conceptions of reality and spirit. "Orthodoxy" has left Christians helpless in real life; therefore, an alternative theology is needed that relates to the entire range of needs that humans have. These include the spiritual but are not limited to abstract, otherworldly, spiritual needs. African religions in general, Christianity included, serve existential needs and relate to everyday issues more than do their Western counterparts. Religion is expected to make life worth living, to maintain and protect life against illness, enemies, and death.

For many African Christologists, healing is the central feature of the life and ministry of Jesus Christ. Aylward Shorter has compared the Galilean healers, whose techniques were adopted by Jesus, with the traditional African medicine men and has discovered many similarities between the two traditions.[15] Both practice a holistic form of healing on the physical, mental, social, and even environmental levels. But in contrast to the healers both of Jesus'

14. See Nyamiti, "African Christologies Today," 6–7.
15. Aylward Shorter, *Jesus and the Witchdoctor: An Approach to Healing and Wholeness* (Maryknoll, N.Y.: Orbis, 1985).

time and in the African context, Christ was the "wounded healer" who became a healer through the pain and suffering of the cross.

Of all Christian traditions, Pentecostalism and later Charismatic movements have focused on the role of Jesus Christ as the healer. A rapidly growing "Pentecostalization" is taking place in Africa, with many traditional churches adopting Pentecostal-type worship patterns, prayer services, and healing ministries. A major attraction of Pentecostalism in African contexts has been its emphasis on healing. In these cultures, the religious specialist or "person of God" has power to heal the sick and ward off evil spirits and sorcery. This holistic function, which does not separate the physical from the spiritual, is restored in Pentecostalism, and indigenous people see it as a powerful religion to meet human needs. For some Pentecostals, faith in God's power to heal directly through prayer resulted in a rejection of other methods of healing. Especially in the so-called African Instituted Churches (sometimes called African Independent Churches), many of which border between Christianity and traditional religions, charismatic healings are an integral part of theology and spirituality.

African Pentecostalism is in constant interaction with the African spirit world. Allan H. Anderson of South Africa (now teaching at the University of Birmingham, England), one of the leading analysts of these indigenous spiritualist movements, contends that in Africa the Pentecostal and Pentecostal-like movements manifested in thousands of indigenous churches have radically changed the face of Christianity. They have done so by proclaiming a holistic gospel of salvation that includes deliverance from all types of oppression such as sickness, sorcery, evil spirits, and poverty. This has met the needs of Africans more fundamentally than the rather spiritualized and intellectualized gospel that was the legacy of European and North American missionaries:

> All the widely differing Pentecostal movements have important common features: they proclaim and celebrate a salvation (or "healing") that encompasses all of life's experiences and afflictions, and they offer an empowerment which provides a sense of dignity and a coping mechanism for life, and all this drives their messengers forward into a unique mission.[16]

Christ, along with his Spirit, the Holy Spirit, is understood as the healer and protector. Healing from and protection against evil forces manifest the power of Christ. With their charismatically oriented Pentecostal-type spiritu-

16. Allan H. Anderson, "The Gospel and Culture in Pentecostal Missions in the Third World" (paper presented at the Conference of the European Pentecostal Charismatic Theological Association, Missionsakademie, University of Hamburg, Germany, 15 July 1999), 11; also published in *Missionalia* 27, no. 2 (1999): 220–30.

ality, many contemporary African healing services sometimes use means such as speaking in tongues as the prelude to a prophetic diagnostic session during which the Holy Spirit reveals to the prophet the cause of a patient's illness. All the symbols used during healing rituals, such as holy water, paper, staffs, and holy cords, symbolize the power of Christ and his Spirit over all destructive forces.

In the prophetic movements of the African Instituted Churches, the activity of the Healer, Jesus Christ, has never been restricted to spiritual matters or even to physical healing alone; he is also the Spirit of justice and liberation. The late bishop Samuel Mutendi of Zion Christian Church in Zimbabwe entered the political arena by opposing the colonial administration on education, land, and religious issues. The spiritual mobilization of the community to take action was effected through sermons, prayer, and a role model, often accompanied with prophecies. The Holy Spirit was depicted as the "guardian of the land" who was directing the liberation fighters. The African way of life is more holistic than that of the West, and therefore, the concept of healing is also related to earthkeeping. In the post-Independence period in Zimbabwe, starting in 1980, many African Instituted Churches increasingly turned their attention to various development projects. For example, several churches started nurseries for exotic fruit and indigenous trees at or near prophetic church headquarters. Jesus Christ's function as healer and life-giver encompassed everything relating to human well-being, including the healing and protection of crops.

Contemporary Challenges for African Christologies

According to Benezet Bujo, with all the positive developments in African theology, there is also a danger: the tendency of theology to dwell exclusively on the African cultural heritage:

> It is of course true that this heritage must be one aspect of a genuinely African theology, and that any attempt to incarnate the Christian message in African culture must take it into account. However, while this tendency speaks of understanding the faith, . . . it ignores the contemporary African context. One must therefore ask whether such a theology can speak seriously of either understanding the faith or of incarnating the message of Christ today.[17]

Indeed, a dilemma is to be found in the development of African Christologies. On the one hand, there is a pronounced need to appropriate cultural elements drawn from the long history of the various peoples of the continent.

17. Benezet Bujo, *African Theology in Its Social Context* (Maryknoll, N.Y.: Orbis, 1992), 15.

On the other hand, as a result of rapid change and a transformation of the societies, often accompanied by a diminishing of traditional beliefs, there is a need to fashion Christologies that speak to contemporary concerns of Africans. Many African Christologies that are authentically African, based on the history and beliefs of past cultures, are no longer relevant to urbanized, modernized Africans, many of whom have received a Western education and are influenced by Western mass media. This is especially the case with regard to youth. Many African Christologies, says Onaiyekan, "are so concerned with the past cultures of Africa that they become irrelevant to our contemporary African needs and concerns." Consequently, it "is possible to end up in a sort of exotic archaeological theology, which may perhaps fascinate foreigners, but has nothing relevant to say to the day-to-day life of our Christians."[18]

One way to avoid this lurking irrelevancy is to pay attention to the contemporary sociopolitical dimension to help restore the needed balance. One of the contemporary images of Christ in Africa is Jesus as the Liberator. While it comes from Latin America, as shown above, the idea of Jesus as the Liberator is not foreign to African soil, and it has taken various forms in the African context. One of those is the South African "black theology" discussed earlier. In some other parts of Africa, the idea of Jesus as the Liberator is concerned with poverty, economic oppression, and a lack of access to education.

Christ as the Liberator is often joined with the idea of Christ as Reconciler, as in the work of the South African Anglican bishop Desmond Tutu. This Jesus is the Jesus of justice and peace. Peace and reconciliation is needed not only in South Africa, with its tragic history of conflict between the dominant white race and oppressed black people, but also in the rest of Africa, where blacks are oppressing other blacks. Many contemporary African rulers, not unlike their colonial white predecessors, have invoked Christian concepts to consolidate and misuse their power over their own people.

Another burning issue in contemporary Africa is the relationship between Christianity and the major religions of the area, especially Islam and traditional African religions. This brings the christological question into focus: What is the role of Christ vis-à-vis the hopes and conceptions of saviors in other religions? In such a context, the universal rule of Christ in relation to the claims of universality made by Islam and other religions has to be carefully considered, as does the saving role of Christ with regard to followers of other religions.

In sum, a genuine, relevant African Christology for the third millennium needs to avoid both a traditionalist attempt to preserve African culture in a mindless fashion and a reformist neglect of African roots.

---

18. Onaiyekan, "Christological Trends," 366.

28

Benezet Bujo

Christ as Ancestor

Christ as the Proto-Ancestor

One of the main images African Christology employs in describing the unique role of Christ is ancestor. According to many African theologians, the conception of ancestor might be the most accurate way of describing the meaning of Christ. Benezet Bujo maintains that in Africa the *gesta* (spirits) of ancestors are constantly reenacted through ritual. This enables an African to recall these *gesta* and to conform his or her conduct to them. This is the starting point for Bujo's reflection on the mystery of Christ, whom he considers the Proto-Ancestor, the unique ancestor, the source of life and highest model of ancestorship.

> Through the incarnation Christ assumed the whole of human history, including the legitimate aspirations of our ancestors. This assumption of the future which the ancestors sought to guarantee is assured because our ancestors' experiences have been made efficacious in Jesus, crucified and risen. Thus the incarnation enables Christ to be the unique and privileged locus of total encounter with our ancestors and allows them to be the locus where we encounter the God of salvation.[1]

1. Charles Nyamiti, "African Christologies Today," in *Faces of Jesus in Africa*, ed. R. J. Schreiter (Maryknoll, N.Y.: Orbis, 1991), 10.

Obviously, the idea of Christ as ancestor is more meaningful to the typical African than, say, *Logos* or Messiah or *Kyrios*. It allows the culture of Africa to have a bearing on the understanding of faith in Christ. When Africans honor ancestors, they are, at least implicitly, also honoring God.

Bujo is not indifferent to the negative sides of pre-Christian traditional religions of Africa and their mistaken conceptions and practices; nevertheless, he believes that an authentically African theology and Christology have to be founded on African culture, just as the early church's understanding of Christ was grounded in the soil of Greek culture. Christ as the *Proto*-Ancestor represents all the good and positive elements of the African cult of ancestors and serves as the critic of its less honorable features. Bujo contends that Jesus Christ as Proto-Ancestor not only brings to realization the ancient African belief in the supremacy of the ancestors but also transcends and refines it in light of biblical revelation.

> If we look back on the historical Jesus of Nazareth, we can see in him, not only one who lived in the African ancestor-ideal in the highest degree, but one who brought that ideal to an altogether new fulfillment. Jesus worked miracles, healing the sick, opening the eyes of the blind, raising the dead to life. In short, he brought life, and life-force, in its fullness. He lived his mission for his fellow-humans in an altogether matchless way, and furthermore, left to his disciples, as his final commandment, the law of love.[2]

To better understand the African idea of Christ as Proto-Ancestor, we need to examine some of the governing background ideas of African thought and belief systems as they are explicated by Bujo in his book *African Theology in Its Social Context,* the name of which emphasizes the communal nature of African Christology. The idea of life as the most profound gift from God is the leading motif, and Christ's role as Proto-Ancestor is integrally related to that idea.

Life as a Gift from God

Life for Africans is so central that it is characterized as sacred. Long before the arrival of Christianity in Africa, African religion recognized God as the source of all life, especially human life. Holistic in their approach, Africans conceive of life not by making distinctions but by seeing all life, whether social, psychological, or spiritual, as constituting an undivided entity. Physical life is not something to be abhorred but something to be cel-

2. Benezet Bujo, *African Theology in Its Social Context* (Maryknoll, N.Y.: Orbis, 1992), 79.

ebrated and honored. Physical life can be considered a dimension of religious faith and patrimony.

For Africans, then, God possesses fullness of life. The Bahema and the Walendu of Zaire call God self-sufficient, in need of no outside support. The Banyarwanda and the Barundi call God the source of life and the one who acts in a living way. God alone is creator; God alone is the source of life, strength, and growth.

Life means participation in God, but this participation is always mediated by one standing above the recipient in the hierarchy of the universe. The hierarchy applies to both the invisible and the visible worlds. In the invisible world, the highest rank is given to God, the source and energy of life. Next are the founding fathers of clans, who participate most fully in the life of God. They are followed by the tribal heroes, deceased elders, other deceased members of the extended family, and so on.

Life is unity for Africans, an insight that carries several implications. There is continuous traffic between the visible and the invisible realms, between the dead and the living. In fact, every member of the clan is expected to maintain and cherish this communication with the dead. Physical death does not mean that ties are cut, as it does in the West. In fact, ancestors live on in their descendents. Life as unity also has a mystical nature in most African cultures. Life is transmitted from God to ancestors to other members of the community. God as the giver of life, with the help of ancestors who are regarded as the models for life, has the prerogative to lay down rules for the life of the community, including various taboos and laws. These are meant for the protection of the community and harmony of life.

Living members of this "mystical communion" have an inalienable responsibility to protect and prolong the life of the community. The responsibility to cherish and protect life, of course, belongs primarily to the leaders and ancestors, but it is also the task of every member of the community:

> Every member of the community, down to the least significant, shares the responsibility for strengthening the force of the tribe or clan and of each of its members. The morality of an act is determined by its life-giving potential: good acts are those which contribute to the community's vital force, whereas bad diminish life. African society is a real "mystical body," encompassing both dead and living members, in which every member has an obligation to every other.[3]

The head of this mystical body is the founder-ancestor (an ancestor who is venerated as a semi-divine figure). It is from him that the life force flows into all the members of the community, and it returns to him. Life can be enjoyed in its fullness only when the ancestors are remembered and honored.

3. Ibid., 22.

The Cult of the Ancestors

The African ancestor cult is not organized around fixed times but is part of everyday life. According to Bujo, communion with the ancestors has both an eschatological and a soteriological dimension:

> Salvation is the concern of both the living and the dead members of the society, for all affect each other and depend upon each other. The dead can only be happy when they live on in the affectionate remembrance of the living; nevertheless, they are stronger than the living, on whom they exercise a decisive influence, since the living cannot hope even to survive unless they render due honour to their dead and continue faithfully along the track laid down by them.[4]

Even though for Africans salvation has to do with earthly happiness and harmony, there is an eternal or eschatological dimension to it; salvation involves participation in the other world, where the "dead live." Funeral rites express Africans' belief in the life after physical death. Strength and life force are expected from those who have already gone to the invisible world. For example, the father who becomes an ancestor bestows on his descendants everything needed for a life of fullness. Fullness of life is available only to persons who look to their ancestors for guidance and protection. The rituals are ways of remembering and reenacting the past, and their repetition constitutes a guarantee of prosperity for future generations.

The importance of the cult of ancestors is enhanced by the fact that ancestors are regarded as models for the living. Success or failure in one's life is based on a personal choice: "In freely recalling the life-giving actions and words of the ancestors, a person is choosing life; but in neglecting these things, that person is choosing death."[5] The particular words, actions, and rituals associated with the ancestors have a deep meaning in the life of African people. They constitute a rule of conduct for the living, and they must be repeated continually.

The story of Jesus washing the feet of his disciples at the Last Supper (John 13) has a particular significance in light of the African conception of Jesus as the Proto-Ancestor. The time he spent with his disciples was like the final hour a parent spends with his or her children before death. He or she gathers the children to give them a blessing and to pronounce the last will. Only those who carry out the terms of the will have life: "Now that you know these things, you will be blessed if you do them" (John 13:17).

4. Ibid., 24.
5. Ibid., 30.

The Unique Ancestorship of Jesus Christ

In his earthly life, Jesus manifested all the qualities and virtues that Africans like to attribute to their ancestors and that lead them to invoke their ancestors in daily life. Positive elements such as hospitality, a sense of family, and care for the elderly, the orphaned, and the unfortunate were taken up by Jesus and brought to completion. As *Proto*-Ancestor, Jesus not only fulfilled the expectations of an ideal ancestor but also transcended that idea and brought it to completion. No other ancestor is capable of such a deed. In Christian theology, Jesus Christ is connected with the imminent rule of God in his kingdom. This internal relation to the kingdom of God distinguishes Jesus from all other ancestors.

According to Bujo, then, the idea of Jesus as the Proto-Ancestor is not a superficial concession to existing cultural need. It is not a cheap technique of contextualization to make Christ relevant to Africans. It is connected to the biblical idea of God's Word becoming human (John 1:14). God assumed human form and became part of this world. "This implies that henceforth God can no longer be the 'Unchangeable One'; God has taken changeableness. . . . The kenosis, the emptying, happened."[6] Incarnation is God's highest self-expression; it is a real meeting place between the divine and the human. Jesus of Nazareth is not only the total and final revelation of God but also of humankind. It is within this perspective that Jesus Christ is the Proto-Ancestor for the African.

> Jesus, the Christ, identified himself with humankind, so that he constitutes their explanation. From now on, Jesus makes his own all the striving of the ancestors after righteousness and all their history, in such a way that these have now become a meeting-place with God of salvation. Above all, Jesus Christ himself becomes the privileged locus for a full understanding of the ancestors. The African now has something to say about the mystery of the Incarnation, for after God has spoken to us at various times and in various places, including our ancestors, in these last days God speaks to us through the Son, whom God has established as unique Ancestor, as Proto-Ancestor, from whom all life flows for God's descendants (cf. Heb 1,1–2).[7]

For Bujo, one of the advantages of speaking of Jesus Christ as the Proto-Ancestor is that African anthropocentrism, manifested in ancestor-oriented patterns of thought, is central for incarnating Christianity in Africa. The starting point is Christology from below, but not to the exclusion of Christology from above. It is crucial that Christianity shows Africans that being truly Christian and being truly African are not opposed to each other. This is

6. Ibid., 82.
7. Ibid., 83.

possible only if Jesus Christ is firmly anchored in the thought forms and patterns of African culture, as he is rooted in other cultures.

A truly African ancestor Christology, as developed by Bujo and others, also brings to the fore the full trinitarian explication of a culturally sensitive theology. Jesus' ancestorship is not just an external feature, for Jesus was the eternal Son of God, totally dedicated to, or initiated into (as Africans prefer to express it), God, and he manifested that dedication in the world. "The Father has the fullness of eternal life and begets the Son. They live for each other in a total and vital union, mutually reinforcing their common life. The vital power goes out from the Father to beget the Son and finally returns to the father."[8] This vital union, which produces the interaction between Father and Son, is nothing other than the Holy Spirit, the bond between the Father and the Son.

If Jesus Christ is the Proto-Ancestor, the source of life and happiness, then the task of his descendants is to bring to realization in their lives the memory of his life, passion, death, and resurrection. The Proto-Ancestor is the goal and criterion of all life, including ethics. Bujo's distinctive contribution to African Christology involves its ethical and social dimensions. For example, with regard to political life, Bujo notes that if Christ as the Proto-Ancestor is given priority, African vices such as corruption, abuse of power, and the like can be overcome. Jesus' life and words as the Proto-Ancestor serve as criticism of unethical and oppressive behavior and attitudes.

Finally, the cross brings to fulfillment the uniqueness of Jesus' ancestorship. The cross will always remain a scandal and folly even for Africans. Only the African who has been converted and has faith will see in the crucified Jesus the Proto-Ancestor with whom he or she can identify. "Jesus is Proto-Ancestor, the eschatological Adam, the life-giving principle (1 Cor. 15:45), only because he passed through death on the cross. It is the remembering of this event, and the retelling of it, that is both liberating and challenging." According to Bujo, this is what "humanizes and purifies the African ethos."[9]

Christ as the Brother Ancestor

Whereas Bujo developed an African ancestor Christology in terms of Christ as the Proto-Ancestor, Charles Nyamiti describes Christ as the Brother Ancestor. He claims that while there is no uniform ancestor religion among the black African tribal societies, enough beliefs are shared by these societies to enable one to affirm the presence of a common ancestral belief. He argues that two elements are characteristic of the African view of ancestorship: a

8. Ibid., 86.
9. Ibid., 91.

"natural" relationship between the ancestor and the living, and a "supernatural" or sacred status acquired by the deceased ancestor. The natural relationship can be based on a blood relationship. To attain the supernatural or sacred status, the dead person must have led a morally holy life that enables him or her to serve as a model for the descendants.

Nyamiti says that according to the cultural beliefs of the African continent, the ancestral relationship between the living and the dead, and sometimes between the Supreme Being and humanity on earth, comprises the following elements:

1. Kinship between the dead and the living. In many cases, the ancestor also has to be the source of life for the earthly relatives.
2. Superhuman status, usually acquired through death, comprising nearness to God, sacred powers, and other superhuman qualities.
3. Mediation between God and the earthly kin.
4. Exemplary behavior in community.
5. Right or title to frequent sacred communication with the living kin through prayers and ritual offerings.

Theologically, it is highly significant that Nyamiti draws parallels between the ancestral relationship on the human level and the inner life of the Triune God. He maintains that there is an ancestral kinship among the divine persons: The Father is the Ancestor of the Son; the Son is the Descendant of the Father. These two persons live their ancestral kinship through the Spirit, whom they mutually communicate to as their ancestral "Oblation" and Eucharist. "The Spirit is reciprocally donated not only in token of their mutual love as Gift but also on behalf of the homage to their reciprocal holiness (as Oblation) and gratitude to their beneficence to each other (as Eucharist, from the Greek: *eucharistein* 'to thank')."[10]

With regard to Christian veneration of ancestors, which is part of the Catholic tradition, Nyamiti distinguishes four types. First, the traditional ancestors (African ancestors in general) take part in the Christian veneration of ancestors in terms of incorporation into the body of Christ (as, for example, in Hebrews 11). Second, the saints in heaven and in purgatory are regarded as brother ancestors. Third, Jesus Christ is considered *the* Brother Ancestor. Fourth, God himself as the Parent Ancestor is the source of all.[11]

Nyamiti offers a detailed comparison between Jesus Christ and African brother ancestors. Commonalities include such aspects as the following:

- blood relationship
- supernatural powers

10. Nyamiti, "African Christologies Today," 11.
11. Ibid., 10–13.

- mediation between the father and his human brothers
- the role of an ethical model
- communication between Christ and his followers through prayers and the mass
- designated places for worship

But there are also divergences, some of which are:

- Christ transcends all limitations of kinship.
- Christ attained to his sacred status by death and resurrection.
- Christ communicates salvation.
- The descent of Christ is divine rather than human.
- The Holy Spirit also has an important role in Christian life.

The Growing Tradition of Ancestor Christologies

Bujo's and Nyamiti's ancestor Christologies, while the best known currently, are not the only versions available in the growing body of ancestor Christologies in Africa. In Muntu Christology, Jesus' words to Thomas, "I am the way and the truth and the life. No one comes to the Father except through me" (John 14:6), bring to mind for a Muntu the persons who are the source of life and obligatory route to the Supreme Being: the ancestors. The saying of the Johannine Jesus about the vine reminds Bantus of the importance of ongoing contact with ancestors for the maintenance of life. The interdependence among the members of a Bantu clan reminds them of a liquid being poured from one to all the others. Life is comparable to such a liquid; the individual receives it from the first vessel, which represents his or her ancestor. For Bantus, then, Christ is the last Adam who gives life (1 Cor. 15:45).

Bujo argues that the real starting point of African theology came from a European Franciscan missionary in the Belgian Congo named Placide Temples. One of his lasting findings was that the African religion and worldview generally centered around "vital force," or "life force." Temples went so far as to claim that for the African, "to be" was the same as "to have life force." Temples linked the African search for life with the Johannine Gospel, in which Jesus said that he had come to bring life and to bring it in abundance (John 10:10):

> If Jesus is truly the Way, the Truth and the Life, then he is the final answer to the aspirations of the whole human race and not only of Africans. All human cultures manifest the human longing for fullness of life. In seeking to christianize these cultures, missionaries must put aside their own Western culture, repu-

diate it even, in order to adapt themselves to their people of adoption. . . . This is how the living Christ encounters the many races and cultures of people, it is thus that Christianity is born, and thus that different people come together to uncover the gospel in common.[12]

In the Bantu tradition, God first communicated the divine vital force to the ancestors. Thus, they constitute the highest link, after God, in the chain of beings. The parallels between such a tradition and Christ have several facets:

1. Life: The primary roles of the ancestors are to transmit and to safeguard life; they are our origins, our sources of life. Christ came to give life and to give it abundantly (John 10:10; 17:2).
2. Presence: The Bantu ancestors are not dead but alive. The European ancestors are a memory; the Bantu ancestors are a presence. While one remembers the former, one invokes the latter. Christ is present always with his own (Matt. 28:20).
3. The eldest: For Bantus, being the eldest child is a place of honor. These children are closer to the source and foundation, to God. Christ, God's only Son, receives the attribute of "eldest" because he is the firstborn (Col. 1:15).
4. Mediation: The African universe is hierarchical: All beings share in the life of the Supreme Being on different levels according to their nature. But this participation is indirect. Bantu ancestors serve as mediators. Christ is the mediator of everything (Hebrews 8).[13]

It was not until the twentieth century that an authentic African theology in general and Christology in particular began to emerge. Various African customs, cultural features, and traditional beliefs play into a distinctive appropriation of the person and work of Christ. Features such as communalism and a desire for healing, typical biblical emphases, are gaining new significance in the renaissance of African Christologies.

Having surveyed both Latin American and African contextualized interpretations of Jesus Christ, it is time to turn to the most populated continent, Asia, and to inquire into the various ways Christology takes shape in that religious and cultural context.

12. Bujo, *African Theology in Its Social Context*, 57.
13. François Kabasele, "Christ as Ancestor and Elder Brother," in *Faces of Jesus in Africa*, 120–26.

29

Christology in Asia

Search for Meaning

The Critical Asian Principle

There is a quiet determination among Asian Christians that their commitment
to Jesus Christ and their words about Jesus Christ must be responsible to the
life they live in Asia today. Such theology is called a living theology. . . . Asian
theology seeks to take the encounter between life in Asia and the Word of God
seriously.[1]

With these words, Kosuke Koyama, one of the best-known Asian theologians from Japan, introduced an anthology of essays on the themes of emerging Asian theologies. While Asia is the cradle of most of the major religions
in the world, it was not until the last part of the twentieth century that contributions to Christian theology began to emerge there on a large scale. What
is distinctive about the Asian context is the continuous correlation between
Christian theology and the pluralism of Asian religiosity. Also, Asian churches
have been on the forefront of ecumenism. The groundbreaking work of the
Ecumenical Association of Third World Theologians (EAOTWT), founded
in 1976, has fostered both interreligious and ecumenical activities.

1. Kosuke Koyama, "Foreword by an Asian Theologian," in *Asian Christian Theology:
Emerging Themes,* ed. Douglas J. Elwood (Philadelphia: Westminster, 1980), 13.

It is not easy to divide Asia, the continent where currently more than half of the world's population lives, into various theological centers. For heuristic reasons, however, that kind of classification might be helpful. Theologically, perhaps the most fertile soil has been India and Sri Lanka, with their strong Hindu influence. Because of the long tradition of English-speaking education, these countries have contributed significantly to emerging international discussions. Another center of theological thinking is rising in Korea, with its phenomenal church growth. Korean theology ranges from fairly conservative evangelical theology that cuts across denominational boundaries to a more liberal strand of Asian pluralism and *minjung* theology (to be discussed). A cluster of Asian countries in which Buddhism has played a major role includes China, Taiwan, Thailand, and Japan. Some Japanese theologians, such as Koyama, have made headway into the international theological academy, as has the Taiwanese Choan-Seng Song. The predominantly Catholic Philippines stands in its own category, as does Indonesia, which is strongly influenced by Islam. Hinduism and Buddhism exert influence in other areas of Indonesia.

In any Asian country, Christians are the minority. This fact has implications for Asian theologies when compared to European and U.S. theologies, which are often written from the standpoint of Christianity being a major force in society. The thrust of Asian theology is to inquire into the identity of Christianity vis-à-vis other religious confessions. Koyama aptly notes the various forces that shape Asian Christianity as Asians address the question, "Who do you say I am?" (Matt. 16:15):

> This question comes to Asian Christians, who live in a world of great religious traditions, modernization impacts, ideologies of the left and right, international conflicts, hunger, poverty, militarism, and racism. Within these confusing and brutal realities of history the question comes to them. Here the depth of soul of the East is challenged to engage in a serious dialogue with the Word of God. Jesus refuses to be treated superficially.[2]

Asia, like Africa and Latin America, is plagued by poverty and social problems such as immense inequality. Ethnic conflicts abound, and some parts of Asia, such as the Philippines, are still politically unstable.

Yin-Yang

Choan-Seng Song from Taiwan, one of the leading Asian theologians, encourages Asians to write "theology from the womb of Asia."[3] His theology,

---

2. Ibid., 14.
3. Choan-Seng Song, *Theology from the Womb of Asia* (Maryknoll, N.Y.: Orbis, 1986).

called "third-eye" theology, is tuned into seeing Christ not only through Chinese, Japanese, and other Asian eyes but also through African, Latin American, and other eyes; "third-eye" refers to the Buddhist master who opens eyes to see areas that have been unknown. The goal of this kind of authentic Asian theology is "the freedom to encounter Jesus the savior in the depth of the spirituality that sustains Asians in their long march of suffering and hope."[4]

Several Asian theologians talk about the "critical Asian principle" as the main guide to their theology. Following this principle, they seek to identify what is distinctively Asian and to use this distinctiveness in judging matters dealing with the life and mission of the Christian church and theology.

One of the distinctive features of Asian thinking is the reluctance to employ the Western either-or dialectic. Instead, most Asians feel comfortable thinking in terms of yin-yang inclusiveness. This term goes back to Taoism and Confucianism in their Chinese forms. According to such philosophies, change is the interplay of yin and yang. These two terms, crucial to much of Eastern thought (and expressed in different Asian languages and thought forms in varying terminology), mean female-male, weak-strong, light-dark, and so on. But these poles are seen not as opposites but as complements. One can easily imagine how this kind of inclusive thinking might affect one's Christology:

> Jesus as the Christ, as both God and man, cannot really be understood in terms of either/or. How can man also be God? In the West we have to speak in terms of paradox or mystery in order to justify the reality of Christ. However, in *yin-yang* terms, he can be thought of as both God and man at the same time. In him God is not separated from man nor man from God. They are in complementary relationship. He is God because of man: he is man because of God.[5]

Christ in the Interpretations of the Neo-Hindu Reform

Christianity and Hinduism have had an unprecedented encounter during the past two or three centuries with the so-called Indian Renaissance or Neo-Hindu reform. During the nineteenth century and the first part of the twentieth century, various Hindu personalities acknowledged Christ in relation to their own religious backgrounds and contexts. Both M. M. Thomas and Stanley Samartha, whose Christology is studied in the following chapter, have written major studies on this Indian Renaissance. Samartha describes the Christ acknowledged by Neo-Hinduism as an "unbound" Christ. While many attach themselves to the person of Jesus Christ, they usually detach that person from the institutional church, which for them does not represent the

4. Ibid., 3.
5. Jung Young Lee, "The Yin-Yang Way of Thinking," in *Asian Christian Theology,* 87.

quintessence of Christ's religion. They often complain that the church of Jesus' followers is either a hierarchical institution or a Western, even colonial, power system:

> The Christ acknowledged by Hinduism is often a churchless Christ. For that matter, the Christ acknowledged by Hinduism is often a Christ delivered from the encumbrances of numerous "bonds" with which he is laden by traditional Christianity—whether it be a matter of applauding his message while reject-ing the Christian claim to his person, or of receiving him as one divine man-ifestation among others in a catalog of divine descents *(avatara)* as varied as it is extensive.[6]

Understandably, the representatives of Hindu Reform have taken various approaches to the person of Christ. For some, the social teaching of Christ serves as an inspiration but does not involve a personal commitment to him. Mahatma Gandhi is an eminent example here. Others, such as Keshub Chun-der Sen, are committed to Christ but not to the institutional church. Finally, there are Hindus who have become Christians but insist they have remained Hindus. The best-known of these is Brahmabandhab Upadhyaya. The fol-lowing survey explores each of these christological approaches.

Mahatma Gandhi's Jesus is an ethical teacher who expresses the ideal of a new community and way of life in the Beatitudes and other teachings. In those teachings, Gandhi saw the same principles that guided his own pacifis-tic fight for the liberation of the Indian people, namely, *satyagraha* (the search for truth) and *ahimsa* (nonviolence). These values, based on the Hindu religion and culture, were similarly presented by Jesus Christ. As deeply committed as Gandhi was to the teaching of Jesus, especially the Ser-mon on the Mount, he was never able to make a personal commitment to the person of Christ, let alone to the community of the Christian church. What mattered to Gandhi was personal sincerity and loyalty to the authentic identity of one's religious tradition. All religions, he believed, are based in faith in the one and same God, and all are of equal value. For Gandhi, Jesus was a model to imitate and a source of inspiration. Gandhi had no problem affirming Jesus as a special divine manifestation; he could not, however, re-gard Jesus as unique in his personhood. Jesus was one among many inspir-ing, divine teachers. When it came to the historical Jesus, Gandhi was not interested. Whether Jesus of Nazareth really lived did not matter; the Ser-mon on the Mount still counted. Gandhi summarized his attitude toward Jesus Christ in this way:

6. Jacques Dupuis, S.J., *Jesus Christ at the Encounter of World Religions* (Maryknoll, N.Y.: Orbis, 1991), 15.

The message of Jesus, as I understand it, is contained in his Sermon on the Mount. The Spirit of the Sermon on the Mount competes almost on equal terms with the Bhagavadgita for the domination of my heart. It is that Sermon which has endeared Jesus to me. . . .

Though I cannot claim to be a Christian in the sectarian sense, the example of Jesus' suffering is a factor in the composition of my underlying faith in non-violence, which rules all my actions, worldly and temporal.[7]

For Keshub Chunder Sen, a Hindu teacher of the nineteenth century, Christ was the focus of personal devotion *(bhakti)*. Sen reminded his hearers of the fact that Jesus was originally Asian, and therefore, it was appropriate for Indians to venerate him. Jesus was no stranger to Asians but was one of them. Sen summed up his Christology as a "doctrine of the divine humanity."[8] He believed that Christ's humanity was not a stumbling block for Indians but rather the Christian claim of the divinity of Jesus. For Sen, the essential component of Christ's divinity was his oneness with the Father. Christ is "a transparent crystal reservoir in which are the waters of divine life. . . . The 'medium' is transparent, and we clearly see through Christ the God of truth and holiness dwelling in him."[9] The transparency of Jesus, which revealed his Father, was seen in Jesus' total self-abandonment to God and his perfect asceticism, according to Sen. This was a life rooted in divinity.

For Brahmabandhab Upadhyaya, who was once a member of the Church of the New Dispensation, founded by his friend Keshub Chunder Sen, and who later became a Catholic by way of receiving an Anglican baptism, the main task of Christology is to find harmony between Hinduism and Christianity. This task has four essential components:

1. the integration of the Indian social structure into the Christian way of life
2. the founding of an Indian Christian monastic order
3. the use of the categories of the *Vedanta* in Christian theology
4. the acknowledgment of the Vedas as a preparation for the gospel in India, analogous to the place of the Old Testament in the West[10]

Upadhyaya's spirituality was based on a deep personal experience of the person of Jesus, the Son of God, who was at once his *guru* and his friend. Whether Jesus was divine or not did not matter; what mattered was that

7. Mohandas K. Gandhi, *The Message of Jesus Christ* (Bombay: Bharatiya Vidya Bhavan, 1963), cover page and 79 respectively.
8. Quoted in Dupuis, *Jesus Christ at the Encounter of World Religions,* 23.
9. Ibid., 24.
10. See ibid., 38.

Christ claimed to be the Son of God. As a monk, Upadhyaya also understood Jesus Christ in terms of *advaita,* the Hindu mystical experience.

The Universal Christ and the Particular Jesus

The approach of the Indian Renaissance to Christology differed from that of the later Indian theologian Raimundo Panikkar, a Catholic priest from India whose father was Hindu and who spoke of *The Unknown Christ of Hinduism.*[11] Significantly, the book on neo-Hindu Christologies by M. M. Thomas is titled *The Acknowledged Christ of the Indian Renaissance.*[12] For Panikkar, God always works in the world through Christ; where God is present, Christ and the Spirit are also present. This Triune God works in all religions and forms the common foundation for all religions. Thus, Christ, the *Logos,* is present in the holy writings of Hinduism. Christ is also present mystically where people reach for union with God. God himself is the Mystery, Absolute, even though he is not so acknowledged. Panikkar sees correspondences and similarities between Christ and Hindu figures such as *Isvara.*

In his earlier works, Panikkar argued that in the historical Jesus the fullness of revelation had occurred, though not in an exclusive way. But in his revised version of *The Unknown Christ of Hinduism,* published in 1981, he moved toward a pluralistic version of Christology. In that book, he rejected all notions of the fulfillment of other religions in Christianity. His reason was simply that the world and our subjective experience of the world have radically changed since the Christian doctrine concerning Christ was first formulated. Because our experience of the world has changed, our understanding should also be modified.

Panikkar's revised understanding was based on the distinction between the universal Christ and the particular Jesus. This was the key to an "authentically universal" Christology. "Christ is . . . a living symbol for the totality of reality: human, divine, cosmic."[13] As such, Christ represents an intimate and complete unity between the divine and the human. Panikkar called this a "non-dualist vision." God and human being are not two realities but one. God and human being presuppose each other for the building up of reality, the unfolding of history. The confession "Christ is God the Son, the Logos" means that Christ is both symbol and substance of this non-dualistic unity between God and humanity.

11. Raimundo Panikkar, *The Unknown Christ of Hinduism* (London: Darton, Longman & Todd, 1973).

12. M. M. Thomas, *The Acknowledged Christ of the Indian Renaissance* (London: SCM, 1969).

13. Panikkar, *The Unknown Christ of Hinduism,* 27.

But what, then, is the relationship between this universal Christ and the historical Jesus? With Catholic theology he affirmed that the *Logos* or Christ was incarnated in Jesus of Nazareth. But he departed from orthodoxy by denying that this incarnation took place solely and finally in Jesus. Contrary to what he argued in the first edition of *The Unknown Christ of Hinduism,* which posited a unity between Christ and Jesus, he stated that no historical form can be the full, final expression of the universal Christ. The universal symbol for salvation in Christ can never be reduced to a historical personhood. Panikkar claimed, "Christ will never be totally known on earth, because that would amount to seeing the Father whom nobody can see."[14] Total identification between the universal Christ and the historical Jesus would lead in Panikkar's understanding to a sort of idolatrous form of historicism. The saving power of Jesus, indeed, is to be found in the fact that he embodies a reality that is beyond every historical form, the universal Christ. On the other hand, as a Catholic theologian, Panikkar was not willing to give up all historical contours. He issued a warning against diluting the Christian belief that Christ appeared in the form of the historical Jesus. The connection, if not the total identity, is to be maintained, but in a way that does not hinder dialogue with people of other faiths, as it tended to do in the past. For Panikkar, this means that a person can make a genuine confession of Christ, the "Supername" (Phil. 2:9), and yet in one way or another acknowledge that all religions recognize and acknowledge Christ.

On the basis of these considerations, Panikkar believes that the various religions are approaching one another, and he expects a convergence, not necessarily at the doctrinal level but at an existential level, in the cave of the heart, as he puts it. Doctrinal conceptions create differences and conflicts, whereas the meeting of hearts fosters unity. This is the call, in Panikkar's words, of "ecumenical ecumenism." This interreligious ecumenism works from a common origin and goal, a "transcendental principle" or mystery, a basis for shared experience active within all religions. Panikkar calls this shared mystery "the fundamental religious fact" that does not lie in the realm of doctrine, nor even of individual self-consciousness, but is present everywhere and in every religion. The purpose of ecumenical ecumenism is to deepen one's grasp and living of this mystery. For this to happen, all religions, Christianity included, have to give up any claim for uniqueness, let alone absolute normativity.

Lotus and Cross

Choan-Seng Song has attempted, among other things, to establish bridges between Buddhist and Christian religions. The key to his theology in general

14. Cited in Paul F. Knitter, *No Other Name? A Critical Survey of Christian Attitudes toward the World Religions* (Maryknoll, N.Y.: Orbis, 1986), 156.

is "transposition"—a transposition from the Israel-centered view of history to the view that regards other nations as constructive parts of God's design of history. In this view, Israel's role as the people of God was symbolic, illustrating the way God would also deal redemptively with other nations. Asian nations have their own specific moments of salvation history parallel to Israel's exodus, giving of the law, captivity, and so on. Furthermore, the savior figures of Asian religions parallel the savior figure of the Christian faith, Jesus Christ:

> The expression of Buddha's compassion for the masses in his vows and the way he toiled unselfishly for their emancipation from pain and suffering are not without redemptive significance. Can we not say that Buddha's way is also a part of the drama of salvation which God has acted out fully in the person and work of Jesus Christ?[15]

Consequently, the task of the proclamation of Christ on Asian soil is not one of conversion but of growing with Asians in their knowledge and experience of God's saving work in the world. The contribution of Christian missions is to inform the Asian spirituality shaped by Asian cultures and religions of the love of God in Jesus Christ. This helps to move Asian society toward freedom, justice, and love.

Several theologians interested in merging Christian theology with Buddhist concepts have paid attention to the *kenōsis*, or self-emptying, of Christ as explicated especially in Philippians 2:7–11. According to Siddhartha Gautama, later known as Buddha, the "Enlightened," there are three marks *(thilakhana)* of existence: all existence is a flux-in-process *(anicca),* having nothing permanent but constant change *(anatta),* and hence it is devoid of any kind of lasting satisfaction *(dukkha).* The term *dukkha,* thus, denotes suffering, anxiety. The self-emptying of Jesus Christ can be seen in the light of these three *thilakhana:* Jesus' self-emptying was the emptying of his divinity but the negation of the self in which the divinity of love was disclosed. "In this self-emptying there is nothing of self to be seen—no notion of I, Me, Mine—but only the Ultimate, Unconditional love of God."[16] The essential principle of the divine *kenōsis* is that Christ negated himself without losing himself.

John Keenan, in his book *The Meaning of Christ: A Mahayana Theology,*[17] attempts to offer a full-scale synthesis of Christology in light of Mahayana Buddhism.[18] He argues that christological insight could profit from engage-

15. Choan-Seng Song, "From Israel to Asia: A Theological Leap," in *Mission Trends,* vol. 3, ed. Gerald H. Anderson and Thomas F. Stransky (New York: Paulist Press, 1976), 212.

16. Lynn de Silva, "Emergent Theology in the Context of Buddhism," in *Asian Christian Theology,* 230.

17. John P. Keenan, *The Meaning of Christ: A Mahayana Theology* (Maryknoll, N.Y.: Orbis, 1989).

18. *Mahayana* (literally, "big chariot") represents the more open-minded, liberal interpretation of Buddhism in contrast to *hinayana* ("small chariot").

ment with Buddhist thought, especially the defining idea of emptiness, foundational to Buddhist ontology. In a Mahayana understanding of the person of Jesus Christ, he is empty of any essence that might identify him and that might serve as a definition of his being. Like human beings, Jesus lacks self (*atman*). This Christology rejects the ontology of classical creeds that emphasizes substance (and consequently, a clearly defined selfhood). The reason is simple: The Gospels do not define Christ. For the Gospel writers, Christ's "being" is constituted by a deep consciousness of the presence of Abba and by a dedication to the rule of God.

In addition to the idea of emptiness, what draws Asians to Christ and his cross is the theme of suffering. According to the analysis of Buddha, the elimination of *dukkha,* suffering, is the focus of religion and ethics (in fact, Buddha did not regard himself as the founder of a religion but of a new ethic; his followers hailed him as a religious figure). What is distinctive about Christ's suffering for Asians is not the idea of vicarious suffering, explicated in classical theology, but the suffering of Christ *with* humans as a fellow sufferer. In Christ, God loves his people so much that God suffers with them and dies with them.

These and other parallels lead many to wonder if the Buddhist lotus and the Christian cross could exist side by side. As the cross of Christ has been the focus of Christian spirituality and theology, so the image of Buddha seated cross-legged on the lotus has symbolized Buddhist devotion. But the symbols differ: The lotus springs from fertile water and symbolizes serenity, while the cross, a rugged piece of wood cut off from its roots and placed on a stony hill, represents cruelty and shame. Yet they are united in that they are responses to the question of suffering: "Asian Buddhists enter human suffering through the lotus, and Christians through the cross."[19]

Asia's Struggle for Full Humanity

Liberation theology and the yearning for freedom are not limited to Latin America, the cradle of liberationism. Asian Christians have joined forces to develop an authentically liberationist Christology and theology. In 1979, the Asian Conference of Third World Theologians held a consultation in Sri Lanka under the rubric of "Asia's Struggle for Full Humanity: Toward a Relevant Theology." The consultation took notice of problems such as poverty, unemployment, child labor, and the exploitation of women and committed to furthering a "radical transformation" of theology. That kind of theology "must arise from the Asian poor with a liberated con-

19. Choan-Seng Song, *Third-Eye Theology: Theology in Formation in Asian Settings* (Maryknoll, N.Y.: Orbis, 1979), 123.

sciousness."[20] What CELAM, the Latin American Catholic Bishops' Conference, was for Latin America, the Asian Conference of 1979 was for Asia. Its point of departure was the Asian context and dialogue with local culture, Asian religious traditions, and the life of the people, especially the poor. The Asian bishops acknowledged that, with the local church as the focus of evangelization and dialogue as its essential mode, they would help Asian Christians work for salvation and solidarity with the poor and oppressed as well as attempt a true dialogue with the ancient religions of the area.

Most Asian countries are poor, with the exception of Japan and South Korea. From the Western viewpoint, it is painful to acknowledge that one—if not *the*—major reason for poverty in too many Asian countries is the tragic history of colonialization. This historical fact should make Western preachers of Christ aware of the difficulty with which many Asians hear their message, the message of their former masters.

The most noted theologian in Asia who has attempted to draw implications from Christology for the struggle of humanization is M. M. Thomas, a layperson of the Mar Thoma Church of southern India. He entered theology through the gateway of political and social consciousness, coming as he did from Marxist philosophy. The title of his main book, *Salvation and Humanization*,[21] reveals the central orientation of his thinking. For Thomas, the validity of Christology is based less on its doctrinal orthodoxy than on its contribution to the human quest for a better quality of life and social justice. In *Risking Christ for Christ's Sake*,[22] Thomas attempted to develop a "Christ-centered humanism" based on a syncretistic view of religions. The source of strength for this risky ecumenical and interreligious work came from the cross and resurrection of Jesus Christ. In it he put forth a liberation theology with the purpose of explicating in real life the implications of faith in Christ.

Thomas's theology recognizes the presence of Christ in all struggles for justice, whether Christian or not. Moreover, it acknowledges the presence of Christ in all spiritualities that inspire struggles for justice. Christ is present in these struggles as the cosmic lord of history. Not only Christianity but also Asian religions provide a spiritual basis for striving for justice. On the basis of Colossians 1 and Ephesians 1, Thomas argues that if Christ as the principle and goal of creation is present in all creation, then every attempt to better creation and the life of creatures is related to Christ, whether so acknowledged or not by the agents of change. There is a curious dialectic in Thomas's un-

---

20. Quoted in Donald K. McKim, *The Bible in Theology and Preaching* (Nashville: Abingdon, 1994), 160.

21. M. M. Thomas, *Salvation and Humanization: Some Crucial Issues of the Theology of Mission in Contemporary India* (Madras: Christian Institute on the Study of Religion and Society, 1971).

22. M. M. Thomas, *Risking Christ for Christ's Sake: Towards an Ecumenical Theology of Pluralism* (Geneva: WCC, 1987).

derstanding with regard to how people recognize the power of Jesus at work in the world: "Christ makes use of worldly and non-worldly forces for this purpose. The notion that Christ is at work only in the church and Christians is foolish and nonsensical. But it is the church and the Christians who can recognize Christ in the efforts and events of our time."[23]

Thomas's Christ, the cosmic lord of history, is not so much related to the mystery of the divine (as in many other Asian interpretations of Christ) as to the historical plane, the struggle for equality, justice, and peace. Thomas's liberation theology is for Asia:

> Thomas' Christology does not deny the importance of history in order to provide a common basis for all religions. Rather, the cosmic lord of history becomes the meeting point of religions as they struggle for justice. Christ is present not so much in ahistorical mystery as in the human quest for a better life. Therefore, for Thomas, the cosmic lord of history and the historical Jesus, who labored among the poor, are one and the same, sharing an identical purpose.[24]

Jesus not only identified with the poor but also suffered and died on the cross to empower his followers to continue the same work.

Another Christologist who has labored in the area of social justice is Aloysius Pieris, a Sri Lankan Jesuit and director of a local research institute that promotes Christian-Buddhist dialogue. Like Thomas, he criticizes other liberation movements for their inability to recognize the liberative force of other religions. Naming Christianity the specifically liberationist religion too easily leads to the implication that other religions are not and thus fosters an unhealthy isolation of Christianity from other religions.

Pieris links Asia's poverty and spirituality to Jesus' "double baptism" in "the Jordan of Asian religions and the Calvary of Asian poverty."[25] Jesus' baptism and death immersed him in the Asian context and life. By submitting to baptism by John the Baptist, Jesus refused the ideology of the Zealot movement, the radical political left wing of his day, and the appeal to power and privileges of other contemporary movements, such as that of the aristocratic Sadducees. Instead, he identified himself with the powerless margins of the society. Jesus pointed to the ascetic John as the archetype of the true spirituality of the kingdom of God and denounced striving for the accumulation of wealth and placing one's trust in mammon. Jesus' radical social program, in Pieris's analysis, led him finally to the cross, on which he was executed by the

23. Cited in Volker Küster, *The Many Faces of Jesus Christ: Intercultural Christology* (Maryknoll, N.Y.: Orbis, 2001), 84.

24. Priscilla Pope-Levison and John R. Levison, *Jesus in Global Contexts* (Louisville: Westminster John Knox, 1992), 73.

25. Aloysius Pieris, *An Asian Theology of Liberation* (Maryknoll, N.Y.: Orbis, 1988), 48.

powerful elite. The powerful crucified him on "a cross that the money-pol-
luted religiosity of his day planted on Calvary with the aid of a colonial power
(Luke 23:1–23). This is where the journey, begun at Jordan, ended."[26]

Christ, *Minjung,* and *Dalit*

Asia's struggle for humanization faces enormous challenges. An authentically Asian Christology cannot help but delve into the suffering and wounds
of Asian people. Chi-Ha Kim, a Korean poet, wrote a play titled *The Gold-
Crowned Jesus.* The scene plays in front of a Catholic Church, where there is
a cement statue of Jesus wearing a golden crown. It is a cold winter day, and
beggars are lying beneath the statue. Looking at the gold-crowned Jesus, one
of them wonders what the relevance of such a savior figure might be for a beggar with no place to go. And after all, how can a Jesus made of cement speak
or feel anything? In the midst of his anguish, the beggar feels something wet,
like small drops falling on his head. When he looks up, he sees the cement
Jesus weeping. Noticing that the golden crown might be of value, the beggar
is about to take it for himself when he hears the voice of Jesus: "Take it, please!
For too long a time have I been imprisoned in this cement. Eventually you
have come and made me open my mouth. You have saved me."[27]

It is the task of Asian Christology to free Jesus for the common people. The
term *minjung* means "mass of people." It is also the name of a Korean liberation movement for people who since the 1960s have lived under a military
dictatorship and have been exploited economically and alienated sociologi-
cally, without due rights for social action. The *minjung* movement stands for
human rights, social justice, and democratization.

Byung-Mu Ahn, the most famous theologian related to this movement, argues that it is time for Christian theology to free Christology of the *kērygma*
from Western enslavement and put the living Jesus in contact with the common people. The living Jesus lived with the poor, the sick, and the women,
healing them, feeding them, and defending them. According to Ahn, Jesus'
action is incessant. Unlike the "Christ of the *kērygma,*" Jesus does not remain
seated, immovable on his unshakable throne within the church. On the contrary, Jesus associates and lives with the *minjung.* The Gospel of Mark especially highlights Jesus' association with the *ochlos* (the Greek term for common people), but the other Gospels have the same emphasis.

The main difference between traditional Christology and *minjung* Christology, as developed by Ahn, is that the former depicts Jesus as the true Mes-

26. Ibid., 49.
27. Quoted in Byung-Mu Ahn, "Jesus and the People (Minjung)," in *Asian Faces of Jesus,*
ed. R. S. Sugirtharajah (Maryknoll, N.Y.: Orbis, 1995), 163–64.

siah in the sense that he obeyed and fulfilled God's will. *Minjung* Christology does not deny this aspect of obedience, but there is another tradition that:

> conveys an absolutely different image of Jesus, who identifies with the cries and wishes of the suffering Minjung. It is particularly the healing-stories that expose this image of Jesus. The Jesus who heals the sick people is by no means described as someone who fulfills a pre-established program. Jesus never seeks for the sick persons voluntarily, nor does he follow an earlier intention (plan) for helping them. On the contrary, the request always comes from the Minjung's side first. And accordingly, Jesus' healing activities appear as him being obedient to the wishes of the patients. . . . Jesus' healing power, which has a functional relation to the suffering of the Minjung, can be realized only when it is met by the will of the Minjung.[28]

Jesus, as the spokesperson for the sick, the poor, the alienated, and women, speaks to God on behalf of the *minjung*. Christian faith does not constitute "a manufactured product" given to human beings from heaven to possess but rather involves the "salvation that Jesus realized in the action of transforming himself, by listening to and responding to the cry of Minjung."[29]

The Japanese theologian Koyama, who has worked with the exploited and poor rural people of northern Thailand, strikes the same chord when talking about the crucified Christ challenging human power. Christ exposes human power, not from the luxury of an armchair but by abandoning himself to human dominance, even to crucifixion. No one can mutilate him, Koyama says, because he is already mutilated. No one can crucify him, because he is already crucified. "In the crucified Christ we are confronted by the ultimate sincerity of God."[30]

Another Asian Christology that focuses on the least in society comes from India. *Dalit* is currently the self-designation of the Indian outcastes. The *dalit* theologian Arvind Nirmal enumerates six meanings of the term: "(1) the broken, the torn, the rent, the burst, the split, (2) the opened, the expanded, (3) the bisected, (4) the driven asunder, (5) the downtrodden, the crushed, the destroyed, (6) the manifested, the displayed."[31] *Dalit* Christology represents a liberation movement for these people at the bottom of society.

Nirmal, who coined the term *dalit* theology at the beginning of the 1980s, argues that Jesus himself was a *dalit*. Jesus identified with the *"dalits"* of his day, and in his "Nazareth Manifesto" (Luke 4:18–19), he promised liberation

28. Ibid., 169.
29. Ibid.
30. Kosuke Koyama, "The Crucified Christ Challenges Human Power," in *Asian Faces of Jesus*, 149.
31. Cited in Küster, *Many Faces of Jesus Christ*, 164.

Christ in the Contemporary World: Contextual Christologies

for the prisoners. On the cross "he was the broken, the crushed, the split, the torn, the driven asunder man—the dalit in the fullest possible meaning of that term." Therefore, it is "precisely in and through the weaker, the downtrodden, the crushed, the oppressed and the marginalized that God's saving glory is manifested or displayed. This is because brokenness belongs to the very being of God."[32]

In the Asian context, Christology interacts with two major challenges: ancient yet still vibrant religious life and utmost poverty. The future of distinctively Asian Christology depends on how well Christian theology succeeds in speaking to these and related contexts. One of the spokespersons in that attempt is Stanley Samartha, whose interpretation of Christ occupies us next.

32. Cited in ibid., 172.

30

Stanley Samartha

Christ as Universal Savior

One Christ—Many Religions

Although most Christians today are unwilling to take a totally negative attitude toward neighbors of other faiths, there seems to be a good deal of hesitation on the part of many to reexamine the basis of their exclusive claims on behalf of Christ. The place of Christ in a multireligious society becomes, therefore, an important issue in the search for a new theology of religions.[1]

Ordained in the Church of South India and involved in theological teaching in his earlier years, Samartha has exercised considerable influence through his post as director of the World Council of Churches Dialogue Programme, which he initiated. Throughout his life, Samartha has advocated dialogue among world religions as the demand of our age. Samartha began his theological thinking with nondogmatic Christocentrism but later moved toward a more clearly pluralistic model. In *One Christ—Many Religions: Toward a Revised Christology,*[2] he argues that Christocentrism is applicable only to Christians; it can never be considered the only way to the mystery of the divine.

1. Stanley J. Samartha, "The Cross and the Rainbow: Christ in a Multireligious Culture," in *Asian Faces of Jesus,* ed. R. S. Sugirtharajah (Maryknoll, N.Y.: Orbis, 1995), 104.
2. Stanley J. Samartha, *One Christ—Many Religions: Toward a Revised Christology* (Maryknoll, N.Y.: Orbis, 1991).

Christocentrism, therefore, cannot be the norm by which various religious traditions are valued. All approaches to the divine have validity.

Samartha observes that a process of rejecting exclusive claims and seeking new ways of understanding the relationship of Jesus Christ to God and humanity is already underway. A shift is taking place from the "normative exclusiveness" of Christ to what he calls the "relational distinctiveness" of Christ. The term *relational* refers to the fact that Christ does not remain unrelated to neighbors of other faiths, while *distinctiveness* denotes the recognition that the great religious traditions are different responses to the mystery of God.

Samartha argues that Hindus and Christians have their own particular contributions to make to the common quest for truth. The problem with religious exclusivism (according to which only those who believe in Christ will be saved) is that it cannot explain why a God whose love and justice are universal would reveal the way of salvation through only one savior, one people, and one book. Samartha wonders why the authority of one book should be binding for faith communities that have their own books, some of which are older than the New Testament. Christians with a limited view argue for that kind of limitation in God's dealing with humankind. The claim for the exclusive truth in Christianity puts religion in the prison of history. According to Samartha, genuine pluralism does not relativize the truth; the only thing that can make the truth relative are the different responses of different people. The truth is no one's privilege. The goal of ecumenism and interreligious dialogue is to create a truly universal community that cuts across boundaries of nations and religions.

The drive behind the interreligious dialogue is twofold: the search for the truth and the worldwide struggle against injustice in which religions have found themselves. Interreligious dialogue must seek after truth not only for its own sake but also to promote justice, peace, and equality. There can be no lasting justice, Samartha envisions, unless it is rooted in divine truth, and there is no authentic divine truth that does not produce the fruit of social justice.

Sense of Mystery

In the context of India, which has a growing sense of religious tolerance but an increased and intensified political and social intolerance, there is a need for a Christology that is based on something other than clearly defined doctrinal formulations, Samartha contends. He adds that in order for Christology to take root in Asian soil, the specific nature of the Asian mind-set has to be taken into consideration. This is where the concept of "mystery" enters his theological discourse. Any attempt to formulate a Christology should take into account at least two factors that have emerged from Asia's long history of multireligious life. One is the acceptance of a sense of mystery, and the other is the rejection of an exclusive attitude concerning ultimate matters. However, the conception of mystery in Asian thought does not denote something that fills the gaps in rational knowledge. Rather, mystery provides the ontological basis for tolerance, which would otherwise run the risk of becoming uncritical friendliness.

> This Mystery, the Truth of the Truth *(Satyasya Satyam)*, is the transcendent Center that remains always beyond and greater than apprehensions of it even in the sum total of those apprehensions. It is beyond cognitive knowledge *(tarka)* but it is open to vision *(dristi)* and intuition *(anubhava)*. It is near yet far, knowable yet unknowable, intimate yet ultimate and, according to one particular Hindu view, cannot even be described as "one." It is "not-two" *(advaita)*, indicating thereby that diversity is within the heart of Being itself and therefore may be intrinsic to human nature as well.[3]

The emphasis on mystery is not meant to be an escape from the need for rational inquiry, but it insists that the rational is not the only way to do theology. The mystical and the aesthetic also have their necessary contributions to make to theology. Samartha believes that mystery lies beyond the dichotomy of theistic versus nontheistic. "Mystery is an ontological status to be accepted, not an epistemological problem to be solved. Without a sense of Mystery, *Theos* [Greek term for god] cannot remain *Theos*, nor *Sat* [Hindi term for god] remain *Sat*, nor can Ultimate Reality remain ultimate."[4]

One strand of Hinduism, for example, has described this mystery as *sat-cit-ananda*, "truth-consciousness-bliss." This is one way of responding to mystery in a particular setting that differs from that of the early Christian centuries. The Christian doctrine of the Trinity, with Jesus Christ as the self-revelation of God, is a way of approaching the mystery in a particular historical context. The terms *Sat* and *Theos* can be regarded as two responses to the same mystery in two cultural settings, Samartha concludes.

The nature of mystery is such that any claim on the part of one religious community to have exclusive or unique knowledge of it is inadmissible. Samartha strongly believes that an exclusive attitude erects a fence around the mystery. Exclusiveness also creates dichotomies between different religious communities and leaves little room for the nonrational elements in religious life such as the mystical, the aesthetic, meditation, and rituals. Furthermore, exclusive claims isolate the community of faith

3. Samartha, "The Cross and the Rainbow," 110–11.
4. Ibid., 111.

from neighbors of other faiths, creating tensions and disturbing relationships within the larger community. But when the distinctiveness of a particular faith is stated in a manner that avoids open or hidden exclusiveness, then meaningful relationships between different communities are possible. As a consequence, Christianity in Asia need not be in competition with the whole range of Asian religions; instead, it can foster cooperation in the common quest for fullness of life. The central effort of theology for Samartha is to acknowledge the mystery of Christ and explain the meaning of the person and work of Jesus Christ for theology and the church. Out of this commitment arises his theocentric pluralistic view of Christ.

Theocentric Pluralism

Samartha is a more moderate theologian of religion than many other pluralists. Like many of his colleagues, Samartha began with the open-minded view according to which the cosmic Christ is acknowledged by all religions. Later in his theological and ecumenical career, however, he moved in the direction of Raimundo Panikkar and others. He became dissatisfied with the idea of "anonymous Christianity" of Karl Rahner and similar ideas that betray an assumption of the normativity of Christianity over other religions. Samartha began to question the absolute finality and universal normativity of Christ. The reason for the shift in his thinking was his theocentric approach to theology in general and Christology in particular: Before the total mystery of God, no religious figure and no single religion can call itself the final and full word. Samartha's reluctance to name Jesus Christ the final revelation was, interestingly enough, based on his understanding of God, and this makes his pluralism distinctive: "The Other [God as the Mysterious Other] relativizes everything else. In fact, the willingness to accept such relativization is probably the only real guarantee that one has encountered the Other as ultimately real."[5] In other words, those who recognize God alone as absolute will recognize all religions as relative.

Clearly, for the mature Samartha, the incarnation is a symbol of the divine rather than a normative historical happening. Also, the death and resurrection of Christ, even though they are revelations of who God is, are not to be treated as a universally valid paradigm. Samartha has no problem affirming the humanity and divinity of Jesus Christ, but he is not willing to affirm the orthodox teaching that Christ is God. The reason is simply that "an ontolog-

5. Stanley J. Samartha, *Courage for Dialogue: Ecumenical Issues in Inter-Religious Relationships* (Maryknoll, N.Y.: Orbis, 1982), 151.

ical equation of Jesus Christ and God would scarcely allow any serious discussion with neighbors of other faiths or with secular humanism."[6]

Samartha, also following Panikkar, relativizes all particular religious expressions and forms in history, the incarnation of Christ included, but is not willing to deny their necessity. The Mysterious Other must confront us through particular mediations. Therefore, Samartha does not naively assume the equality of all religions. What he claims is that each and every religion and its figures are limited: "A particular religion can claim to be decisive for some people, and some people can claim that a particular religion is decisive for them, but no religion is justified in claiming that it is decisive for all."[7]

For Samartha, classical theology runs the danger of "christomonism" in its insistence on the absolute finality of Jesus Christ. It turns Jesus into a kind of "cult figure" over against other religious figures. Instead of a christomonistic approach to other religions, Samartha advocates a theocentric approach, which is more consistent with the God-centered message of Jesus of Nazareth. He tries to hold in tension the normative significance of Christ as the revelation of God and the need for openness in relation to other faiths:

> No one could have anticipated in advance the presence of God in the life and death of Jesus of Nazareth. There is an incomprehensible dimension to it. That Jesus is the Christ of God is a confession of faith by the Christian community. It does indeed remain normative to Christians everywhere, but to make it "absolutely singular" and to maintain that the meaning of the Mystery is disclosed *only* in one particular person at one particular point, and nowhere else, is to ignore one's neighbors of other faiths who have other points of reference. To make exclusive claims for our particular tradition is not the best way to love our neighbors as ourselves.[8]

This kind of nonnormative Christology, in Samartha's view, allows Christians to hold their personal commitment to Christ and even their belief in his universal meaning, though not in an exclusive way. For Christians, Christ represents the fulfillment of God's promises. "But such an announcement will be an enthusiastic *witness* to their own revealer, *not* a denigrating *judgment* about other revealers."[9] Consequently, "whether it is in the attempts to redefine the goals of life or in the effort to meet human needs in the dust and heat of the plains, wherever two or three Hindus and Christians are gathered

6. Stanley J. Samartha, "The Cross and the Rainbow: Christ in a Multireligious Culture," in *The Myth of Christian Uniqueness,* ed. J. Hick and P. Knitter (Maryknoll, N.Y.: Orbis, 1987), 80.

7. Samartha, *Courage for Dialogue,* 153.

8. Samartha, "The Cross and the Rainbow," in *Asian Faces of Jesus,* 112.

9. Paul F. Knitter, *No Other Name? A Critical Survey of Christian Attitudes toward the World Religions* (Maryknoll, N.Y.: Orbis, 1986), 159, italics in text.

together in his name, there one need not doubt the presence of the living Christ in the midst of them."[10]

Buddha, Rama, and Krishna

In one of his main theological works, Samartha studies the interpretations of Christ in the Hindu Renaissance, showing a clear preference for the *advaita* philosophy of Shankara.[11] In an interesting analysis, he regards the Upanishads as Protestant movements within Hinduism that sought to liberate the essence of religion from the authority of the church and old-fashioned modes and practices. Samartha sees a parallel to this in the early church as it struggled its way through the challenge of expressing the gospel in Greek thought forms. By adopting the categories of *advaita* in its classical and modern interpretations in the Hindu Renaissance, "Samartha wants to make room for faith in Jesus Christ in Indian pluralism and overcome the traditional claim of Christianity to absoluteness. . . . Christology and advaita are to be mutual correctives."[12]

In the Indian context, Samartha sees no way to avoid the comparison between Jesus Christ and the savior figures of Hinduism and other religions of the area. Samartha cites Buddha, Rama, and Krishna as examples and argues that no credible Christology can be constructed in an Asian context without relating Christ and these figures to one another. Many things unite these three saviors with Christ. In the life and work of each of them, revelation and liberation stand in a direct connection. Each of these savior figures experienced—according to their followers' interpretation—a development from original humanity to later deity.

Rama and Krishna are household words in India and are at the center of theistic *bhakti* (devotional religion), at times merging into the larger horizon of *advaita*. The question of the historicity of Rama and Krishna has always been a complex one, but Samartha does not give too much attention to it, given that the quest for the historical foundations of the founder of a religion is a recent phenomenon. The quest of the historical Jesus did not arise until

10. Stanley J. Samartha, "Unbound Christ: Towards Christology in India Today," in *Asian Christian Theology: Emerging Themes,* ed. Douglas J. Elwood (Philadelphia: Westminster, 1980), 146.

11. Stanley J. Samartha, *The Hindu Response to the Unbound Christ* (Madras: Christian Literature Society, 1974). *Advaita* literally means "not two." According to this philosophy, reality is characterized by unity, non-dualism, and therefore, the goal of Christian life is to be immersed in the Absolute.

12. Volker Küster, *The Many Faces of Jesus Christ: Intercultural Christology* (Maryknoll, N.Y.: Orbis, 2001), 89.

the emergence of the Enlightenment in the eighteenth century; before that time the historicity of Jesus of Nazareth was taken for granted.

Samartha believes it is easier to talk about Buddha and Christ together, partly because the case for the historicity of each is strong, and partly because both Buddhism and Christianity have transcended their particularities and have become universal in the sense that they are at home in different countries and cultures. For Samartha, the key to the similarities between Buddha and Christ lies in their role as liberator. During the past few centuries, the life and work of Jesus of Nazareth has provided both an inspiration and an example for reformers working for the liberation of the poor and oppressed in Asian society. In more recent years, Buddha has provided both a shelter *(saranam)* and a dynamic source of power for missions to *dalits* (the lowest class of people, the "class-less"). Millions of *dalits* have adopted the religion of Buddhism in India and have rebelled against the ruling Hindu caste system. Christ can be an inspiration for the followers of Buddha, Samartha argues, but a "Christology of domination" is not good news for Buddhists. In this context, Samartha quotes with approval Aloysius Pieris, who has argued that an Asian theology of liberation evolves into a Christology that does not compete with Buddhology but complements it by acknowledging:

> The one path of liberation of which Christians join Buddhists in their *Gnostic detachment* (or the practice of voluntary poverty) and Buddhists join Christians in their *agapaeic involvement* is the struggle against forced poverty. . . . It is only at the end of the path, as at Emmaus, that the path itself will be recognized by name (Luke 24:31).[13]

In summing up his consideration of these four savior figures—Buddha, Krishna, Rama, and Christ—Samartha argues that the theory of multiple *avatara* (incarnations) seems to be theologically the most accommodating attitude in a pluralistic setting, one that permits recognition of both the mystery of God and the freedom of people to respond to divine initiatives in different ways at different times.

---

13. Samartha, *One Christ—Many Religions*, 126.

Epilogue

The Future of Christology

The great Christian novelist of the seventeenth century John Bunyan struggled with the devil, who assailed him with painful questions about the truth among religions and the role of Christ with regard to other savior figures:

> How can you tell but that the Turks had as good Scriptures to prove their Mahomet the Saviour, as we have to prove our Jesus is; and could I think that so many ten thousands in so many Countreys and Kingdoms, should be without the knowledge of the right way to Heaven . . . and that we onely, who live but in a corner of the Earth, should alone be blessed therewith? Everyone doth think his own Religion rightest, both Jews, and Moors, and Pagans; and how if all our Faith, and Christ, and Scriptures, should be but a thinks-so too?[1]

Many and varied have been the challenges facing Christian theology in its painful yet exciting task of accounting for the person and work of the founder and center of the faith, Jesus of Nazareth. None, however, can compete with the urgency and seriousness of the question of the theology of religions, namely, the relation of Christianity to other religions. This question, of course, focuses on Jesus Christ and his role with regard to religion in general and to concrete forms of religions in particular.

Long before Bunyan's struggle, Christian theology faced the question of who Jesus Christ is in relation to other saviors. Christianity was born and took its initial form in a polytheistic environment, as did its Old Testament predecessor, the Jewish faith. Therefore, the excitement of theologians and students of religions over the newness and freshness of this challenge is not always historically well informed. Early apologists spoke of the "seeds of *Logos*" sown in

---

1. John Bunyan, *Grace Abounding to the Chief of Sinners,* ed. Robert Sharrock (New York: Oxford University Press, 1962), 31.

the rich soil of religions, and several medieval heroes such as Peter Abelard, who wrote *Dialogue of a Philosopher and a Jew and a Christian,* and Ramon Llull, who wrote *Book of the Gentile and the Three Wise Men,* challenged the limits of Christian exclusivism. A more recent example from the beginning of the last century is the Scottish Protestant missionary to India, John Farquhar, for whom Christ was *The Crown of Hinduism* (1913).

In light of these and many other historical examples, one wonders if characterizations such as a "monstrous shift" (Langdon Gilkey), a "fundamental revision" (Gordon Kaufman), a "genetic-like mutation" (Raimundo Panikkar), a "momentous kairos" (Paul Knitter), a "Copernican revolution" and "radical transformation" (John Hick), and a "crossing of a theological Rubicon" (Claremont Graduate School Conference of March 1986) are overstatements with regard to the present and future states of Christian faith and theology. Nevertheless, there is no denying "that the future of Christian theology lies in the encounter between Christianity and other faiths," as Alan Race contends in his widely used textbook on the relationship between Christianity and religious pluralism.[2] Race and many others, however, do not see this state of affairs necessarily in negative terms. In fact, he states that Christian theology "ought to rejoice at being at the frontiers of the next phase in Christian history."[3]

Some students of Christian theology who have spent considerable time living among other religions even see pluralism as an integral part of Christian faith. Such is the dream of a theological moderate, the Catholic Jacques Dupuis, S.J., who wants to see a shift toward a Christian theology of religious pluralism.[4] Not insignificantly, his earlier book was titled *Jesus Christ at the Encounter of World Religions.*[5]

Indeed, of all the turns in Christian theology in general and the study of Christology in particular, the "turn to other religions" will be the most scary but at the same time potentially the most fruitful with regard to the continual mission of the Christian church. No doubt, it will add to the fragmentation and divisions of both Christian churches and Christian theologies; yet the challenge is to be faced.[6]

Another challenge for the study of Christology and Christian theology concerns the question of contextual theologies. As this book has shown, Christian theology has already begun to tackle this issue. An exciting, rich

2. Alan Race, *Christians and Religious Pluralism: Patterns in the Christian Theology of Religions* (Maryknoll, N.Y.: Orbis, 1982), xi.

3. Ibid.

4. Jacques Dupuis, S.J., *Toward a Christian Theology of Religious Pluralism* (Maryknoll, N.Y.: Orbis, 1997).

5. Jacques Dupuis, S.J., *Jesus Christ at the Encounter of World Religions* (Maryknoll, N.Y.: Orbis, 1991).

6. For starters, see my textbook, *Christian Theology of Religions: An Introduction* (Downers Grove, Ill.: InterVarsity, 2003).

array of contextual or global—sometimes ironically yet fittingly called "lo-cal"—interpretations of Jesus Christ are emerging in various contexts of our world. These interpretations not only add to the mosaic of christological tra-ditions and so speak to varying needs and desires but also have the potential to correct one-sided classical Western views. They have also helped classical theology to acknowledge its own dependence on context. All theologies are shaped and conditioned by their intellectual, social, psychological, and reli-gious environments.

The challenges of both contextualization and other religions raise anew the question of the relationship between Christ's work and his person, in other words, the relationship between soteriology and Christology proper. Here, as in any other area, the necessity of speaking to the various and changing needs of specific contexts is urgent. Addressing that challenge requires a continuous dialogue between biblical and historical traditions and contemporary con-texts. A promising example of such dialogue is found in a recent textbook by two evangelical scholars, Joel B. Green and Mark D. Baker: *Recovering the Scandal of the Cross.*[7] Their work is a careful reappraisal of biblical testimonies and traditional atonement theories (shorthand for the work of Christ) accom-panied by an inquiry into contextual needs of Asian cultures, feminism, West-ern youth cultures, and so on. Methodologically, this is a preferred direction for Christology in general: Speaking either to other religions or to other con-texts is not helped by neglecting the traditions developed (mainly) in the West during the first two millennia of Christian thought. A *Christian* theology of religions will not become more appealing by overthrowing its distinctively Christian heritage, as some theologians too hastily seem to be doing, nor are contextual Christologies made more contextual just by rejecting existing Western views and uncritically adopting any kind of new framework. Some contextual Christologies have become prisoners—though to a new context instead of the traditional Western theology—and parochial from the outset.

The development of a distinctively Christian Christology in all its various colors and shades—we do not want to suppress plurality for the simple reason that the Bible, the foundational source of all Christian theology, embraces a variety of approaches to who Christ is and what he has done—requires pains-taking dialogue between the biblical texts, historical developments, and varied current contexts. There is no easy way, no miracle solution. Doing Christian Christology is a global, intercultural exercise, transcending ecclesiastical and theological boundaries. The end result is not one Christology but a variety of rich voices, not unlike the Gospels, yet voices that share a common focus.

The study of Christology has yet another dimension. The great Catholic theo-logian of beauty, Hans Urs von Balthasar, in his spiritual reflections on the Cre-

7. Joel B. Green and Mark D. Baker, *Recovering the Scandal of the Cross: Atonement in New Testament and Contemporary Contexts* (Downers Grove, Ill.: InterVarsity, 2000).

ator Spirit, issued a warning that has to do not only with pneumatology; it is also appropriate for the study of the Second Person of the Trinity: God, the source of life and beauty, is never an "object" to be studied but rather a Subject who grants us the needed, albeit necessarily limited, lenses to look at him. If the Spirit, according to the vision of von Balthasar, is the "seeing eye of grace," the Third Unknown who turns our eyes to the Son and the Father in the blessed Trinity, then "in the same way the Son neither wishes nor is able to glorify himself but glorifies only the Father (John 5:41; 7:18)."[8] What Balthasar reminds us of is twofold. First, everything we say about Jesus Christ is conditioned by and related to the doctrine of the Trinity, the specifically Christian understanding of the Godhead. Consequently, though for pedagogical reasons this introductory text has focused on Jesus Christ alone, we cannot disassociate the person and work of Jesus Christ from the Christian understanding of God as triune. Second, von Balthasar underlines the ancient—albeit too often forgotten—conviction that the study of theology in general and Christology in particular is always an exercise in "spiritual things." Despite what a careful, painstaking study gains, much is always left unexplained. More importantly, the "kernel" lies somewhere behind the "husk" of scientific inquiry. Even if it is neither feasible nor desirable to go back to the pre-Enlightenment idyllic mind-set, students of Christology need to remember that Christian theologians have always approached their task of inquiring into Christ with reverence and anticipation.

At the end of the day, Jesus of Nazareth, whom Christians confess as Lord and Savior, searches the depths of our lives and hearts. When the dilemma of faith and history is overcome—so the Christian church confesses—the "seeing eye of grace" will allow us to behold the beauty of the Savior. With Melanchthon and a host of other witnesses, we will grasp the depths of the dictum, "To know Christ is to know his benefits."[9]

8. Hans Urs von Balthasar, *Explorations in Theology*, vol. 3, *Creator Spirit* (1967; reprint, San Francisco: Ignatius Press, 1993), 111; see also 106–7.
9. Wilhelm Pauck, *Melanchthon and Bucer*, Library of Christian Classics, vol. 19 (Philadelphia: Westminster, 1969), 21–22.

Subject Index

Scripture Index